# Beachheads

## ASIA/PACIFIC/PERSPECTIVES

**Series Editor: Mark Selden**

*Crime, Punishment, and Policing in China* edited by Børge Bakken
*Woman, Man, Bangkok: Love, Sex, and Popular Culture in Thailand* by Scot Barmé
*Making the Foreign Serve China: Managing Foreigners in the People's Republic* by Anne-Marie Brady
*Marketing Dictatorship: Propaganda and Thought Work in China* by Anne-Marie Brady
*Collaborative Nationalism: The Politics of Friendship on China's Mongolian Frontier* by Uradyn E. Bulag
*The Mongols at China's Edge: History and the Politics of National Unity* by Uradyn E. Bulag
*Transforming Asian Socialism: China and Vietnam Compared* edited by Anita Chan, Benedict J. Tria Kerkvliet, and Jonathan Unger
*Bound to Emancipate: Working Women and Urban Citizenship in Early Twentieth-Century China* by Angelina Chin
*China's Great Proletarian Cultural Revolution: Master Narratives and Post-Mao Counternarratives* edited by Woei Lien Chong
*North China at War: The Social Ecology of Revolution, 1937–1945* edited by Feng Chongyi and David S. G. Goodman
*Little Friends: Children's Film and Media Culture in China* by Stephanie Hemelryk Donald
*Beachheads: War, Peace, and Tourism in Postwar Okinawa* by Gerald Figal
*Gender in Motion: Divisions of Labor and Cultural Change in Late Imperial and Modern China* edited by Bryna Goodman and Wendy Larson
*Social and Political Change in Revolutionary China: The Taihang Base Area in the War of Resistance to Japan, 1937–1945* by David S. G. Goodman
*Islands of Discontent: Okinawan Responses to Japanese and American Power* edited by Laura Hein and Mark Selden
*Women in Early Imperial China, Second Edition* by Bret Hinsch
*Civil Justice in China: Past and Present* by Philip C. C. Huang
*Local Democracy and Development: The Kerala People's Campaign for Decentralized Planning* by T. M. Thomas Isaac with Richard W. Franke
*Hidden Treasures: Lives of First-Generation Korean Women in Japan* by Jackie J. Kim with Sonia Ryang
*North Korea: Beyond Charismatic Politics* by Heonik Kwon and Byung-Ho Chung
*Postwar Vietnam: Dynamics of a Transforming Society* edited by Hy V. Luong

*The Indonesian Presidency: The Shift from Personal toward Constitutional Rule* by Angus McIntyre
*Nationalisms of Japan: Managing and Mystifying Identity* by Brian J. McVeigh
*To the Diamond Mountains: A Hundred-Year Journey through China and Korea* by Tessa Morris-Suzuki
*From Underground to Independent: Alternative Film Culture in Contemporary China* edited by Paul G. Pickowicz and Yingjin Zhang
*Wife or Worker? Asian Women and Migration* edited by Nicola Piper and Mina Roces
*Social Movements in India: Poverty, Power, and Politics* edited by Raka Ray and Mary Fainsod Katzenstein
*Pan Asianism: A Documentary History, Volume 1, 1850–1920* edited by Sven Saaler and Christopher W. A. Szpilman
*Pan Asianism: A Documentary History, Volume 2, 1920–Present* edited by Sven Saaler and Christopher W. A. Szpilman
*Biology and Revolution in Twentieth-Century China* by Laurence Schneider
*Contentious Kwangju: The May 18th Uprising in Korea's Past and Present* edited by Gi-Wook Shin and Kyong Moon Hwang
*The Inside Story of China's High-Tech Industry: Making Silicon Valley in Beijing* by Yu Zhou

# Beachheads

## War, Peace, and Tourism in Postwar Okinawa

Gerald Figal

ROWMAN & LITTLEFIELD PUBLISHERS, INC.
*Lanham • Boulder • New York • Toronto • Plymouth, UK*

Published by Rowman & Littlefield Publishers, Inc.
A wholly owned subsidiary of The Rowman & Littlefield Publishing Group, Inc.
4501 Forbes Boulevard, Suite 200, Lanham, Maryland 20706
www.rowman.com

10 Thornbury Road, Plymouth PL6 7PP, United Kingdom



British Library Cataloguing in Publication Information Available

**Library of Congress Cataloging-in-Publication Data**
Figal, Gerald A., 1962–
Beachheads : war, peace, and tourism in postwar Okinawa / Gerald Figal.
p. cm. — (Asia/Pacific/perspectives)
Includes bibliographical references and index.
ISBN 978-1-4422-1581-8 (cloth : alk. paper) — ISBN 978-1-4422-1583-2 (electronic)
1. Tourism—Japan—Okinawa Island—History—20th century. 2. Tourism—Government policy—Japan—History—20th century. 3. Reconstruction (1939-1951)—Japan—Okinawa Island. 4. Okinawa Island (Japan)—History—20th century. I. Title.
G155.J27F55 2012
952'.294—dc23

2011051862

∞™ The paper used in this publication meets the minimum requirements of American National Standard for Information Sciences—Permanence of Paper for Printed Library Materials, ANSI/NISO Z39.48-1992.

Printed in the United States of America

# Contents

# Illustrations

# Acknowledgments

The idea for this book began in a cafe on Kokusai Dōri in Naha in June 1995. There, while I was enjoying the laid-back atmosphere of Okinawa compared to the hustle and bustle of Tokyo and wishing I had reason to spend more time on the island, friend and anthropologist Linda Angst suggested that I consider doing a study of Okinawa tourism. Still in the midst of finishing my first book, I filed this idea away, intrigued by the implicit tensions in a place so actively cultivating an image of tropical leisure tourism while so steeped in wartime legacies. A short recon trip to Okinawa a couple years later paved the way for six months of research there from February through July in 2001, supported by a generous Japan Foundation research fellowship that allowed for the real work behind this book to begin.

That work comprised extensive archival research, interviews, and on-site fieldwork enabled by a veritable *champuru* of contacts and connections, some planned but many more serendipitous. The chance online meeting of U.S. Air Force nurse Sandra Dickinson while I was casting about for housing before my research trip led to invaluable logistical support and numerous kindnesses from her and her Marine Intelligence Officer husband, both stationed in Okinawa. Thanks to Sandra, I also gained access to Kadena Air Base for firsthand observations on several occasions. On the other side of the fence, I owe much gratitude to Ishihara Masaie of Okinawa International University for serving as sponsor for my Japan Foundation fellowship and for providing materials, contacts, and encouragement. Former archivist and Okinawa researcher Genka Yoko introduced me to the beautiful Okinawa Prefectural Archives, whose diligent and patient staff aided me on a daily basis for several months, acquiring and copying the documents that form the core of this project. Staff at the Prefectural Library and the University of the Ryukyus Library likewise made the gathering of materials easier, while the dedicated crew at the Okinawa Prefecture Peace Promotion Division took out an afternoon to field questions and dig up reports on its surveys of the Thirty-second Army Headquarters Cave over the years. I greatly profited from multiple visits to the old and the new Haebaru Culture Center, which has spearheaded battlefield archaeology in Okinawa through its work on the nearby Army Field Hospital Cave. The center's curator, Taira Tsugiko, was especially generous with her time and knowledge of the center's history and continuing efforts to excavate, preserve, and publicly display these war ruins. And like many pilgrims to the war sites on the island, I, in the company of Mark Selden, also paid respects at Chibichirigama, guided by Chibana Shoichi, who always seems to find time he doesn't have to show inquisitive foreigners the cave and to tell its story.

Historical testimonies and on-the-ground insights into the development of postwar Okinawa tourism were graciously shared with me by former bus guide veteran and bus guide trainer Shiroma Sachiko of Okinawa Bus Company and old-timer Mr. Takushi of the Okinawa Convention & Visitors Bureau. Longtime Okinawa resident Betty Hoffman—whose kind graces, hospitality, and island-wide connections are legendary—introduced me to Vicky Obayashi, president of the Southeast Botanical Gardens. I have Julia Yonetani to thank for taking me to Ōta Masahide's National Diet seat election campaign launch party, where I had the privilege and pleasure of dancing *kachāshī*—on camera—with him. Julia also deserves thanks for sharing her own fine work on the politics of war history and memory in Okinawa and braving the heat and mosquitoes on our joint visit to the Kenji-no-tō. Similarly, I owe much to Okinawa resident and scholar John Purves for his keen perspective on Okinawan issues, for research leads, for long conversations into the night, and for the welcoming warmth he and his wife, Rachel, showed me on many visits (including the party they hosted where my then two-year-old daughter Safa broke her arm). Back in the States, I benefited from discussions of my project with good friend Alan Christy of the University of California, Santa Cruz, who also knows a thing or two about Okinawa. These and many unnamed others with whom I had spontaneous on-the-spot interviews and from whom I gained leads and bits of information—the tour bus guide leading a group of students to Anpo no Oka, the clerk at the Navy Underground Headquarters, the performers at Ryukyu Mura, the docent at the Himeyuri Memorial Museum, the *obā-san* at a souvenir shop on Kokusai Dōri, the potter at Yachimun no Sato, and the numerous tour groups I stalked with cameras in hand—all helped direct my own circuitous tour through the past and present of a place so perplexingly shaped by wartime memories and tropical dreams.

Once the writing began in the inspiring new study architect John TeSelle designed and contractor Bill Lawrence built, my wife, Sara, kept it going with unlimited love and unflagging faith in my follow-through. Her patience and understanding in allowing me both to babble about the latest section I was working on one day and to hole up in seclusion in the safe house that is my study the next banished any doubts about the value of the project and made completing it a sure bet.

# Note on Romanization and Abbreviations

I have included macrons on long vowels in romanized Japanese words except in those cases where the word is commonly seen in print in English without macrons (Tokyo, Osaka, etc.). I also have followed this practice with Okinawan words whose long vowels are often romanized with double vowels rather than a macron over a single vowel (*gōyā* rather than *gooyaa*). In the case of the word *Ryūkyū*, I have omitted macrons except in the romanized Japanese-language titles, in the romanization of quoted Japanese text, and in a quotation of English text that has already included macrons.

Common abbreviations in the text and notes derive mainly from standard practices during the American occupation (1945–1972) and subsequently continued in the literature related to that period—for example, USCAR (United States Civil Administration of the Ryukyu Islands); GRI (Government of the Ryukyu Islands); GOJ (Government of Japan). I frequently refer to the Okinawa Kankō Kyōkai (Okinawa Tourism Association) as OTA. Additionally, documents from the Okinawa Prefectural Archives appearing in notes are identified by their record locator number in the format OPA xxxxxxxx.

# Prologue

## "Mensōre, *Welcome to Okinawa!*"

It's June 1995. I am sitting in a Japan Air Lines (JAL) 747 on a flight from Tokyo to Naha City, located on Okinawa Island, the largest of the string of about 160 small islands of the Ryukyu archipelago comprising Okinawa Prefecture. The flight will take about two hours to cover the fifteen hundred southbound kilometers from national to prefectural capital. This is my first trip to Okinawa, site of the bloodiest land battle of the Asia-Pacific War. Of the more than two hundred thousand deaths in that battle, the majority were Okinawan civilians, most of whom died in the barrage of American naval bombardment, artillery, gunfire, flamethrowers, and phosphor bombs used to asphyxiate the enemy hidden within the island's hundreds of caves. Some, however, took their own lives, and some had their lives taken from them by "friendly" Japanese forces who questioned the loyalty of these recently assimilated Japanese imperial subjects whose Japaneseness—ethnic, cultural, historical, ideological—had been a subject of debate ever since the Japanese government forcibly dissolved the Ryukyu Kingdom in 1879 and brought it within the national polity. I'm going to Okinawa for the fiftieth anniversary of the end of that infamous battle, so I'm thinking about these things. I am likely solitary in my thoughts, for the plane—a special Okinawa summer vacation model with a fuselage spangled with tropical-colored Disney characters bedecked in beachwear—is filled predominantly with mainland Japanese tourists whose thoughts are likely on white-sand beaches, scuba diving, golf courses, and exotic drinks, not the atrocities of war. Feeling restrained from discussing the battle's anniversary with my cabin mates, I make small talk with a flight attendant. She's twenty-something, thin, brightly smiling, and probably from the Tokyo area:

"Is this your regular route, Tokyo to Okinawa?"
"Yes, that's right."
"Do you get the chance to spend time on the island?"
"Oh, yes. I love Okinawa!"
"Really? Could you maybe recommend places to eat local food?"
"Oh, I don't like Okinawan food."
"Why not?"
"It's too oily."
"Well, then, what do you like about Okinawa?"
"The beach."

Her reply disappoints but doesn't surprise me. I note it for possible future use in an Okinawa-related project.

Cut to January 2002, during my fourth trip to Okinawa. This time I'm going to do research on that project I imagined in 1995. I'm in a hotel in downtown Naha, listening to a recently purchased CD of Okinawan/Hawaiian fusion, Hirayasu Takashi and Bob Brozman's *Nankuru naisa*. One song, the medley "Mensōreyo/Toshin doi" is Hirayasu's cleverly updated version of a traditional folk tune, "Toshin doi," typically sung now (far too frequently) to welcome visitors and invite them to join in *kachāshī*, a form of group dancing often performed at parties and at the end of festive events. Hirayasu prefaces his version of "Toshin doi" in the first half of the medley with a fast-paced welcome (*mensōre*) to the "real" Okinawa. Translated from Okinawan into English, one part of Hirayasu's song goes something like this:

When you come to Okinawa
Please come to the market in Naha City
We'll welcome you with many good things

Ribs, trotters, boiled fish paste, *gurukun* fish
Please come to find what you want
Ladies and gentlemen
Please come to buy and enjoy

If you understand Okinawan culture
You must eat Okinawan food
You can then make friends

Sautéed *gōyā*, boiled sponge gourd
Please come check it out, thank you, see you soon

To the JAL flight attendant, this Okinawa would likely be very distasteful. Abhorring the food, she would never be able to "understand Okinawan culture."

The disjuncture between the flight attendant's Okinawa and Hirayasu's might simply be viewed as the difference between an outsider's and insider's position. To the extent that growing up with a particular regional cuisine shapes one's tastes and distastes and cuisines become representative of local cultural authenticity, it is reasonable to take this view. But if we extend this question of the production and consumption of different Okinawas more broadly over time, specifically from the Asia-Pacific War (1931–1945) to the present, we find a far more complex situation where an easy division of authentic insider and superficial outsider views only goes so far as an analytical framework. When the messiness and particulars of historical conditions are brought into the picture, generalizations about peoples and places become strained. What might first appear natural and unchanging is revealed as a contingent product of a tangle of forces—political, economic, social, cultural—and a mix of peoples—Okinawan, Japanese, Chinese, American—whose individual actions cannot always be reduced to their supposed identity group and its supposed interests.

English-language research on Okinawa has markedly increased over the last fifteen years and has yielded many noteworthy works that tackle the complexities of the people and the place from different disciplinary stances. Drawing tactically on such traditional discipline-based research and widening the scope of analysis between archive and fieldwork, a study of tourism in Okinawa—a seemingly peripheral if not frivolous topic—offers perhaps one of the best possibilities to capture the historical contingencies and the multifaceted forces that have structured the development of Okinawa since the end of war. By its nature, tourism embraces political, economic, social, and cultural issues. It often uses (and abuses) historical knowledge. As a worldwide phenomenon generated by advanced capitalist societies, it is bound up with problems of modernity and globalization. So constituted, it fundamentally involves sites of production and consumption, frequently entailing the marketing of "authentic" experience of the unfamiliar or of a nostalgic longing for an imagined past. Viewed in this light, the status of tourism in general moves from peripheral to central. This recognition parallels tourism's steadily increasing centrality in Okinawa's economy since the prefecture's reversion to Japanese rule in 1972. With this economic rise of tourism, however, have come political and social tensions within Okinawa Prefecture, between Okinawans and their American "guests," and between Okinawa and mainland Japan. Since its earliest stirrings in the 1950s, the manufacture of "Tourist Okinawa" as cultural product predicated on the promotion of peace and leisure has been ceaselessly engaged with the Battle of Okinawa and its abiding legacies, even when such engagement is unstated. Damaged natural and cultural assets, prolific war memorialization, ongoing debates over Japanese wartime conduct in Okinawa, prolonged U.S. occupation, and concentrated militarization have all—directly and indirectly, positively and negatively—shaped Tourist Okinawa, which for many visitors is synonymous with Okinawa.

The deep connections—sometimes obvious, sometimes not—among war, peace, and tourism and their widespread manifestations across postwar Okinawa's human, cultural, and natural landscapes form the topic of this book. Demonstrating these connections and their unshakable traces not only restores and underscores oft-ignored historicity; it restores meaning to the cliché "the profound impact of war." In the case that I will make in this book, the development of Tourist Okinawa into the billion-dollar business it is today would not have happened without Okinawa's history of war and occupation. This is not to claim that war and occupation have had a silver lining. Neither is it to claim that tourism in Okinawa is an unalloyed good. Rather, it is to focus on the historical conditions of late-twentieth-century Okinawa and how Okinawans have faced them; it is to extend the exploration of what Glenn Hook and Richard Siddle have usefully framed as "structure and subjectivity" in Okinawa.[1] In other words, a wide view of the production and consumption of tourism encompasses historical, environmental, and institutional structures and the human interactions (reactive and generative) with those structures. Structures shape parameters of human actions, but human actions also shape structures. At the risk of appearing reductive (or perhaps stating the obvious), I think it is fair to say that whether through embrace or erasure, the war and its legacies have been especially formative in the "structure and subjectivity" of postwar Okinawa. This book's proposition is that the depth and breadth of this phenomenon is best seen not in another study of the U.S. military base issue or the Reversion movement or the political wrangling between Naha and Tokyo—as important as those are—but rather in a historically informed analysis of the culture and politics of tourism from the end of the Asia-Pacific War to the present. Discussing tourism in Okinawa before the advent of beach resorts that rode the wave of Japan's bubble economy of the late 1980s might raise some eyebrows, especially if that discussion is extended back before Reversion, back to the early postwar years of war-torn Okinawa Island. Yet it is my contention that it is only through such a perspective that the structure and subjectivity that inform present-day Tourist Okinawa make any sense.

It follows that a concomitant concern of this study is the extent to which Tourist Okinawa has insinuated itself—has been naturalized—into the makeup and identity of Okinawa at large, rendering redundant "Okinawa" and "Tourist Okinawa." After all, the tour guidebooks, the websites, the billboards, the costumed performers at the airport and at Ryukyu theme parks all greet visitors with "Welcome to Okinawa," not "Welcome to Tourist Okinawa." Even if such greetings might be self-conscious put-ons (we're really welcoming you to the Okinawa of your tourist imagination, not the real thing of our daily lives), in the realm of consumer capitalism in which these utterances circulate, the commodification they connote is an unavoidable component of modern daily life in Okinawa. This issue necessarily broaches the problem of authenticity, not in the sense of judging between "real" and "fake" Okinawas but rather in examining the contexts and agents involved in the manufacture and marketing of what is put forth and consumed as authentic Okinawa. In other words, the activities of commodification cannot be discounted from the activities of daily life as somehow inauthentic when daily life is shot through with—even depends on—the kind of commodification that modern tourism demands. Erve Chambers usefully notes that the question of authenticity in tourism is often misguided insofar as we assume that "the real is a thing of the past" or that the past is "more real" than the present. Instead of using an imagined past ideal as the measure of present authenticity, Chambers emphasizes the ever-changing nature of culture and the degree of autonomy a community has over deciding those changes (or deciding to resist change). As he puts it, "Without significant degrees of autonomy, any notion of authenticity is meaningless." This focus on autonomy as a criterion for authenticity opens up the view that, for example, "a community that has the ability to decide to tear down all its historic buildings in order to construct a golf course for tourists is more authentic than is another community that is prohibited by higher authorities from doing the same thing in order to preserve the integrity of its past."[2] While this example might strike us as extreme—even scandalous—the move away from the assumption that preserving the past always enhances authenticity and, in contrast, serving the present always threatens authenticity helps clear the ideological ruts that commonly clog discussions of traditional culture in modern times. Declaring, as the prefectural government did, that Okinawa will be Japan's "Tourism Prefecture" implicates Okinawa in the active transformation of Okinawan culture and identity within a national framework, often against the will of individuals who fear the erosion of natural landscapes and "traditional" local practices in the face of beach resort development and the theme-parkization of Ryukyuan history and culture as Okinawan heritage tourism. One might still rightfully deplore resort development and commodified culture, but to do so out of hand on the grounds that such activity is necessarily inauthentic (i.e., "bad") obscures the complex relationship among cultural production, tourism development, and consumer capitalism and slights the question of local autonomy and subjectivity. In fact, it limits local actors to only one "authentic" role, that of resisters to development and change, often, ironically, at the behest of outsiders.

The imbroglio of authenticity, tradition, and consumer capitalism—emblematic of the modern condition in general—stands out sharply in tourism, making tourism an especially rich field of inquiry into the production and consumption of historical and cultural identity. The symbolic dimension of commodities is highly charged in tourism, which explicitly attaches commodified meanings to material objects, places, and experiences to promote the rationalization of tourism as a self-enriching, value-added experience of "history," "culture," and "nature"—a triad that is especially prominent in Okinawa tourism. Indeed, the material goods of tourist consumption are commonly valued more as signs and symbols than as material objects in and of themselves. Symbolic content, in turn, is seldom fixed; it is produced between the intentions of hosts and the desires of guests and is changeable through consumption. Nevertheless, some signs, through repetition and dissemination in mass media, accrue commonly understood meanings verging on cliché. The word "Okinawa" itself has stood for different things to different people over time; for most mainland Japanese visitors, it has increasingly shifted from a sign of "tragic war history" to a sign of "tropical paradise" while maintaining the connotation of "U.S. bases" and, by association, "foreign" or "not entirely Japanese."

The sign that has been hanging from the ceiling of the baggage claim area of Naha International Airport's impressive new domestic terminal (opened in May 1999) greets visitors with a panoply of present-day clichés of (Tourist) Okinawa, but it would have been unimaginable before the Asia-Pacific War, or even before Okinawa's reversion to Japan in 1972 after twenty-seven years of U.S. occupation (see figure P.1). Where a domestic Japanese traveler would normally see *yōkoso* (welcome), this sign uses the Okinawan word *mensōre* written in hiragana script above its English equivalent, "welcome," thus signaling two sources of "foreign." The word is framed in the background by what have become visual icons of Okinawa: tropical fish, tropical flora (palm trees and hibiscus most prominent), sea shells, billowing clouds, Shuri Castle's famed Shureimon (Gate of Courtesy), and an early modern Chinese tribute ship. The English word is flanked by cartoony hands while one of the flowers, a hibiscus, stands out red in the foreground. The impossibility of this sign in prewar Okinawa lies in the immense historical gap between then and now, a period cleaved by the war and the subsequent U.S. occupation. The political, economic, and sociocultural conditions in prewar Okinawa precluded the imagination's producing—and consuming—this sign. The public use of Okinawan language, embodied in the greeting *mensōre*, was circumscribed under the assimilation policies of Imperial Japan before becoming outright criminalized during the war.[3] Whether judged a separate language or a dialect of Japanese, any of the many forms of Okinawan spoken throughout

**Figure P.1.** "*Mensōre*, Welcome to Okinawa!" sign in baggage claim area of Naha International Airport. *Source*: Gerald Figal.

the Ryukyu Islands were, like dialects in provincial mainland Japan, marks of backwardness, of a premodern past, that were not yet packaged as exotic and nostalgic tourist product.

Similarly, the gesture toward Okinawa's premodern relationship with China, embodied by the tribute vessel and Shureimon (originally built in the early fifteenth century to greet Chinese envoys on their way to Shuri Castle), would have fallen flat as a tourism advertisement to the mainland Japanese. In fact, it would likely have been viewed as suspicious if not unpatriotic since it implied something less than Japan's exclusive claims to the Ryukyus. On the other hand, U.S. political and cultural policy in Okinawa during occupation highlighted the Ryukyus' historical and cultural ties to China, its existence as an independent kingdom before Japan's annexation of it in 1879, and its peripheral status within Imperial Japan. Ironically, this American distancing of Okinawa from Japan—and exoticization represented by the U.S. military presence itself—would lay the groundwork for an important strand in the marketing of the place during the "Okinawa boom" of the late 1980s and early 1990s, when the trappings of the Ryukyu Kingdom were fashionable in the wake of the Japan Travel Bureau's "Exotic Japan" domestic tourism campaign and in the midst of Japan's rediscovery of non-Japanese Asia. The Japan

Broadcasting Corporation's (NHK) 1992–1993 television drama *Ryūkyū no kaze* (Winds of the Ryukyus, discussed in chapter 4) marked the height of this boom and introduced to many Japanese for the first time Okinawa's "Chinese past," complete with a full-scale replica of a Chinese vessel and a re-creation of the Chinese settlement of Kume on Okinawa Island. All Nippon Airways (ANA), owner of major beach resorts in Okinawa, was among the prominent advertisers tied to *Ryūkyū no kaze,* and it ran one print ad in conjunction with the television program that ends with an invitation to discover this foreign past within Okinawa: "It's the Ryukyu Spirit itself that allows you to sense a new Okinawa because it reveals to you the Okinawa you didn't know until now." "The Okinawa you didn't know until now" begs the question, What Okinawa was known until now?

Although known for its verdurous subtropical flora, the landscape of Okinawa Island did not exist in prewar popular Japanese imagination as a tropical paradise of swaying palm trees and Hawaiian-like hibiscus highlighted on the "Welcome to Okinawa" sign in baggage claim. On the contrary, it was imagined as a forbidding environment full of tropical disease and poisonous snakes. Tall palm trees did not exist natively on Okinawa Island, and hibiscus were associated with graves. The *sotetsu* (*Cycas revoluta*, a type of cycad) was probably the most common floral image, made famous in the phrase *sotetsu jigoku* (sotetsu hell) when desperate Okinawans turned to boiling the plant's potentially poisonous pulp for sustenance during the lean years following the 1920–1921 sugar market crash that hollowed out Okinawa's principal source of prewar revenue. In general, the positive tropicality—sunbathing, swimming, and scuba diving—symbolized in the welcome sign would have struck prewar Japanese (and prewar Okinawans as well) as alien. The most well-known sea-related image of Okinawa then was arguably the fishermen of Itoman and their wives, the object of study for researchers intrigued by the distinctive political economy of the Itoman fisher community. In the context of such prewar studies of Okinawan society—including the "dialect debate" among scholars during the interwar period[4]—and in the interest taken from the mid-1920s to renovate cultural properties attached to the Shuri Castle complex and designate them National Culture Treasures, accounts of the islands by well-heeled travelers, anthropologists, and ethnographers had begun to circulate an appreciation of Okinawa's natural and cultural assets by the 1930s, when passenger steamship service was expanded before being abruptly abandoned upon the outbreak of war. After the war, a growing number of middle-class Japanese tourists by the 1960s began to desire "Tropical Paradise Okinawa," but such a place existed only in the most vivid imaginations and in the most ambitious tourism development plans. Not until considerable Japanese capital investment from mainland-based companies from the mid-1970s did these tropical dreams—for better or for worse—find meager manifestations in reality. Tellingly, much of the early tourism promotion produced within Okinawa was directed toward Okinawans themselves, who could scarcely believe that their war-scarred, militarized, and generally poor island could possess any appeal for outside visitors. By the early twenty-first century, however, Okinawa Island and its neighboring smaller islands had become the tourist destination of choice for nearly 6 million visitors per year by 2010, over 95 percent of whom hailed from the mainland and returned home with gifts, photos, and memories of Okinawa as tropics.[5] This postwar tropicalization of the Okinawan landscape within a growing hospitality industry forms a central object of analysis of this study.

What is notably absent from the tropicalia and Ryukyuania of the "Welcome to Okinawa" sign that greets these visitors from the mainland is any sign of Okinawa's significant war history and continuing U.S. military presence. They are, however, present in their absence as the negative space that foregrounds positive highlights. War history has produced peace tours; military bases have spawned palm trees. Given the abundance of battle sites and war memorials on Okinawa Island, war history is difficult to ignore completely, even if the focus is on beaches and not beachheads. Present-day Tourist Okinawa incorporates this prominent aspect of the local landscape, but in contrast to the earliest tourism promotion in Okinawa, it does so in highly circumscribed ways. War history is physically and narratively contained in typical mainstream tour packages. Promotional literature generally caters to images of the Battle of Okinawa preexistent among mainland Japanese (if they know about the battle at all), although actual on-site presentations at war-related destinations might nowadays confound rather than confirm these images. In other words, local manifestations of war history and memory can create dissonance with prestructured tour "packages." Canned war history starts to leak. Still, war memorials—the founding landmarks of early tourism to Okinawa examined in the first part of this book—are no longer featured among the flashy signs, posters, and pamphlets dominated by tropical tropes and reveries of Ryukyu.

Officially, the sixteen U.S. military installations that cover about 18 percent of Okinawa Island do not exist in Tourist Okinawa. Unofficially, they have been among the most popular tourist attractions since the 1960s. Met with pressure from antibase activists and tempered by a sense of propriety, the Okinawa tourism industry has understandably been reticent to promote bases openly as tourist sights despite manifest interest in them. Yet such a prominent physical presence in the central section of Okinawa Island easily falls within the tourist gaze and becomes part of the experience and identity of the place that is related to the folks back home. Tour bus guide and taxi driver narratives deliver short histories, statistics, and anecdotes about the bases; some stop at Anpo no Oka (Japan-U.S. Security Treaty Hill) on the perimeter of Kadena Air Base to watch jet landings and takeoffs; some mingle among (or gawk at) U.S. military personnel and their families at the "American Village" shopping and entertainment district; some shop at the many military surplus stores on the island for that unique Okinawa souvenir (ammo cartridges, dog tags, unit insignia patches, Zippo lighters, bomber jackets, aviator shades, camouflage mini-tees); and thousands participated in the annual festivities of Open Base Day on Kadena Air Base before the event was temporarily suspended post-9/11. Further from the public eye, there are also nonmainstream guidebooks to base town brothels written for mainland Japanese men and nightclubs known to attract Japanese women seeking to meet American men.[6] In spite of the official line on the bases, which does not include them in the tourist landscape, they and their personnel remain de facto attractions and another instance of the war's impact on the production and consumption of Tourist Okinawa. In the same turn, U.S. military personnel in their off-base leisure time form a special class of tourists, a class not recognized in most industry statistics but one that nonetheless must be reckoned with. Thus, the last part of this book takes up bases and beach resorts together as sites/sights of occupation.

The gateway for virtually all of those millions who annually visit Okinawa now is the Naha International Airport's domestic terminal. Accordingly, I introduce it here following Chambers's observation that terminals are "among the best places to confront the confluence between the universal and the particular. They are built to accommodate travelers who might not be familiar with local customs or values, and yet they invariably reflect the places of their origin."[7] Beyond the encapsulation of "Okinawa" represented in the baggage claim area welcome sign, the entire terminal offers a prelude to present-day Tourist Okinawa, deserving at least a thumbnail analysis. It demonstrates a sometimes concordant, sometimes discordant overlapping of international standards, Japanese expectations, and local initiative and "color." Pausing to take a quick glance at the airport terminal presents us with an appetizer for this book's main course, Okinawa's transformation from battle site into tourist site, or, more generally, its transformation from *place* into *destination* in the aftermath of war.[8]

Unlike any other domestic airport terminal in Japan, Naha's is ethnically themed as if it were on quasi-foreign territory, which, in a sense, it is. In fact, the *domestic* terminal strikes the user as much more like an *international* terminal in the manner it greets travelers. In contrast, the sorely neglected international terminal (the old domestic terminal) makes little effort to distinguish itself for the relatively small (but lately increasing) numbers of travelers it handles from Taipei, Shanghai, Hong Kong, Seoul, and, since 2011, Beijing. This ethnic theming that is aimed at mainland Japanese partakes in and goes beyond the display of local arts, crafts, performances, foodstuffs, and natural assets that make up the *meibutsu*, or "famous things," that are commonly showcased as souvenirs and tourist attractions as well as badges of regional identity in cities, towns, villages, regional airports, and train stations throughout Japan. Within the usual structure of *meibutsu* marketing that decades if not centuries of Japanese tourists have come to expect, Naha's airport terminal—and Okinawa at large—inserts an ethnic element in the form of "Ryukyuan" to mark a special difference (the particular) within Japanese citizenship and nationhood (the universal in this context).[9] Other marks of cultural otherness within the familiarity of the Japanese exist for tourist consumption in Okinawa—most notably the foregrounding of *champuru*, or "mixed," culture stemming as much from the postwar American presence as from Ryukyu Kingdom trading contacts with China and Southeast Asia—but it is the suggestion of ethnic difference indexed to the history and culture of an independent, pre-Japanese Ryukyu Kingdom that forms the core of Okinawa's distinct and marketable "heritage." In short, heritage and heritage tourism in contemporary Okinawa mean "Ryukyu."[10] Ryukyu signifies "traditional Okinawa." But "Ryukyu" and "Ryukyuan" are signifiers with complex and contested histories, which have been at the heart of cultural politics in modern Okinawa. Carrying a derogatory nuance of "not quite Japanese" (i.e., uncivilized) in Imperial Japan, these terms were resuscitated by Okinawans in the late twentieth century as signs of regional identity and ethnic nationalism.[11] In the time between, they were the terms—instead of "Okinawa" and "Okinawans"—that U.S. authorities insisted on using during their occupation, while, as the Reversion movement grew in the late 1960s, pro-Reversion Okinawans insisted on calling the territory "Okinawa Prefecture."[12] None of this ambiguity of things Ryukyuan comes across in the airport terminal today because of the aestheticization and commodification of "Ryukyu" into the "Ryukyuesque." In other words, within the marketing spectacle that welcomes and sends off travelers in the terminal, Ryukyu exists as a consumer cultural product, not as overt political statement.

And yet, that Naha Airport is ethnically themed—even as object of consumer desire—when other Japanese airports are not is noteworthy. Placed in that larger national context and linked to other assertions of local voice and color in the 1990s, the political message of Naha's airport terminal begins to emerge. The planning, construction, and opening of the new domestic terminal paralleled the governorship of Ōta Masahide (1990–1998), who was a strong proponent of enhancing Okinawa's local political and economic autonomy while raising awareness of Okinawan history and culture (and raising the political hackles of Tokyo in the process). He saw U.S. base reduction and Okinawa tourism development, among other initiatives, as means to these larger ends. While unsuccessful in realizing his vision of the airport as a true regional hub less dependent on mainland connections and a Tokyo-based tourist industry, he excelled at promoting at least the veneer of an independent identity in public projects like the airport that showcased local form and content.[13] Quotations of the Ryukyu limestone ramparts of Shuri Castle, the seat of the premodern Ryukyu Kingdom, are prominent throughout the terminal, as are images of the rebuilt castle itself, which opened to visitors in 1992 (the topic of chapter 4). Similar "neo-Ryukyuesque" architecture is taken to greater degrees in two of Ōta's major pet projects: the new Peace Memorial Museum (opened on April 1, 2000, two years after the end of his tenure as governor) and the Okinawa Prefectural Archives, a gorgeous facility opened in 1995 upon which much of this book depends. A scholar before a politician, Ōta put much attention into establishing the museum and archives and spared no expense wrapping modern amenities and the latest technology in local color. Also a survivor of the Battle of Okinawa, he took personally the founding of a distinctively Okinawan contribution to World War II memorialization, the Heiwa no Ishiji (Cornerstone of Peace) monument that is adjacent to the museum in the Peace Memorial Park at Mabuni, site of the last organized resistance against U.S. forces on the southern tip of Okinawa Island in June 1945.[14] While recently built edifices such as Naha's new domestic terminal, the Okinawa Prefectural Archives, the Peace Memorial Museum, and Shuri Castle Park physically connote Ryukyu as Okinawan heritage, war/peace memorial sites such as the Cornerstone of Peace join a long and tangled postwar history of trying to represent the particularity of Okinawan relationships to the war. What links these different forms of asserting local identity is the self-conscious attempt to present difference from mainland Japan, and this is where their political dimension emerges. The extra labor and money spent on emulating Ryukyu limestone and laying costly red-tiled roofs are investments in cultural political capital. They serve to remind Tokyo that Okinawa does have its own peoples, histories, and cultures, even as they have been subject to assimilationist policies and a militarization not of their own making. The "foreignness" that greets Japanese travelers in Naha Airport's domestic terminal thus operates on at least two levels: it is cultural exotica served to fascinate and cash in on that fascination but also a mark of historical visions and political ambitions.

By no means is everything in the terminal's gift shops, restaurants, and design elements cast as Ryukyuesque; many treats, trinkets, and decorations are variations on common themes, particularly the tropical. But against the bland backdrop of globalized travel standards, ethnicized items stand out: from *sātā andagī* (Okinawan donuts) and *awamori* (Okinawan liquor) to the *ufujishi* (Okinawan lions) and Ryukyu dance performers (ending, of course, with "Toshin doi") that greet visitors in the central Welcome Hall.[15] Such items are verbally and visually identified with the Ryukyu Kingdom period qua traditional Okinawa, much in the same way as items from Tokugawa-period Japan (1603–1868) are commonly taken as the content of "traditional Japan." In most cases they are domesticated for the mainland audience—song and dance performances in the Welcome Hall are medleys of excerpts, ranging from slow-paced court dance to fast-paced popular dance adapted from the repertoire used to greet Chinese envoys; lyrics of songs are largely translated into standard Japanese, with just a dash of local language to give it flavor; local foods for sale as souvenirs and immediate sustenance are those made most palatable to mainland tongues. This tailoring of the form and content of local cultural production for tourist consumption has been one of the most debated issues within tourism studies in general and the principal focus of questions of authenticity. Okinawa's case is no different in this regard, but debating whether such cultural products set before the tourist gaze are "authentically" Ryukyuan or not misses much of the point. Their importance lies in their symbolic value as signifiers of a Ryukyuan past that is on display and for sale while they also function as sources of local historical, cultural, and political identity. If, as signifiers, they are successful in making the association with the Ryukyu Kingdom, then they are on that level "authentic." Asserting local identity while serving consumer tastes might appear to be a regrettable compromise for the former, but it might also be the only way to construct and circulate widely any sense of identity in a "posttraditional" consumer culture.

Signifiers of (post)traditional Okinawa as Ryukyu, however, compete with those more clearly fabricated from sources nonspecific to the place. Grafted onto the Ryukyuesque in the terminal and throughout tourist areas in Okinawa is the tropical in the form of clichés internationally popularized by Hawaiian and South Seas travel. After the fish, palm trees, and hibiscus of the baggage claim area sign, one encounters a large aquarium of real tropical fish and planters of live tropicalesque flora bordering walkways. The Welcome Hall itself features several tall nonnative palm trees that flank the area where the welcoming dances take place. Indeed, the Naha Airport website ends its description of the Welcome Hall by pointing out that "palm trees tower over this expansive space, allowing you to savor the atmosphere of tropical [*nangoku* = literally, 'south country'] Okinawa."[16] Before Ryukyu Kingdom Okinawa became hip, *Nangoku* Okinawa ruled, and it still strongly shapes the Okinawan touristscape. As the second section of this study documents, the first concerted efforts at reshaping Okinawa for tourism in the early 1960s involved looking to Hawaii and listening to mainland Japanese who desired a more "*nangoku* feel" to the place. *Nangoku*—the Japanese word most frequently used in Okinawa tourism promotion to signify "tropical"—goes beyond simply gesturing to Hawaii and its booming international tourism of the 1960s.[17] In the Japanese case, a more literal rendering of "south country/island" (that is, south sea islands) comes into geographical play and raises questions about the image of the south sea islands of the former Empire of Japan. Both as a launch point of the empire's southern colonial expansion and a nostalgic vestige of its loss, *Nangoku* Okinawa unintentionally evokes memories of wartime geography and landscape as it conjures images of serene tropical scenery. The literally constructed nature of the tropical in Okinawa comes to the fore once one recognizes the extent to which tropical flora nonnative to Okinawa (which is technically in a subtropical climate zone) has been increasingly used in Okinawan landscapes, especially in tourist-exposed areas, over the last forty years. But the issue of authenticity has even reached flora. As I discuss in chapter 3, the Greenery Promotion Division of the prefectural government is currently attempting to re-create in certain areas the flora of the Ryukyu Kingdom, ironically using the catalog of botanicals and preserved specimens Commodore Matthew C. Perry's mission gathered during its sojourn in the Ryukyus on the way to Japan in 1853. Thus, the identification of Okinawan heritage with Ryukyu comes to embrace historical, cultural, and natural assets—or at least some of them.

Like the welcome sign, travel posters, brochures, and Okinawa tourism websites, the airport terminal does not acknowledge war history or the island's militarization as part of Okinawa's identity or "heritage." In fact, Okinawa's modern history since annexation to Japan in 1879 is difficult to find on explicit display among the gift shops, restaurants, banners, and design elements throughout the terminal unless one considers the modern inventions of traditional Okinawa as such. The absence of signs of imperial subjectification, war, and militarization from representations of Okinawa is unsurprising but striking given that historical discrimination under Imperial Japan, unique wartime experience, and the postwar burden of U.S. bases are central to claims of difference and identity from the rest of Japan. This erasure is reflected writ large in what constitutes cultural heritage tourism throughout Okinawa. Of course, displays of Okinawa's modern and war-related history exist—most notably at the Prefectural Peace Memorial Museum, the Himeyuri Peace Memorial Museum, and among the many memorial sites discussed in part 1 of this study—but they are never identified in tourism promotion as part of Okinawa's "heritage," as what makes up Okinawan cultural and historical identity. With rare exception, Okinawa's war legacies are treated as anomalies imposed by outsiders, not as part of the contemporary cultural fabric that they have arguably become. Thus, while peaceful relations with outsiders during the Ryukyu Kingdom period dominate the rhetoric of Okinawa's heritage, wartime relations with outsiders are accorded a separate status in mainstream tourism promotion. Only in pockets of turbulence at the edges of the mainstream do the war and its legacies bubble up.

When flying into Naha Airport in June 1995, I experienced some of this war-related turbulence although I didn't know it at the time. At a notably far distance from the airport, we were approaching the island at an unusually low altitude. Whitecaps were not exactly lapping at the plane's underbelly, but it seemed as if one could almost touch the East China Sea below. The view was stunning, clearly intended, I thought, to whet the appetite of the tourists onboard. As we headed down the east coast of Okinawa Island, the recently built beach resort compounds that anchor Onna Village's coastline came conspicuously into view, followed a few minutes later by the signal light towers that emanate from the departure end of Kadena Air Base, cross the main north-south artery, Route 58, and gesture over the East China Sea. If commercial jets from Japan approached any higher, they would be directly in the flight path of jets taking off from Kadena. The low approach, which I thought might have been designed to benefit the view of airline passengers, was actually the product of airspace control agreements negotiated between the U.S. and Japanese governments upon Okinawa's reversion to Japan in May 1972. U.S. control of Okinawan territory ascended into the space above, up to 6,096 meters in a 92.6-kilometer radius from Kadena Air Base, bending the flight paths of commercial aircraft unless they expressly request permission from the Radar Approach Control (RAPCON) at Kadena Air Base to enter U.S.-controlled airspace.[18] The procedure pilots and air traffic controllers must follow to get commercial flights in and out of Naha Airport in coordination with Kadena RAPCON are complicated, potentially confusing, and have, according to one report, led to about 40 percent of Naha air traffic controllers experiencing "hair-raising experiences" every year.[19] Unbeknownst to most travelers, such restricted and fragile conditions under which tourism in Okinawa exists today epitomize the conditions under which it and Okinawa in general have developed historically since the end of the war. That invisibly distorted flight path—now depositing nearly 6 million Japanese tourists per year onto a tarmac shared by Japanese Self-defense Forces aircraft and channeling them into an anomaly of a domestic air terminal—can well be taken as a metaphor for the not-so-obvious impacts of war legacies and the attempts to cope with them in postwar Okinawa. When Okinawa welcomed me that first time in June 1995, I barely sensed the depth of these impacts and the extent of the scaffolding behind what I saw. Where does wartime end and peacetime begin? Where does Okinawa blur into Tourist Okinawa and back again?

Having been there and back again several times since 1995, I now aim to make some sense of the connections among war, peace, and tourism in postwar Okinawa. As I conceive of it, a multidimensional study of the formation of Tourist Okinawa brings into tight focus interrelated issues of historical and cultural self-representation, local political autonomy, economic sustainability, interregional and international relations, and Okinawa's role as a global "cornerstone of peace" while it burdens under the legacies of war. Taking a broad definition of tourism, this book encompasses war/peace tourism, cultural heritage tourism, and beach resort tourism, which have proliferated in postwar Okinawa. It also considers U.S. military bases and personnel as tourist sights. From this perspective, the development of tourism—at old battlefields, new beach resorts, and restored sites of premodern Ryukyu culture—becomes an effective object through which to examine contemporary Okinawa's relationship to and use of its wartime past and militarized present, its premodern heritage, and its natural resources. My effort here draws on insights derived from the theory and practice of tourism studies as developed largely among anthropologists and sociologists, but grounds itself within a historical framework often lacking in analyses of contemporary tourism. It also benefits from secondary work across several disciplines within Okinawa studies, an area studies field that has rapidly been coming into its own in recent years. Both Japanese- and English-language research in the history, anthropology, sociology, economics, politics, art, music, and literature of Okinawa inform this present work, but the heart of it is formed around archival research and fieldwork conducted largely from that first visit in June 1995 to June 2004, with one last brief trip in November 2009 to visit newly established war memory sites. The sensorial, performative, and material aspects of tourism are difficult to reproduce adequately within traditional publishing formats, but I have done what I can through the reproduction of images, original photos, and rich textual descriptions. Like popular culture in general, tourism is full of ephemera, a fact that becomes more apparent when a study of it goes beyond the present (which is too often ahistorically generalized into the past). What has come and gone—or never materialized—in Okinawa tourism over the past sixty years tells a history of hopes and frustrations, dreams and schemes, creativity and catastrophes. Certain tropes—such as "bloody battle site" and "tropical paradise"—have had, however, longer lives, although they too have changed in form over time. It is this change over time—this history of transformation of Okinawa the place into Okinawa the destination—that we must acknowledge and contemplate before generalizing from the present scene.

To capture this sense of history across the multiple dimensions manifested in Okinawa tourism, I have adopted a generally chronological organization over three thematic parts comprised of two chapters each. That said, this is a book of short stories as much as it is of a larger narrative. These short stories sometimes parallel the larger chronology as they advance it and can perhaps be read as discrete essays. The whole, however, is, I hope, greater than the sum of its parts. By no means do I intend this work to be a comprehensive history of postwar Okinawa or even a comprehensive history of tourism development in postwar Okinawa. Rather, these are historical analyses and contemporary critiques of how issues of war and peace have shaped Okinawa's identity as a tourist destination and how tourism development has dealt with war history and peace promotion as it puts forth a marketable product. What drives much of the smaller stories and overarching narrative that follow is the inherent tension in trying to fashion an attractive destination from a place that harbors a horrific war history and everyday reminders of that history in the form of battlefield ruins, monuments, memorial rites, refugee caves, the bereaved, and the continued presence of the foreign military who conquered the place in 1945. Big plans and little money form a secondary motif in the story of early tourism in Okinawa, while big money and little planning emerge as a motif in the story of later decades.

Part 1, "Graves and Caves," begins among the ruins wrought by war. Its two chapters excavate the foundations of Okinawa tourism—pilgrimages to battle sites, war ruins, and memorials. Not long after the American occupation of mainland Japan ended in 1952, Japanese veterans and the bereaved began visiting landmarks of the Battle of Okinawa, particularly the memorial markers (*irei-tō*) and ossuaries (*nōkotsu-dō*) that Okinawans had set up out of necessity since the end of war. Many of these memorials originated as mass grave sites established during cleanup of areas on the southern end of Okinawa to which U.S. authorities had relocated locals in order to clear the way for base construction in the central area of the island. The growing popularity of such pilgrimages throughout the 1950s and into the 1960s catalyzed the growth of a nascent tourism infrastructure. It also led to the gradual commercialization (secularization) of memorial sites considered sacred, one of the major points of controversy surrounding the transformation of war memorials into tourist sites. Another major point of controversy tied to the growth of battle site tours is the representation of the war at memorials, by tour guides, and in related literature. The physical path taken; the form, content, and authorship of monuments and memorial practices; the framing of the tour by guides and governing authorities; the use of the site; and the way visitors consume it all figure in how the war is represented and remembered. Part 1 concludes by following from the end of the war to the present the fate of caves that have been objects of historical and archeological study, tourist fascination, war dead enshrinement, and peace promotion.

Emerging from the graves and caves of part 1, part 2, "Creations and Recreations," details aspects of Okinawa's makeover and branding as "tropical paradise" and "Ryukyu Kingdom." These transformations have both physical and discursive dimensions. It doesn't do simply to call subtropical Okinawa "tropical"; it must look it and feel it. Here is where practical postwar reforestation programs merged with the interests of a mainland Japanese tourism industry that aimed to turn Okinawa into "Japan's Hawaii" and largely succeeded in convincing local interests to follow suit. The creation of a tropical image involved replanting sections of Okinawa Island with imported tropicalesque plants, most notably palm trees and exotic flowers, while redefining the cultural meaning of existing flora, most prominently the hibiscus. Landscape—natural and cultural—underwent dramatic changes that began in the 1960s and rapidly accelerated in the wake of Reversion and the Japanese investment that came with it. Tropical tropes did not determine all such landscaping in Okinawa, but it was the dominant trope put forth as the public persona of Okinawa's natural environment, as what defined the place as a destination. The "paradise" part of "tropical paradise" has been a harder sell. Wartime devastation—physical and emotional—was more than a memory in postwar Okinawa. Indeed, for some people, "postwar" was and still is a misnomer given the abiding effects of the Battle of Okinawa. Not only did Okinawa Island require vast rebuilding and reforestation, but the ensconced U.S. military presence there did not connote paradise. Even looking past U.S. bases and the problems they have brought, "paradise" means more than palm trees, hibiscus, and beaches to the modern tourist. It means combining an escape from the bustle of modern life with a level of fairly priced modern accommodation that has often fallen short in the opinion of Japanese tourists to Okinawa. Whether it be transportation infrastructure, hotel service, cuisine, local souvenirs, or general guest amenities, overcoming deficiencies in Okinawa's fledgling hospitality industry proved challenging. Before training to host and serve travelers on vacation, most Okinawans needed convincing that their poor and war-torn home could approximate a "paradise" as outsiders might envision it. Once that was accomplished, the best-intentioned plans could go unrealized for want of money. A dearth of capital and U.S. restrictions on Japanese investment in Okinawa before Reversion hamstrung the fulfillment of both the tropical and the paradisiacal. Post-Reversion, the problem became too much Japanese capital investment, government subsidies, and the strings back to Tokyo that came with them. "Tropical paradise" could now be funded, but at what cost to local autonomy and identity?

Part 2 ends with an analysis of the assertions of local autonomy and identity through cultural heritage tourism that has attempted to coexist with the touristic tropical. Shurijō Kōen (Shurijo Castle Park),[20] the main section of which opened in 1992 on the site of the old castle, resuscitates the history and culture of the Ryukyu Kingdom and is now the heart of Okinawa heritage tourism. A full-scale replica of the seat of government for the unified kingdom as it existed in the early eighteenth century rather than as it existed just prior to its wartime destruction, it represents a self-conscious attempt to recapture and display the glory of Ryukyu while downplaying the castle's ignominious modern history. The NHK television drama series *Ryūkyū no kaze* cited above and several other Ryukyu theme parks also aid and abet this "Ryukyu restoration." The latter often feature "living history" or "living museum" exhibits pitched to offer a live experience of *furusato* (old village, hometown) Okinawa. The entire small island of Taketomi in the Yaeyama Islands of the southern Ryukyus (taken up briefly in the epilogue) is also usefully considered a kind of living museum (and theme park) by virtue of the community's decision to preserve within everyday life the look and feel of traditional homes and gardens. The problem of including outlying Taketomi within the Ryukyu/Okinawa cultural and political orbit notwithstanding, it exists in tourist literature and by reputation as the best place to experience authentic "Okinawaness."

In contrast, while the U.S. military presence in Okinawa is commonly treated as a distinguishing trait of the place, it is predictably discounted as part of "Okinawaness." This issue occupies the first half of part 3. Here I demonstrate the long-standing tourist appeal of the U.S. military in Okinawa, from the spectacle of the bases and their hardware to the personnel themselves. While such fascination is often parlayed into advancing education about Okinawa's situation as principal host to U.S. forces in Japan, it also carries consequences for Okinawa's reputation, inhabitants, and environment. Treating bases as tourist sights in turn opens the way to see high-end beach resorts as types of "bases"—established beachheads, if you will—that launch their own kind of invasion upon Okinawan physical and cultural space. Although their guests, like those at military bases, rotate in and out, the physical and institutional presence of beach resorts is, since the resort-building boom of the late 1980s and early 1990s, virtually permanent and ironically complements U.S. military installations.

Traversing this complex and varied territory winds together scarcely acknowledged connections among the material and discursive dimensions of war, peace, and tourism in postwar Okinawa. One surprising discovery is the depth of Okinawa tourism's dependency on its history of war and occupation even as tourism promotion has increasingly absented both from its view. Tourism's relationship to peace promotion is equally tangled. On the one hand, tourism has long been advertised as a "peace industry," one that fosters hospitable relations among hosts and guests and, in former war zones, serves to redeem wartime losses as well as to stimulate an ailing local economy. On the other hand, in its efforts to put on a perpetually happy face—especially for mainland Japanese tourists—Okinawa tourism has been open to criticisms that it willfully marginalizes or misrepresents the war, U.S. occupation, and the current militarized situation of Okinawa Island. The social, environmental, and even negative economic impact of steadily increasing tourism is also a target of criticism that ironically recalls, albeit in attenuated form, the devastations and displacements caused by war and occupation.

And yet, amid much gloom, the narrative that follows contains stories of economic growth, cultural revitalization, deep historical consciousness, and community action. To bash tourism development in Okinawa as an unmitigated blight or to embrace it uncritically as an unproblematic panacea fails to appreciate the historical conditions, political regimes, and consumer capitalism under which Okinawa has labored. Such extremes also blinker us from what makes a study of tourism in postwar Okinawa so fascinating: the built-in tensions, messy compromises, and unresolved ambiguities that are sure signs of real structures rubbing up against real subjectivities and vice versa. Viewed in this light, even the "Welcome to Okinawa" sign in Naha Airport's baggage claim begins to look authentic.

## NOTES

1. Glenn D. Hook and Richard Siddle, eds., *Japan and Okinawa: Structure and Subjectivity* (London: RoutledgeCurzon, 2003).

2. Erve Chambers, *Native Tours: The Anthropology of Travel and Tourism* (Prospect Heights, IL: Waveland Press, 2000), 98–99.

3. Alan Christy, "The Making of Imperial Subjects in Okinawa," *Positions: East Asia Cultures Critique* 1, no. 3 (1993).

4. See Hugh Clarke, "The Great Dialect Debate: The State and Language Policy in Okinawa," in Elise K. Tipton, ed., *Society and the State in Interwar Japan* (New York: Routledge, 1997), 193–217.

5. Tourism Policy Division, "2010 Nyū-iki kankōkyaku tōkei gaikyo," Okinawa Prefecture, http://www3.pref.okinawa.jp/site/view/contview.jsp?cateid=233&id=24177&page=1 (accessed July 20, 2011).

6. Linda Isako Angst, "In a Dark Time: Community, Memory, and the Making of Ethnic Selves in Okinawan Women's Narratives" (PhD diss., Yale University, 2001).

7. Chambers, *Native Tours,* 1.

8. At its most fundamental, tourism is about turning a place that locals use into a destination that nonlocals use in conjunction with locals who are now hosts as well as inhabitants. For discussions on the theory and practice of touristic transformations of place, especially with regard to cultural or heritage tourism, see, for example, Barbara Kirshenblatt-Gimblett, *Destination Culture: Tourism, Museums, and Heritage* (Berke-

ley and Los Angeles: University of California Press, 1998); Chris Rojek and John Urry, eds., *Touring Cultures: Transformations of Travel and Theory* (New York: Routledge, 1997); and what are now considered founding texts of tourism studies, Dean MacCannell, *The Tourist: A New Theory of the Leisure Class* (New York: Schocken Books, 1976; reprinted by University of California Press, 1999), and Valene L. Smith, *Hosts and Guests: The Anthropology of Tourism* (Philadelphia: University of Pennsylvania Press, 1977). Also of note in this context is John Urry's influential book *The Tourist Gaze: Leisure and Travel in Contemporary Societies* (London: Sage Publications, 1990; 2nd ed., 2002). On the construction of themed environments as tourist sights and more generally as consumerscapes, see Sharon Zukin, *Landscapes of Power: From Detroit to Disney World* (Berkeley and Los Angeles: University of California Press, 1991) and *The Cultures of Cities* (Cambridge, MA: Blackwell, 1995); and Mark Gottdiener, *The Theming of America: American Dreams, Media Fantasies, and Themed Environments* (Boulder, CO: Westview Press, 2001).

9. On the history and role of *meibutsu* in Japanese tourism, see Nelson H. Graburn, "The Past in the Present in Japan: Nostalgia and Neo-traditionalism in Contemporary Japanese Domestic Tourism," in Richard Butler and Douglas Pearce, eds., *Change in Tourism: People, Places, Processes* (New York: Routledge, 1995).

10. "Heritage tourism" has recently been one of the fastest growing areas of tourism. It is usually associated with tourist sites that focus on the particular history and culture of a locality, but expanded definitions also include local natural assets while stressing the preservation, restoration, and conservation of such community assets. The National Trust for Historic Preservation, pioneer in the promotion of heritage tourism in the United States, defines "cultural heritage tourism" as "traveling to experience the places, artifacts and activities that authentically represent the stories and people of the past and present. It includes cultural, historic and natural resources." See "Heritage Tourism," National Trust for Historic Preservation, http://www.preservationnation.org/issues/heritage-tourism (accessed September 15, 2010). So-called ethnic tourism—tours specifically aimed to "experience" other (typically "nonmodern") cultures, such as hill tribes of northern Thailand—is a notable subcategory of heritage tourism. The literature on heritage tourism is vast and growing fast, much of it being of the how-to variety. For a discussion of ethnic tourism in the Asia Pacific, see Michel Picard and Robert E. Wood, eds., *Tourism, Ethnicity, and the State in Asian and Pacific Societies* (Honolulu: University of Hawaii Press, 1997).

11. For a concise English-language discussion of Ryukyuan/Okinawan identity over time, see Koji Taira, "Troubled National Identity: The Ryūkyūans/Okinawans," in Michael Weiner, ed., *Japan's Minorities: The Illusion of Homogeneity* (New York: Routledge, 1997). Japanese-language studies of Okinawan identity vis-à-vis Japan abound; the most notable include Oguma Eiji, *"Nihonjin" no kyōkai: Okinawa, Ainu, Taiwan, Chōsen shokuminchi shihai kara fukki undō made* [Boundaries of the Japanese: Okinawa, Ainu, Taiwan, Korea from Colonial Rule to Reversion Movements] (Tokyo: Shinyōsha, 1997); Tomiyama Ichirō, *Kindai Nihon shakai to "Okinawajin": "Nihonjin" ni naru to yū koto* (Tokyo: Nihon Keizai Hyōronsha, 1990), and Tomiyama Ichirō, "The Critical Limits of the National Community: The Ryūkyūan Subject," *Social Science Japan Journal* 1, no. 2 (October 1998): 165–80. One accessible,

locally produced work on the topic is Okinawa Chiiki kagaku kenkyūjo, ed., *Okinawa no kenmin zō: Uchinanchu to wa nani ka* [A Portrait of Okinawans: What Are "Uchinanchu"] (Naha: Hirugisha, 1997).

12. For an English-language discussion of the buildup of the Reversion movement, see Christopher Aldous, "Achieving Reversion: Protest and Authority in Okinawa, 1952–70," *Modern Asian Studies* 37, no. 2 (2003): 485–508.

13. This focus on "veneer" is not to detract from Ōta's hardcore political actions, most notably his principled stance in going toe-to-toe with Tokyo over the issue of base leases.

14. For analyses of the Cornerstone of Peace and of the controversy surrounding the Peace Memorial Museum, see Gerald Figal, "Historical Sense and Commemorative Sensibility at Okinawa's Cornerstone of Peace," *Positions: East Asia Cultures Critique* 5, no. 3 (Winter 1997); "Waging Peace on Okinawa," in Laura Hein and Mark Selden, eds., *Islands of Discontent: Okinawan Responses to Japanese and American Power* (Lanham, MD: Rowman & Littlefield, 2003); and Julia Yonetani, "On the Battlefield of Mabuni: Struggles over Peace and the Past in Contemporary Okinawa," *East Asian History* 20 (December 2000): 145–69.

15. Video clips of the latter are available on the event gallery page of the Naha Airport website at http://www.naha-airport.co.jp/event (accessed July 20, 2011).

16. Op. cit.

17. *Nettai*, or "tropics," is a more specialized term used more often to describe climate zones, flora, and fauna, although it is also used at times to evoke "tropical" in general. The English word "tropical" and its Japanese form *toropikaru* are probably used in print media as much as *nangoku* in recent years.

18. A fifty-five-kilometer radius fifteen hundred meters high from Kume Island, due west about one hundred kilometers from Naha over the East China Sea, has also been under U.S. military air traffic control. It was made public on December 4, 2004, that the United States had agreed to return all air traffic control rights over Okinawa Prefecture to Japan by the end of fiscal year 2007. However, due to delays in the training of Japanese air controllers, the transfer was rescheduled for the end of March 2010. Demands for the return of airspace control heated up after a near miss between an Air Nippon plane and a U.S. fighter jet on February 4, 2000.

19. *Asahi Shimbun*, February 18, 2000, 36.

20. Despite the redundancy of "Shurijo" (Shuri Castle) and "Castle," that is the official English translation of the name. The macron is also left out over the "o."

# Part I

# GRAVES AND CAVES

# 1

# Tours among the Ruins

## THE MIGHT HAVE BEEN

Okinawa tourism was born in the ruins of war. In the immediate aftermath of the battle that put Okinawa Island on the map and in the minds of international observers, tropical leisure and rich cultural displays seemed unimaginable, even sacrilegious. Rather, what was palpably real and gave the place its identity was the massive destruction and loss of life that took place between April 1 and June 23, 1945, and dominated Okinawan social life well past the end of war. The American preinvasion bombardment of the island's west coast by an unprecedented support force of 564 carrier-based aircraft, 10 battleships, 9 cruisers, 23 destroyers, and 177 gunboats initiated the indiscriminate flattening of built and natural environments and the killing of the island's inhabitants and defenders.[1] The nearly three months of kill-or-be-killed engagement of approximately three hundred thousand U.S., Japanese, and Okinawan personnel further pummeled the pockmarked landscape south from the beachheads at Yomitan to the Kyan Peninsula (Suicide Cliff) at Mabuni, littering it with rubble, shattered coral, splintered trees, trampled cane fields, wrecked equipment, spent ammo shells, unexploded bombs, dead animals, and tens of thousands of rotting human bodies that transformed into hundreds of thousands of weather-bleached bones. One of the high-ranking Japanese survivors of the battle, senior staff officer Colonel Yahara Hiromichi, captured this cruel metamorphosis of southern Okinawa thus:

> When we first reached Mabuni, the area had received little war damage. There were only a few large ground craters where random bombs had fallen. The fields had still glistened with beautiful shades of green. Two weeks of fierce battle changed the scenery completely. Hills were flattened and reshaped by tanks and bombardments. It was now a wasteland, the darkened terrain exposing a gateway to hell.[2]

Kinjō Fumi, one of thousands of Okinawans who participated in postwar bone-collection campaigns initiated by her father and Mawashi Town mayor Kinjō Washin, remembered the landscape thus: "Corpses bleached by wind and rain were scattered all over along walls and roads and in fields and caves. We respectfully picked them up while clasping our hands together in prayer at one body after another."[3] While the northern half of the island was largely spared such destruction, the southern half of Okinawa Island was rendered a place of death and decay; it was here that Okinawa tourism would be born. It would take a radical reshaping of the island and recovery of the local population to fashion anything resembling a "tropical paradise" for leisure travel, but in the meantime battle site markers, grave sites, and monuments raised for the war dead attracted U.S. servicemen stationed in Okinawa and war veterans and bereaved family members from mainland Japan, the first appreciable tourists to postwar Okinawa.[4]

It did not have to be this way. There were signs that if not for the war and subsequent American occupation, Okinawa might have developed into a very different kind of destination for travelers from mainland Japan and possibly from other countries as well. From the time of the Ryukyu Kingdom's "disposal" (*Ryūkyū shobun*) and incorporation into the Japanese state as Okinawa Prefecture in 1879 to its falling into American hands in 1945, leisure travelers to Okinawa were relatively few, although steamship transport to Okinawa, mostly from the ports of Osaka, Kobe, and Kagoshima, steadily increased. Osaka Shōsen Kaisha (Osaka Mercantile Steamship Co.), founded in 1884, virtually monopolized shipping lines to and from Okinawa from 1885. From 1929, the *Shuri Maru*, named after Shuri Castle, was among the ships serving the Kagoshima-Naha route that had opened in 1916. It was in August 1937, however, that Osaka Shōsen introduced two new ships on a three-day, two-night Osaka-Naha route, which was explicitly tied into tourism-promotion campaigns. One of the ships, the *Naminoue Maru*, took its name from one of Okinawa's top famous places of the time. Articles on sightseeing in Okinawa conjointly appeared in journals such as the *Gekkan Ryūkyū* from 1937 to 1940, while the Osaka Shōsen publication *Okinawa e* (1939) described the "exoticism" of this "virgin territory for tourism" with its tropical fruit, potters, *sanshin* players, and curious dialect.[5] Before this concerted effort to draw leisure travelers to sightseeing in Okinawa, most traffic to and from the island was comprised of government officials, businessmen, and soldiers, while significant numbers of Okinawans left for urban areas in mainland Japan (Osaka in particular) and immigrated to spots outside Japan (Hawaii and North and South America in particular). Nevertheless, prewar academic interest in Okinawa's natural and cultural heritage and local boosterism by civic and business leaders led to the promotion of Ryukyu/Okinawa *meisho* (famous places) and the preservation of cultural assets. These were the seeds of what might have blossomed into full-scale tourism development by the 1960s when leisure travel began to reach the Japanese middle class and was hitting its stride internationally. But the war that reached the island in 1945 dispelled the possibility of this imagined trajectory.

Ethnologists such as Yanagita Kunio, who in 1920 trekked down the Ryukyu archipelago in search of the origins of human migration to mainland Japan, may not have been typical travelers, but they did raise awareness among Japanese of Okinawa's geography and cultural attributes beyond the general subjective perception of Okinawa as backward, premodern, and lacking in natural resources.[6] He and others who followed during the 1920s and 1930s helped shape popular images of Okinawa, but the best visual sense of prewar Okinawan *meisho* is obtained not from the likes of Yanagita, whose writing on Okinawa tends to abstract the landscape from its physical presence, but rather from the picture postcards produced then.[7] Many of these postcards existed in series explicitly labeled *Ryūkyū meisho* or *Okinawa meisho*.[8] Among premodern cultural properties, Shuri Castle and its environs, such as the nearby Ryūtan Pond, the Buddhist temple Enkakuji, and the Ryukyu royal prayer site Sono Hyan Utaki, figure prominently in such cards. So do the Ryukyu royal retreat park, Shikina, and the traditional Okinawan "turtleback" tombs that are more akin to Chinese rather than Japanese burial practices (and thus proved to be interesting sights for Japanese visitors). Atop a coral cliff above Wakasa beach on Naha's coast, Naminoue Shrine, one of the eight Ryukyu shrines and the only Japanese government–supported edifice in prewar Okinawa, held a central place in the mainland Japanese image-repertoire of Okinawa. Containing within its complex the Okinawa Go-kokuji (Protect-the-Nation Temple for the worship of those who died in Japan's wars), Naminoue was invariably one of the first stops of any mainland visitor before and after the Asia-Pacific War.[9] Consequently, Okinawa's first tourist hotels opened in the Naminoue area, which also hosted Naha's pleasure quarters in the nearby Tsuji district. Alongside premodern cultural properties, photos of government buildings that signified Okinawa's modernization and scenes of local markets and customs (*fūzoku*) that often seem to signify Okinawa's "primitive" authenticity if not "backwardness" make up other categories of popular postcards.

Notable among *fūzoku* postcards are those of "Okinawa Beauties" from the Tsuji district, suggesting a Japanese preoccupation with the food, drink, sex, and entertainment provided there. Images of Okinawan nature, such as the distinctive cliffs of Manzamō or specimens of subtropical flora, compose a final general category of the picture postcards a visitor might purchase. In most if not all of these instances it is clear that the fascination a particular scene captures issues from a mainland Japanese gaze. I hesitate to identify it fully as "the tourist gaze" as John Urry has developed the concept because of the ethnographic quality of some of these images that attempt to evoke a nontourist experience of the scene.[10] Still, these are images produced as enticements and mementos for mainland consumers in prewar Japan. With the exception of virtually unchangeable natural sites such as Manzamō, the image set of postwar Okinawa became radically different as a result of wartime devastation; images such as those mentioned above took on a cast of nostalgia and elegiac loss even in the cases of those whose subjects were rebuilt. It is no wonder that Nonomura Takao's edited volume of Yamasaki Masatada's photo record of his 1932 trip to Okinawa is titled *Natsukashiki Okinawa* (Nostalgic Okinawa). Yamasaki's own photos largely mimic picture postcards, the only main difference being that he is posed—in decidedly dapper, modern dress—in front the landmarks that his companion, *Kyūshū Nichi Nichi Shimbun* photographer Tsuru Taiichi, photographed.[11]

While published travel accounts, news reports, and postcards informally contributed to the formation of a canon of notable Okinawan landmarks, more formal actions to qualify certain sites as noteworthy within a Japanese national framework took place as well. Mainland scholars and government officials, under the 1897 Old Shrines and Temples Preservation Law and especially under its successor, the 1929 National Treasures Preservation Law, were keen on having historically and culturally significant Okinawan buildings and artifacts registered as Japanese National Treasures.[12] The principal instance of this type of *meisho* designation involved the Shuri Castle complex and nearby sacred sites, a topic I take up in detail in chapter 4. Just twelve years after seven items encompassing nineteen points were designated National Treasures and after the Main Hall (Seiden) of Shuri Castle was restored as Okinawa Shrine Worship Hall (Okinawa Jinja Haiden) in 1933, all were destroyed or severely damaged in the Battle of Okinawa. These same sites were among the first to be rebuilt, but they followed war memorials as the principal tourist attractions in the early postwar period. In other words, what conferred on Okinawa the status of "destination" was the product of the wartime transformation of the place: fields into battlefields, ground into sacred ground. It is in this grim geography that our stories of war, peace, and tourism in postwar Okinawa must properly begin.

## THE COLLECTION OF BONES AND CONSOLATION OF SPIRITS

"War memorial" connotes different images and ideas to different people (to the winners, the losers, Europeans, Americans, Asians), so it is important to make clear what it meant in early postwar Okinawa.[13] Although literal translations of "war memorial/monument" (*sensō kinenhi*; 戦争記念碑) and "war dead memorial" (*senbotsusha kinenhi*; 戦没者記念碑) exist, the most common Japanese word used to denote a marker for the war dead is *ireitō* (慰霊塔) or *irei-no-tō* (慰霊の塔), literally "spirit consolation tower."[14] In other words, the emphasis in the word *ireitō* is on a site for the consolation of the souls of the war dead rather than on the remembrance of war per se. This function took on special significance in Okinawa because it was the only site of a direct land engagement between Japanese and Allied forces in Japan's home islands (Okinawa's peripheral status therein notwithstanding), which left just over two hundred thousand dead combatants and noncombatants combined.[15] This fact has become an oft-repeated mantra in practically all claims to Okinawa's distinct historical experiences and in its self-promotion as an international "cornerstone of peace," which I discuss in the following chapter. Although comparative statistics are elusive, Okinawa can probably claim to have the largest number of war memorials per square kilometer on earth. On Okinawa Island alone there are over three hundred monuments to the war dead, ranging from elaborate marble art pieces constructed by mainland prefectures to simple roadside markers placed by locals.

As one of only 159 survivors of 385 students recruited into the Okinawa Normal School Student Imperial Blood and Iron Corps (*Tekketsu Kinnō Shihantai*; 鉄血勤皇師範隊) that fought alongside Japanese soldiers, university professor and former Okinawa governor Ōta Masahide has had a personal relationship with Okinawa's *ireitō*, especially the one—the Okinawa Shihan Kenji-no-tō—dedicated to his 289 fellow students and 18 staff members of Okinawa Normal School (Okinawa Shihan Gakkō) who died in battle as members of the Student Corps.[16] This personal experience and his longstanding academic interest in the Battle of Okinawa manifest themselves throughout his voluminous writings, which include a catalog of and reflection on Okinawa's war memorials. In the preface to this work, Ōta poses the question, "What does the consolation of spirits mean?" (*Irei to wa nani ka*).[17] Ideally, he states, it means to grant the spirits of the dead a peaceful resting place by expressing their remorse to later generations. In this sense, these war memorials act naturally as peace memorials, as does practically any grave where, for the souls of the dead, to "rest in peace" is the stated or unstated wish. This interpretation of *irei* is colored by Ōta's own politics and view of the war—namely, that the war is regrettable and Japanese should display remorse for it—and is clearly intended to counter displays of *irei* that imply the righteousness of Japan's war effort. He suggests that those who lived through the war easily understand the meaning of *irei* as an expression of remorse, although he is probably too quick to assume that all of those with direct war experience as well as die-hard patriots would naturally express remorse. Ōta is more concerned, however, about the future of war memorialization. Over the years, the meaning of *irei*—and of the war defeat itself—has changed for those whose experience of war is distant or lacking, so that mourning the war dead risks slipping into their patriotic celebration. This concern is the basis of Ōta's critique of the message that the mainland prefectural war memorials on Mabuni Hill impart in their general praise of the "heroic spirits" (*eirei*) who died in service of the emperor. He extends this critique to his principal concern—the relative disregard for the deaths of Okinawan civilians, which the focus on the patriotic memorialization of Japanese military war dead implies. To understand the proper historical meaning embodied in the war memorials scattered across Okinawa, to try to appreciate the changing connotations of *irei*, one must go back to their practical local roots in the immediate postwar before they became points of pride and competition among mainland Japanese prefectures and before the Southern Battle Sites Tour (Nambu Senseki Meguri) catered too much to mainland visitors.

Unlike war monuments (*sensō kinenhi*) built apart from the site of war deaths, early war memorial building in Okinawa was synonymous with bone collecting and interment. The cleanup of corpses of the war dead—*ikotsu shūshū,* or bone collection—has a distinct place in postwar histories of Okinawa and is alien to tourist images of today's Okinawa.[18] Bone-collection campaigns of the late 1940s and 1950s are part of the lore of the postwar generation of war survivors, graphically depicting the extent of human devastation the war brought as well as demonstrating the depth of community action to rebuild the island. Like the tree-planting campaigns that followed to replenish Okinawa's greenery (see chapter 3), bone-collection campaigns brought hundreds of volunteers of all ages together for a common purpose—physical and spiritual hygiene. It was not enjoyable work as tree planting could be, but it was still something that Gushiken Kanehiro could reminisce over as a childhood memory:

> Immediately after the end of war, soon after I had moved up to Naha High School, we students carried out bone collection work at Mabuni. With no bus or other transportation networks at the time I don't remember how we got there. . . .
>
> As far as the eye could see it was a treeless stretch of ruins, but the places where *kaya* and pampas grass were cut had become conspicuous small heaps of dry bones. After gathering these, we picked up shards of human bones that looked like coral. The buckets were filled in no time at all.[19]

Little did Gushiken and fellow Okinawans know that they were laying the foundations for Tourist Okinawa. Although the bulk of war remains were recovered through these kinds of bone-collection campaigns before Reversion, organized groups still to this day annually find dozens of bones still buried since the war. Those groups and unwitting individuals have also discovered military gear, clothing, medicine bottles, personal items, and the occasional unexploded ordnance. All serve as visceral reminders of a war past that seethes just below the surface of an apparently peaceful present, sometimes causing clashes between sacred ground and secular life. Shima Tsuyoshi's 1973 short story "Bones," for example, captures this clash exquisitely when a construction crew building a new tourist hotel during the rush of post-Reversion development turns up a pit of thousands of bones, which literally raises the war dead to the surface and complicates matters for resort development as depicted in the story.[20]

Long before the post-Reversion construction of resort hotels, the construction of U.S. bases in immediate postwar Okinawa complicated matters for thousands of Okinawans. The occupation redrew living and dying space for most Okinawans, especially those in the central and southern portions of the island. To clear areas for bases, U.S. authorities relocated civilians from refugee camps in central Okinawa to the recent war-riddled battlefields in the south. These refugees undertook the earliest bone-collection efforts as much out of hygienic necessity as for the pacification of spirits of the war dead. Arriving in areas still littered with remains, their first task was to clear them to make the place livable. Between 1946 and 1955 approximately 135,000 remains were collected and either cremated on the spot or deposited in the over one hundred hastily built ossuaries scattered throughout the region.[21] The Kyan Peninsula area alone, within the former administrative unit of Miwa Village (1946–1961), was reckoned to contain 76,706 war remains in ossuaries, according to a 1953 survey.[22] In most instances memorials were erected at the collection spots. The most celebrated of such cases is that of the approximately forty-three hundred residents of Mawashi Village who were ordered on January 23, 1946, to move to Komesu in Miwa Village, an area of some of the heaviest concentrations of casualties. Led by U.S.-appointed village mayor Kinjō Washin, the villagers were greeted by a gruesome mess of bones, some still bearing flesh and hair.[23] After securing, with difficulty, permission from U.S. authorities to gather the remains, the group proceeded to amass thousands of bones of Okinawans, Japanese, and likely some Americans as well, which they first brought to the beach for washing before depositing into a mass grave. Lacking proper materials to complete the ossuary, they acquired cement and old bed frames from the U.S. military, to which they added coral rock to cap Okinawa's first memorial to those who died in the

Battle of Okinawa, Konpaku-no-tō. In the years that followed, a total of over thirty-five thousand remains were deposited within it. In the process of this bone-collection campaign, the caves of the ill-fated Imperial Blood and Iron Youth Corps in Mabuni and the Himeyuri Student Nurses Corps in Komesu were discovered and subsequently became Okinawa's second and third major war memorial sites: the Himeyuri-no-tō (established February 1946) and the Kenji-no-tō (established March 1946) (see figure 1.1).

Of these two memorials, the Himeyuri-no-tō and its adjoining Peace Museum have become the more popular tourist destination, with the tragic story of the young battlefield nurses capturing the imaginations of mainland Japanese as *the* icon of patriotic Okinawan sacrifice and women's wartime experience, despite survivors who contest this nationalistic co-optation of their wartime experience.[24] Kinjō Washin, whose daughters died in battle as field nurses, was also instrumental in establishing the memorial cave site at which *irei* for the elite 219 Himeyuri students takes place. He was recognized for this work and his lobbying on behalf of Okinawa's bereaved families by being awarded the *Okinawa Times*'s first annual Service to Society Award in 1957.[25] He took many trips to Tokyo to argue for equal care and benefits for Okinawan war dead under Japan's Relief and Compensation Law and fought to have the war dead of the Imperial Blood and Iron Youth Corps classified as regular combatants for compensation purposes. Kinjō later became a central figure in the Okinawa Izoku Rengō Kai (Okinawa Bereaved Families Federation; 沖縄遺族連合会), serving as its head from 1966 to 1977.[26]

This initial phase of establishing a commemorative center for the Battle of Okinawa war dead on the Kyan Peninsula was largely ad hoc, volunteer, and born of local Okinawan initiative, necessity, and respect for the dead. The traditional Okinawan burial practice of bone washing (Okinawan: *shinkutsi*; Japanese: *senkotsu*, 洗骨), by which the bones of deceased family members are, after several years, taken from family tombs, cleansed, and reentombed, might well have prepared locals for the grim work of bone collection.[27] As was the case for Konpaku-no-tō and the majority of the over two hundred memorials established throughout Okinawa Island by 1962, these monuments also served as ossuaries (*nōkotsudō*, 納骨堂). In other words, (mass) graves and memorials were one and the same. It would be fitting to call this type of memorialization "organic," given the conditions in which it was undertaken. It was very much rooted in the sense that bodies and spirits permeated the ground, as Kinjō Washin suggested in comments he made in 1962 after spending several years gathering war remains and guiding mainland visitors on tours of the southern battlefields:

**Figure 1.1.** Okinawa's original war memorial trio: Konpaku-no-tō, Himeyuri-no-tō, Kenji-no-tō. *Source*: Gerald Figal.

> Okinawa is now putting a lot of effort into the tourism industry. The number of tourists is also increasing. What are we showing these tourist groups? Mostly battle sites. And when we say battle sites, it's only the places where monuments are standing.
>
> But where monuments are standing aren't the only battle sites. Remains could also be taken back and buried in one's birthplace, collected and laid to rest there. But what became of the uncollected scattered flesh and blood of soldiers? They all turned into Okinawan soil. Even when I myself give tours of the southern battle sites, my skin crawls at the thought of stepping on soil that's the flesh and blood of soldiers. It's difficult to get this feeling across to tourists from the mainland [*naichi*]. However, the bereaved families get it.[28]

This palpable sense that corpses of the war dead really have turned into Okinawan soil and have consecrated the ground has been too widespread among Okinawans to ignore; it is not merely a metaphor or hyperbole used to emphasize the great loss of life in the Battle of Okinawa. The long history of bone collection from 1945 to the present is witness to the physical fact of the flesh of thousands of corpses having decomposed into the soil, thus changing the very nature—physical and spiritual—of the ground itself. Physically, for example, it was believed that the unusually large vegetables harvested immediately after the battle were the result of extra fertilizer the soil absorbed in the form of decomposed corpses of the war dead. Spiritually, this ground was the place of ghosts, only to be trod upon carefully and with respect, or not at all.[29]

While all of Japan remained under U.S. occupation until 1952 and Okinawa remained war-torn and poor, locally conducted bone collection, burials, and memorial building by Okinawan volunteers was probably all that one could expect. Dozens of communities throughout the island had by the early 1950s established their own small ossuaries and memorials, but Konpaku-no-tō—the "tomb of the unknowns"—and the nearby Himeyuri-no-tō honoring the student nurses became the original geographic focus of war memorialization in the Komesu area. The later buildup of mainland Japanese prefectural memorials on Mabuni Hill, a few kilometers to the east and the site of the Kenji-no-tō, diminished this focus as it drew increased numbers of visitors to that area. This shift of attention, while never complete, was accompanied by a corresponding tension between local and national determination of the site and shape of war memorialization in Okinawa. In short, what we witness during the run-up to and the period after Reversion is an effective nationalization of memorial space on Okinawa, presaged by Japanese interest and activity in its former prefecture and World War II battle site almost as soon as the occupation of Japan ended in 1952. By the 1960s, this mainland invasion of the island strained local resources and tested local patience, but it was the catalyst for serious consideration to develop Okinawa as a tourist destination.

Mainland Japanese memorialization activity in Okinawa and elsewhere throughout the former Japanese Empire could not properly begin until the end of occupation on April 28, 1952, when the San Francisco Peace Treaty, signed on September 8, 1951, went into effect. Auxiliary to the main treaty were agreements between Tokyo and Washington concerning the disposition of yet-to-be-returned Japanese war dead, many of them still in Okinawa and in the Trust Territory of the Pacific Islands (TTPI) in Micronesia (the former League of Nations mandates previously administered by Japan), administered by the United States from July 18, 1947, to November 3, 1986. Arrangements for the return or on-site interment of Japanese war remains in U.S.-controlled areas took place throughout 1952, with Okinawa being treated as a case separate from those in the TTPI. All dealings between the Government of Japan (GOJ) and the Okinawan Government of the Ryukyu Islands (GRI, founded under U.S. authority on April 1, 1952), including the handling of war remains, had to go through the newly established Government of Japan Nanpō Liaison Office in Naha (Naha Nihon Seifu Nanpō Renraku Jimusho, established on July 1, 1952).[30] Although U.S. authorities in Okinawa were suspicious of any Japanese aid or intervention coming into the Ryukyus, it was politically difficult to deny the proper collection, return, and burial of war remains. Sensing an opportunity, the GOJ, with the support of local bereaved family associations, stepped up efforts to play a role in war memorialization in Okinawa.[31]

The first manifestation of Japanese involvement in Okinawan memorial space came in the form of the Shikina Central Ossuary, built with Tokyo money and Okinawan labor. Unveiled on July 31, 1957, it was the result of protracted negotiations between Japanese and reluctant American authorities. While Japanese officials emphasized the practical need for a centralized interment of war dead remains for the convenience of bereaved families and others to pay proper respects to relatives and comrades, it was not simply to streamline the travel of mainland visitors to Okinawa that they fought to have the Central Ossuary established. Politics clearly motivated efforts to assert some form of official Japanese presence in U.S.-occupied Okinawa.[32] In an assertion of its so-called "residual sovereignty"[33] over Okinawa, Tokyo initiated the long process of reorganizing the local memorialscape within a national imaginary. The first step was the transfer of unidentifiable war remains from local ossuaries to the Shikina Central Ossuary, while identifiable Japanese remains were to be shipped back to the mainland. As it turned out, a very small percentage of remains could be adequately identified for transfer to mainland Japan, leaving the vast majority for interment in Okinawa. The transfer of bones to the Central Ossuary was an ongoing process as new bones were discovered over the years. The unknown remains interred at Konpaku-no-tō, however, were not moved, thus producing two very differently oriented centers of memorial focus. While the Shikina Central Ossuary had the imprimatur of "official" and "central" and hosted annual organized memorial services attended by dignitaries, it was less directly connected to battleground soil and, in a real sense, was a more artificial repository for the bones transferred there from local ossuaries that in many cases literally sprang from sites where deaths had occurred. In other words, as "sacred ground," the Central Ossuary lacked organic roots; its "sacredness" was largely conferred upon it by state ceremony, which is precisely why U.S. authorities opposed its establishment under Japanese auspices. Organic roots did not figure in the planning for the Central Ossuary. On the physical front, convenience to hotels and roads in Naha for Japanese visitors and a well-kept structure befitting the dignity of Japanese remains were the primary concerns. On the political front, mainland Japanese presence at Shikina was foremost an expression of sovereignty when none other was practically available under U.S. occupation.[34]

The inaugural memorial service for this ossuary exemplifies its political aspect as it continued the controversy concerning Japanese influence in U.S.-controlled Okinawa. Held finally on January 25, 1958, the island-wide memorial service for the war dead interred at Shikina had been postponed for over a month because of a dispute over which mainland representatives would be allowed to attend. Ultimately, three representatives from Yasukuni Shrine, two diet members, and a representative from the Prime Minister's Office were approved by High Commissioner Lieutenant General James E. Moore.[35] The attendance of the Yasukuni Shrine representatives cheered the Okinawa Bereaved Families Federation whose platform included closer relations between Okinawan war dead and Yasukuni Shrine in addition to support for the reestablishment of national government subsidies for and official visits to Yasukuni, the central and controversial Japanese site for the enshrinement of the spirits of the war dead.[36] Once the GRI instituted in 1961 an official Memorial Day (Irei no Hi, June 22, and then changed to June 23 in 1966), controversies over Japanese invitees to the ceremonies broke out annually with American authorities.

## WAR TOURISM FOR PEACE: THE SOUTHERN BATTLE SITES TOUR PACKAGE

The establishment of the Shikina Central Ossuary offered a new anchor point for the typical tour routes for mainland visitors to Okinawa in these early postwar years when few considered the island outside its association with the war and U.S. military occupation there. Tourist Okinawa as such was merely an adjunct to Irei Okinawa and existed more as idea than reality.

Before the boom in visitors and new war memorial building in the mid-1960s, the greatest efforts to organize war-related sights within a broader package of experiencing Okinawa's cultural and natural attributes came from the Okinawa Tourism Association (Okinawa Kankō Kyōkai; OTA). Founded in 1954, the OTA had an original membership of fifty-two men who represented a range of Okinawa businesses and civic leaders with interests in developing the place into a tourist destination. At its inaugural meeting on January 9, 1954, founding member and first director Tōma Jūgō noted that the Battle of Okinawa had put an unprecedented global spotlight on the place, one that presented an opportunity to turn that attention from wartime Okinawa to Tourist Okinawa. In addition, he described the island as being forever burnished in the minds of the bereaved, who now desired to conduct pilgrimages (*irei ryokō*, "consolation trips") for the repose of the souls of the war dead. The consolation of the war dead, Tōma suggested, could be parlayed into the peacetime and peaceful industry of tourism at large. The idea of tourism as a "peaceful industry" (*heiwa sangyō*) that could transform and redeem a war-torn territory existed in the pitch for tourism from the beginning in postwar Okinawa.[37] In this very direct way, the war and the dead resulting from it rationalized and catalyzed tourism development, resulting in Okinawa's first notable postwar attraction packaged by the OTA, the Southern Battle Sites Tour (Nambu Senseki Meguri) that looped down the west coast from Naha to the southern tip of the island to hit the major memorial and battlefield sites before turning back up the east coast on the return (see figure 1.2).

As memorial markers—from Konpaku-no-tō to the Shikina Central Ossuary—were being erected throughout the late 1940s and 1950s, the OTA, tour guides, and visitors began to connect them physically and discursively into routes that formed the backbone of early Okinawa tourism and still exist today. Physically, memorial sites that had sprouted organically from where bones had been collected and interred—sometimes in hard-to-reach places—required access for pilgrims making consolation trips and for general tourists interested in the history of the battle. Among the very first tasks the OTA set out for itself in 1954 was the repair and extension of access roads to war memorials, specifically Konpaku-no-tō, Kenji-no-tō, Reimei-no-tō, and the Protect-the-Island Memorial.[38] In the early 1950s, before enhanced mainland Japanese interest in Okinawa, U.S. military personnel and bereaved Okinawan families on weekend tours constituted the majority of the traffic to the former battle sites on the south side of the island, but they were not consciously viewed as tourists needing extensive facilities.[39] The rudimentary road building and repair that the GRI—with United States Civil Administration of the Ryukyu Islands (USCAR) support—conducted and that laid the foundations for later tourist routes are best considered within the context of general rebuilding of war-damaged

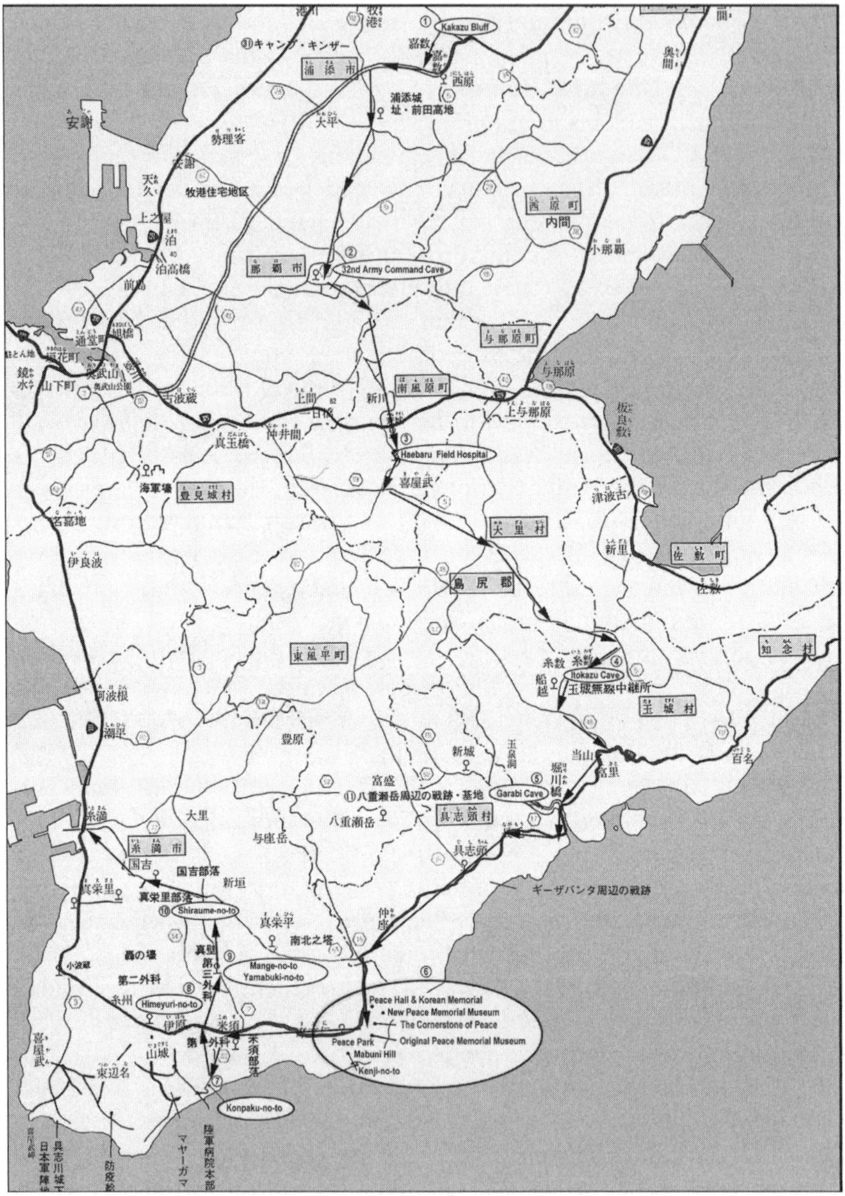


**Figure 1.2.** Map for the Southern Battle Sites Tour. *Source*: *Aruku, miru, kangaeru Okinawa*, adapted courtesy of Okinawa Jiji Shuppan.

infrastructure and providing for resettled local inhabitants. As numbers of outside Japanese visitors increased throughout the late 1950s and early 1960s, however, so did complaints about infrastructure and facilities, which in turn stimulated the need for what OTA members frequently referred to as "tourism consciousness" (*kankō ishiki*) among the local population; in other words, Okinawans needed to view physically and conceptualize discursively their island in terms consonant with the expectations of outsider visitors. Besides the foreign nature of this tourist gaze, what made the generation of tourism consciousness problematic for the OTA was the very thing that had given Okinawa tourism its jump start—former battle sites and the war dead memorialized there. Connecting these sites with roads and signposts was relatively easy if funds were available to do so; the more difficult work existed in defining and packaging grave sites as destinations within broader conceptions of Tourist Okinawa, especially when few Okinawans thought that their poverty-stricken, foreign-occupied, war-ravaged homeland had anything of value or interest to offer visitors. After they recognized this problem, it is understandable why the OTA exerted much of its energies producing tourism-promotion literature directed at Okinawans themselves to enhance tourism consciousness among them as a prerequisite to developing tourism at large.

While we cannot ignore the perennial, practical problem of funding tourism development in U.S.-occupied Okinawa, it is the connection between the physical and discursive development of Tourist Okinawa that deserves particular attention in this early period as it presents a fascinating case of self-definition of a place that strains against definitions thrust upon it by others and by structures beyond local control. This tension is readily discernible in the way the OTA sought to organize tourism by taking advantage of the pilgrim draw to war-related sites while expanding the range of destinations for both pilgrims and general tourists. Despite the impression that they were merely cataloging and formalizing what naturally existed as tourist attractions in Okinawa, their own inside inventions were mixed with outside interventions—some invited, many not—to transform war memorial grounds into battlefield tours grafted to circuits of other cultural and natural sites. In this process, not only was "sacred ground" placed within secular circulation (the focus of the following chapter); what was culturally and naturally noteworthy was also being transformed and (re)defined.

As part of its campaign to raise tourism consciousness and to give shape to destinations in Okinawa, the OTA began in 1955 the publication of the magazine *Kankō Okinawa* (Sightseeing Okinawa), which ran in its original form until 1966. Explicitly conceived to educate Okinawans about tourism, it presents a hodgepodge vision of Okinawa tourism in pre-Reversion Okinawa.[40] During the late 1950s and early 1960s a noticeable amount of space was given over to tours of war memorial sites even as the OTA strived to expand the horizons of sightseeing in Okinawa. It is this suturing of dour war memory with hopeful visions of peacetime progress, culture, and natural beauty that renders the construct "Kankō Okinawa" a particularly valuable object for the analysis of Okinawa's general postwar condition. In its repeated pitches to local government officials and others for institutional and financial support, the OTA quite literally yoked together in the same sentences natural beauty and comfortably warm temperatures with the idea that Okinawa had also become "an island of pilgrimage and an island of memories for over 200,000 bereaved families due to the recent war."[41] That any appreciable numbers of visitors to the island in this period were pilgrims to grave sites and not vacationers to beaches bespeaks the unfortunate reality that much of Okinawa's "natural beauty" had been compromised by war and occupation. It was clear that any hope to form a sustainable tourist industry relied upon steering war site pilgrimages into the "peaceful industry" of general leisure tourism.

An examination of the publication *Kankō Okinawa* in tandem with the record of the OTA's ideas and activities during this period reveals the strategies aimed to accomplish the transformation of pilgrims into tourists. The weaving of war traces, postwar recovery, and "peaceful" nature and culture dominate the presentation of what is deemed worth viewing and experiencing in Okinawa. While the rhetoric of tourism as a peace industry was widespread internationally, in the recent war zone of Okinawa, its deployment had the particular effect of blunting and neutralizing the image of the place as one large blood-soaked battlefield dotted with hundreds of war monuments. And yet, it is the image of war monuments and the international notoriety of the Battle of Okinawa that local boosters counted on to provide the initial pool of tourists. The problem that developed was the need to balance war reminders with vacation escape, reverence with recreation.

A key aspect to the solution of this problem of balancing reverence with recreation turned around the use of Okinawan women as mediums through which to soften war history and memories and smooth over the transition from war to peace. The female roles that were most conspicuously featured in this context were local tour bus guides and traditional dancers; only much later would they include bikini-clad sunbathers from the mainland. Both bus guides and dancers served as cultural ambassadors and figures of hospitality for "foreign" visitors from mainland Japan, but it was the figure of the bus guide that sustained the reputation of early postwar tours of Okinawa. As narrators of the war history behind the monuments and battlefields, tour bus guides constituted the principal direct interface between sights and sightseers, sympathetically modulating that history in what were viewed as dramatic performances. The OTA first began to organize the training and promotion of local bus guides in 1955, sponsoring training sessions throughout the year and hosting annual bus guide contests from 1956 to 1963. The first applicants had to be under twenty-two years old and in good health and to pass oral and written tests on basic local geography and history.[42] Bus guide contests, in which the young women selected a portion of a typical route and narrated it on stage in front of judges and an audience, were consciously designed as a way to enhance tourism consciousness among the local population and to encourage improvement through competition. Local winners competed as Okinawa's representative at the national contest in Tokyo. In contests and as part of their job routine, bus guides also typically sang local folk songs along routes, heightening the dramatic effect and inspiring the nickname "Ugisu-san" (Ms. Bush Warbler), a tribute to their reputed songbird-like voices.

The first issues of *Kankō Okinawa* reflect this activity, featuring articles, reports, and photos about the state of tour bus guide education and typical tours, especially the Southern Battle Sites Tour (Nambu Senseki Meguri), which formed the core of three of the first four tour routes (for half-day, one-day, two-day, and three-day visits) that the OTA had defined in 1954. Reportage and advertisement for the Southern Battle Sites Tour are often difficult to differentiate; pages of the magazine are interspersed with photos of war memorials and young female bus guides, short descriptions of sights, articles on tour bus development, and ads for the Showa Bus Company, whose tour guides dominated the annual contests. It is also sometimes difficult to distinguish tourism promotion from simple development promotion, as many of these early tour routes included sights such as the latest "modern" government building or new local factory. The second issue (February 1956) of *Kankō Okinawa* is exemplary in this regard. Its cover showcases five "sightseeing bus guide girls" lined up in front of the latest model Showa Bus Company tour bus parked on the bluff of Naminoue (over the waves), the historically important Okinawa religious spot previously mentioned that is known in modern times for its views of and swimming access to the East China Sea. Located adjacent to the teahouses and Okinawan-style restaurants of the Naminoue district of Naha and not far from hotels and bus terminals, it was, as the magazine cover suggests, a common starting point for the Southern Battle Sites Tour. The caption to the photo also links Okinawa's postwar recovery with the appearance of leisure zones and sightseeing spots, enumerating parks and sites of natural beauty alongside tours of battle sites, an ad for which appears at the bottom of the page (see figure 1.3). This association between typical leisure tourism sights and modern development appears within this and subsequent issues of the late 1950s and early 1960s, which are sprinkled with photos and short stories extolling the latest Western-style hotels, shops, restaurants, dams, and roads.[43]

# 観光沖縄

2号

一九五六年二月一日発行
発行所 沖縄観光協会
那覇市役所勧業課内
〔電話一番〕
編集責任者 與那國善三
印刷所 沖縄印刷所
〔電話六三九番〕

伸び行く沖縄の人口と共に住民の福祉に緊密な關係を待つているものは 娯楽観光地である。その中で最も多くの住民及観光客に使用されている処は、中城公園、萬座毛、とどろきの瀧、波之上、南部せん蹟地であろう。

特に波之上では春から夏にかけ、沖縄で最も賑わう娯楽観光地として有名、押迫る春の観光シーズンと共に観光バスも登場ーーーーーーーー美しい聲をマイクに乗せて各所に點在する名所旧蹟並に戦蹟地を訪れ一日の清遊を満契することも現代文化人のたしなみの一つーーーーーー

〔写真は那覇随一の観光地波之上神社前に並んだ観光バスのガイド嬢達〕

島尻一周 南部戦せきめぐり

バスガイドが沿線案内を行います

毎土曜 ———— 午後1時発

毎日曜 午前9時発 午後1時発

(約4時間の行程)

御一人当り70圓

御一人でも乗れる昭和観光バスを御利用下さい

尚 團体貸切にも御希望に應じガイドを御供させます

御問合せ御申込は

昭和産業株式会社
(昭和バス)

電 326 332 931



1956 2月

**Figure 1.3.** Tour bus guides and ad for the Southern Battle Sites Tour. *Source*: *Kankō Okinawa*, February 1956.

Accounts of the annual bus guide contests and feedback gathered from visitors who took the Southern Battle Sites Tour confirm that it was not merely the bare physical presence of war memorials themselves that imbued them with meaning; the discursive embellishment—tragedy and pathos—that tour bus guides produced in their presentations of war history is what captured the hearts of visitors and made their time in Okinawa memorable. While visitor surveys gave low marks to nearly all creature comforts and conveniences—transportation schedules, hotel service, cuisine, souvenir selection, and so on—bus guides consistently ranked at the top of the favorable aspects of Okinawa tours. Survey respondents noted how moving their narratives of the battle sites were. That bus guides were always young, unmarried women in their late teens and early twenties enhanced the sense of pathos while offering a pretty face to an otherwise ugly story of merciless slaughter.

This emotional effect was especially true at what became the centerpiece of the Southern Battle Sites Tour, the Himeyuri-no-tō, or Maiden Lily Memorial. As Linda Angst has forcefully argued, the privileged status of the Himeyuri story in mainland Japanese imagination as a story of patriotic sacrifice hinges on the framing of these schoolgirls as both childlike "virginal victims" and as womanlike heroic battlefield nurses.[44] Angst relates a tour to the present Himeyuri Peace Museum on a bus chartered by the Himeyuri Dōsōkai (Maiden Lily Alumni Association) and guided by one of its members, who struck a dramatic "onstage" presence when narrating her personal wartime ordeal as a Himeyuri nurse. While noting that the Himeyuri guide, microphone in hand, echoed the form of the typical tour bus guide, she contrasts this evocative narration with the "canned description" of the young, attractive uniformed bus guides: "The Himeyuri 'tour guides' told their stories as part of a special commemorative ceremony, dressed in warm, comfortable clothing and footwear as they retraced their arduous nocturnal wanderings on the Kyan Peninsula, constantly under allied military attack from air and sea, some fifty years earlier."[45] However, all accounts suggest that the early Okinawan tour bus guides were closer in dramatic spirit if not in historical experience to present-day Himeyuri Dōsōkai tour guides. Being of similar age as the Himeyuri student nurses (although a few years older), of the same unmarried status, and not too temporally removed from the war, the first tour bus guides were easily identifiable with them. Through their own heart-stirring narratives and physical presence, tour bus guides could provide an experience for tourists/pilgrims that vividly evoked this particularly well-known episode in the Battle of Okinawa and do so in a way that redeemed it of the severity of the actual event. As themselves childhood survivors of the war, tour bus guides in effect stood in for the Himeyuri schoolgirls; those of whom who survived did not begin leading their own tours until many years later when they began to talk more publicly about their wartime experiences.

Direct records of the actual content of early battlefield tour narratives no longer exist, but indirect accounts suggest that rather than providing nuanced and historically reflective content, they reinforced mainland Japanese expectations of a harrowing but patriotically redeemable story of loyal Okinawan sacrifice in which even schoolgirls from Japan's periphery willingly served and died for the fatherland.[46]

It is precisely this kind of war memorial tour narration that historians, peace activists, and some Himeyuri Dōsōkai members would in later years challenge as a whitewashing of civilian war experience and as a ready acceptance of the Japanese state's rationale for war and, in particular, its use (sacrifice) of Okinawa to stall the Allies in their advance upon the mainland. Such uncritical packaging of war history, however, to attract and meet the expectations of mainland Japanese visitors is not surprising in the context of a nascent tourism industry within a struggling Okinawan economy. Hosts were not going to insult guests by questioning the wartime actions of their fathers, sons, and brothers who died for their country. With former battlefields and war memorials constituting the principal draw in early postwar Okinawa, this aspect of the tourist gaze had to be catered to and fulfilled lest guests stopped coming. Young female tour guides fulfilled this role admirably, educating and entertaining visitors in ways deemed appropriate for the state of Okinawa tourism at the time. As OTA officials summed them up, "Bus guides stand on the front line of tourism."[47]

The satisfaction tour bus guides provided with their narratives, songs, and comforting presence buoyed an otherwise complaint-ridden Tourist Okinawa during the early pre-Reversion years. Complaints were important, however, in the general transformation of Okinawa from a place into a destination and in its particular transformation from a place of wartime death into a destination of peacetime leisure. With complaints came the provocation of a self-consciousness of the place and what shaping was needed in its topography, infrastructure, and accommodations to attract visitors and investors. Editorials in *Kankō Okinawa* often expressed insufficiencies in Okinawa's tourist infrastructure and hospitality services as a whole; the internal record of OTA activity to improve the situation is even more revealing. Until the GRI finally formed a government Tourism Division in 1961, under which systematic visitor surveys were later conducted and Japanese tourism consultants hired, these two sources provide the best sense of an outside critical view of Tourist Okinawa and how local tourism promoters responded to it.

Out of the ruins of war, basic amenities might seem luxurious to Okinawans, but for Japanese visitors of a fast-aspiring middle-class, what Okinawa had to offer frequently fell short. Mainland Japanese visitors sounded concerns about sanitation and hygiene throughout the island, but their complaints existed against a backdrop of mainland stereotypes about the cultural "backwardness" of Okinawans in general. Sensitive to such criticism (some of which has persisted to this day), the OTA set out to upgrade Okinawa's image and substance; it is likely the reason behind a compulsion to include signs of "modern" progress (new buildings, roads, and factories) within tour guide pamphlets. In addition to the installation of public toilets and shaded rest areas on tour routes, the OTA planned and oversaw the inspection and approval of sanitation and hygiene at inns and restaurants, inspected the quality and packaging of local goods, and sponsored beautification campaigns along tourist routes and around sightseeing spots, particularly war memorials, the bedrock of early Okinawa tourism.

A confluence of activity significantly transformed that bedrock in the 1960s, challenging the integrity of Okinawa's memorialscape, its "sacred ground," and complicating the ability to broaden Okinawa's appeal to would-be tourists. The relatively steep rise in the number of visitors from mainland Japan from the early to late 1960s, combined with more serious interest on the part of American authorities to support tourism development as one way to stimulate the lagging Okinawan economy, led to an unanticipated problem: the overdevelopment of the Southern Battle Sites Tour in a way that put Okinawan economic concerns at odds with Japanese expectations for "sacred ground." Japanese expectations for Okinawa tourism in general and tours of war memorials in particular were themselves full of contradictions typical in the commercialization of destinations for public consumption. The aggressive mid-1960s boom in mainland-sponsored monuments made these contradictions even more overt, bringing to the surface latent problems in the development of sacred ground within a broader tourist industry that needed to sustain a stream of visitors from abroad, regardless of their motivation to visit. Even the Japanese visitor whose primary purpose was pilgrimage to war memorials expected a level of diversion (eating, shopping, entertainment) to make this "overseas" trip complete. As the decade wore on, demands for quality diversions grew, taxing local capacity to meet them on top of tending to memorials that were sprouting like mushrooms on Mabuni Hill. In this period of flux before Okinawa's reversion to Japan, respect for the dead, recreation for the living, and the imperatives of American military presence posed new tensions for Okinawa and fledgling Tourist Okinawa alike. The touristification of sacred ground would not come easily.

## NOTES

1. George Feifer, *Tennozan: The Battle of Okinawa and the Atomic Bomb* (New York: Ticknor & Fields, 1992), 135.
2. Yahara Hiromichi, *The Battle for Okinawa*, trans. Roger Pineau and Masatoshi Uehara (New York: John Wiley & Sons, 1995), 135.

3. Okinawa Taimususha, ed., *Okinawa no shōgen, jōmaki* (Naha: Okinawa Taimusu, 1971), 131.

4. Kitamura Tsuyoshi points out that many of the first explanatory plaques found at memorial sites in the early 1950s were in English, catering to the American soldiers and their families who visited sites of the recent battle, especially those in Mabuni. That and testimony from local residents in Mabuni led Kitamura to identify American servicemen as the first to turn these memorial sites into tourist sites (*kankōchi*). Japanese visitors would soon follow. See Kitamura Tsuyoshi, *Sensha-tachi no sengoshi: Okinawa senseki o megure hitobito to no kioku* (Tokyo: Ochanomizu Shobo, 2009), 282–84.

5. Osaka Shōsen, *Okinawa e* (Osaka: Osaka Shōsen, 1939), cited by Kanda Kōji, "Senzenki no Okinawa kankō o meguru imēji to aidentiti," in Kanda Kōji, ed., *Kankō no kūkan: Shiten to apurōchi* (Tokyo: Nakanishiya Shuppan, 2009), 211. Kanda also cites a 1925 literary travelogue that enumerates a similar list of exoticisms, which is summed up as "nangoku ['south country,' i.e., tropical] Ryūkyū" (213).

6. Alan Christy, "Representing the Rural: Place as Method in the Formation of Japanese Native Ethnology, 1910–1945" (PhD diss., University of Chicago, 1997), 312–19.

7. Yanagita's *Kainan shoki* (Record of the South Seas, 1925) is based on his winter 1920–1921 trip through the Ryukyu Islands. In typical fashion, Yanagita's descriptions of natural environment, while often captivating, are ultimately abstracted in the service of his trademark method of linguistic association aimed at demonstrating the origins and diffusion of customs and beliefs. His protracted discussion of the *birō* (Okinawan: *kuba*) tree, for example, has less to do with the actual tree than with its naming and connections with other things and places which that naming possibly indicates. See Yanagita Kunio, *Kainan shoki*, in *Yanagita Kunio zenshū* (Tokyo: Chikuma Bunko, 1989), 1:483–519. For an incisive analysis of Yanagita's abstraction of Okinawa's actual material present to create a genealogy of Japan and Okinawa's shared past, see Alan Christy, "A Fantasy of Ancient Japan: The Assimilation of Okinawa in Yanagita's *Kainan Shoki*," *Productions of Culture in Japan, Select Papers* 10 (1995): 61–90. On Yanagita's and others' impact on the formation of early-twentieth-century images of Okinawa, see Tada Osamu, *Okinawa imēji o tabisuru—Yanagita Kunio kara ijū būmu made* (Tokyo: Chūō Kōron Shinsha, 2008).

8. Itō Kenichi, ed., *Ehagaki ni miru Okinawa: Meiji, Taishō, Shōwa* [Okinawa as Seen in Picture Postcards: Meiji, Taisho, Showa] (Naha: Ryūkyū Shimpōsha, 1993), reproduces a representative cross section of prewar Okinawa postcards.

9. Naminoue and Go-kokuji are the first stops, for example, of the Kumamoto physician Yamasaki Masatada on his 1932 tour of Okinawa. See the summary of his trip in Nonomura Takao, *Natsukashiki Okinawa: Yamasaki Masatada ra ga aruita Shōwa shoki no genfūkei* (Naha: Ryūkyū Shimpōsha, 2000), 158. "A southern battle sites tour begins at Go-kokuji" became a common saying by the 1960s.

10. John Urry, *The Tourist Gaze: Leisure and Travel in Contemporary Societies* (London: Sage Publications, 1990; 2nd ed., 2002). In this seminal work in tourism studies, Urry develops the concept of a "tourist gaze"—that is, an outsider's vision of a place that is socially constructed and systemized through difference with nontourist

experience. I will return to this concept in my discussion of the tropicalization of the postwar Okinawan landscape in chapter 3.

11. Nonomura, *Natsukashiki Okinawa*, 142–51, relates the background to Yamasaki's trip.

12. See Tze May Loo, "Treasures of a Nation: Cultural Heritage Preservation and the Making of Shuri Castle in Prewar Japan" (PhD diss., Cornell University, 2007), ch. 6.

13. The literature on war memorials, war and memory, and commemorative practices has become quite extensive, especially in the run-up to and in the aftermath of the fiftieth anniversaries associated with World War II.

14. Kitamura, *Sensha-tachi no sengoshi,* 30, usefully distinguishes war monuments (*kinenhi*) from war memorials (*ireitō*) by emphasizing that *ireitō* implies a site where bones are or were interred. In other words, as I discuss below, ossuaries (*nōkotsudō*) and *ireitō* were one and the same in the context of bone collection and memorial building in early postwar Okinawa.

15. Statistics for war dead are notoriously difficult to pinpoint. In the case of the Battle of Okinawa, the lines between regular Okinawan military personnel, civilian conscripts, and general civilians were often blurry. Nevertheless, the official figures published by the Relief Section of the Okinawa Prefecture Department of Welfare is 200,656, of which 94,000 are identified as "general civilian population"; 28,228 as Okinawan military personnel or civilians attached to the military; 65,908 as non-Okinawan Japanese military personnel; and 12,520 as American military personnel. These statistics do not reflect the deaths of other non-Japanese and non-American nationals; nor do they include colonial subjects such as the several thousand Koreans estimated to have perished in the conflict. Okinawa-ken Seikatsu Fukushi-bu Engo-ka, ed., *Okinawa no engo no ayumi: Okinawasen shiketsu 50 shūnen kinen* (Naha: Okinawa-ken Seikatsu Fukushi-bu Engo-ka, 1996), 56.

16. For an account of Ōta's life, politics, and relations to issues of war and peace in Okinawa, see Julia Yonetani, "Making History from Japan's Margins: Ōta Masahide and Okinawa" (PhD diss., Australian National University, 2002).

17. Ōta Masahide, *Okinawa sen senbotsusha o inoru irei-no-tō* (Naha: Naha Shuppansha, 1985), 17–29.

18. Popular "people's histories" of postwar Okinawa invariably include a section—often with photographs—on bone collection campaigns. See, for example, the oral histories in Okinawa Taimsusha, ed., *Shomin ga tsuzuru Okinawa sengo seikatsushi* (Naha: Okinawa Taimsusha, 1998), 39–44. Kitamura includes several exemplary photos and sketches the practice and product of bone collection campaigns (front matter, 56, 78, 85, 90).

19. Gushiken Kanehiro, "Shirokotsu no yama to natta nanbu senseki," in Okinawa Taimsusha, ed., *Shomin ga tsuzuru Okinawa sengo seikatsushi*, 41.

20. Shima Tsuyoshi, "Bones" [*Hone*], trans. William J. Tyler, in Michael Molasky and Steven Rabson, ed., *Southern Exposure: Modern Japanese Literature from Okinawa* (Honolulu: University of Hawaii, 2000), 156–70.

21. Ōta, *Okinawa senbotsusha o inoru irei-no-tō*, 30–36.

22. Kitamura, *Sensha-tachi no sengoshi,* 76.

23. Okinawa Taimsusha, ed., *Shomin ga tsuzuru Okinawa sengo seikatsushi*, 41.

24. See chapter 3, "Gendered Nationalism: Roles, Representation, and Meanings of Himeyuri, 1945–1995," in Linda Isako Angst, "In a Dark Time: Community, Memory, and the Making of Ethnic Selves in Okinawan Women's Narratives" (PhD diss., Yale University, 2001). Kitamura provides a history and analysis of the image of the Himeyuri in chapter 2 of *Sensha-tachi no sengoshi.*

25. Okinawa Izoku Rengo Kai, ed., *Okinawa Izoku Rengo Kai 25-nen no ayumi* (Naha: Okinawa Izoku Rengo Kai, 1977), 18.

26. Okinawa-ken Seikatsu Fukushi-bu Engo-ka, ed., *Okinawa no engo no ayumi*, 56–58; Ōta, *Okinawa senbotsusha o inoru irei-no-tō*, 30–33. See also Kitamura's account of the Okinawa Bereaved Families Federation (*izokukai*) in chapter 3 of *Sensha-tachi no sengoshi* for Kinjō Washin's role in it.

27. Bone washing is typically considered women's work and is fast disappearing in modern Okinawa where crematories have replaced the practice. For a discussion of the cultural and gendered meanings of *senkotsu*, see Noriko Kawahashi, "Seven Hindrances of Women? A Popular Discourse on Okinawan Women and Religion," *Japanese Journal of Religious Studies* 27:1–2.

28. Kinjō Washin, "Seinen-bu no arikata" (1962), reprinted in Okinawa-ken Izoku Rengō Kai Seisōnen-bu, ed., *Wakatake sōshūhen: Sōritsu 25 shūnen kinenshi* (Naha: Okinawa-ken Izoku Rengō Kai Seisōnen-bu, 1985), 87.

29. Medoruma Shun's chilling short story "Droplets" (*suiteki*) neatly combines this sense of supernatural growth and the supernatural appearance of the war dead in the figure of the protagonist's fantastically swollen, gourdlike leg and the ghosts of the war dead drawn to drink the drops of liquid oozing from it. The story is translated by Michael Molasky in Molasky and Rabson, *Southern Exposure*, 255–85.

30. In the context of U.S.-occupied Okinawa, Government of Japan (GOJ) was the usual designation for the mainland Japanese government in official U.S. correspondence discussing the relations among Japan, the United States, and the Ryukyu Islands. Similarly, once established in 1952, the Government of the Ryukyu Islands (GRI) designated the Okinawan civilian government that presided under USCAR and, from 1957, the U.S. High Commissioner (HICOM). Relations between the GOJ on the one hand and the GRI and USCAR on the other took place through the Japanese Government Liaison Office (JGLO) in Naha and its corresponding bureau in the prime minister's office in Tokyo.

31. For a detailed analysis of this nationalization of Okinawan memorial space, see Gerald Figal, "Bones of Contention: The Geopolitics of 'Sacred Ground' in Postwar Okinawa," *Diplomatic History* 31, no. 1 (January 2007): 81–109.

32. Figal, "Bones of Contention," 92–96.

33. This formulation of "residual sovereignty"—crafted by John Foster Dulles and arrived at after debates between the U.S. Joint Chiefs of Staff and the State Department over the nature of U.S. occupation of the Ryukyus—was the basis for any future return of the islands to Japan. See Robert D. Eldridge, *The Origins of the Bilateral Okinawa Problem: Okinawa in Postwar U.S.-Japan Relations, 1945–1952* (New York: Garland Publishing, 2001), 314–28.

34. See Figal, “Bones of Contention,” for a fuller discussion of the political maneuvering between American and Japanese authorities over the question of war memorialization as an act of sovereignty in pre-Reversion Okinawa.
35. Okinawa Izoku Rengō Kai, ed., *Ni jū go nen no ayumi* (Naha: Okinawa Izoku Rengō Kai, 1977), 19–20.
36. This sentiment is seemingly still alive and well among Okinawa bereaved families today if their positive reaction to Prime Minister Koizumi’s intention to visit Yasukuni in August 2001 is any indication. Koizumi made it a point to attend Okinawa’s Memorial Day (Irei no Hi) services at the Peace Park in Mabuni on June 23, 2001, and reiterate his intention to visit Yasukuni in an official capacity that August 15 (the anniversary of the end of war). That mention in his address (which I attended) in Okinawa drew applause from the Okinawa bereaved families in attendance. Pressured by domestic and international criticism, however, Koizumi ultimately visited Yasukuni on August 13 and did not call the visit “official.” For the controversy over Yasukuni Shrine, see John Nelson, “Social Memory as Ritual Practice: Commemorating Spirits of the Military Dead at Yasukuni Shrine,” *Journal of Asian Studies* 62, no. 2 (May 2003); Joshua Safier, “Yasukuni Shrine and the Constraints on the Discourse of Nationalism in Twentieth-Century Japan” (master’s thesis, University of Kansas, 1997).
37. Yamashiro Zensan, ed., *Okinawa kankō kyōkai shi* (Naha: Okinawa Kankō Kyōkai, 1964), 10.
38. Yamashiro, *Okinawa kankō kyōkai shi*, 16.
39. Yamashiro, *Okinawa kankō kyōkai shi*, 15.
40. Yamashiro, *Okinawa kankō kyōkai shi*, 21.
41. Yamashiro, *Okinawa kankō kyōkai shi*, 23.
42. Yamashiro, *Okinawa kankō kyōkai shi*, 30.
43. *Kankō Okinawa*, no. 2, front cover.
44. Angst, “In a Dark Time,” 141–43.
45. Angst, “In a Dark Time,” 158.
46. Kitamura, *Sensha-tachi no sengoshi,* 161, quotes portions of tour bus guide scripts, particularly for the Himeyuri-no-tō, that were used in 1971. Okinawa Bus scripts that I read in 2001 and live on-site performances I witnessed were also generally dramatic and emotion driven, but markedly less patriotic in their focus. The sacrifice (*gisei*) of the girls did not have their selfless love of country as its frame. Rather, there was a critical tone directed at the forces that involved these schoolgirls in the war.
47. Yamashiro, *Okinawa kankō kyōkai shi*, 30.

# 2

# The Touristification of Sacred Ground

## MEMORIAL BOOM AND ECONOMIC BUST

On January 26, 1962, the *Asahi Shimbun* evening edition reported that, for the sake of preserving natural landscapes and slowing down a "memorial boom" (*ireitō buumu*) that had burst forth on Okinawa, the Government of the Ryukyu Islands (GRI) had decided to deny new requests from the mainland for memorial construction.[1] At the time there were only three of forty-six mainland prefectures with large-scale monuments already on Okinawa (Hokkaidō and Wakayama at Komesu; Akita on Mabuni Hill), but other prefectures were poised to join in the willy-nilly construction of war monuments. As one member of the Okinawa Bereaved Families Federation later described the situation on the newly designated Memorial Day of June 23, 1966, "Lately, Mabuni Hill looks like a memorial competition rather than hallowed sacred ground, and I resent that it's being turned into a tourist site."[2] The GRI's position was, as it turned out, sensationally reported. It never intended to end the building of memorials, only to regulate the process so that they might be built in a safe, legal, and orderly fashion. The Government of Japan's Naha liaison reported back to Tokyo the GRI's valid concerns: an inability to provide proper ongoing maintenance; an inability to keep up ceremonial observances over the long term; harm done to scenic beauty; and termite infestations in monuments made of wood.[3] In April 1962 the Prime Minister's Office relayed these concerns to all prefectural governors and outlined procedures that they would have to follow. In short, the prefectures would have to make their requests to the GRI through Japan's Naha liaison office and coordinate the execution of plans with local groups so as to alleviate the problems Okinawans had cited. This included having the Okinawa Bereaved Families Federation purchase land by proxy for mainland groups given that American authorities forbade Japanese from purchasing land in the Ryukyus. Once this procedure was set, the rush was back on among Japanese prefectures to stake memorial claims in Okinawa.[4]

The resentment of the Okinawa Bereaved Families Federation member cited above is revealing. It suggests that by the mid-1960s pilgrims to memorial sites had transformed into tourists and that the land itself—at least Mabuni Hill—was transforming from a place of mourning into a commercialized tourist attraction.[5] The small mainland groups of surviving relatives and veterans chartering a Southern Battle Sites Tour had given way to larger groups whose members were less likely to have personal ties to the war dead as bereaved families did. But attracting bigger crowds was precisely the goal of the Okinawa Tourism Association (OTA), which was now receiving more active support from the United States Civil Administration of the Ryukyu Islands (USCAR) to promote tourism as one of many economic initiatives in a cash-strapped Okinawa. With pilgrim-tourists to war sites as the core, the OTA sought to expand the appeal of Okinawa as a vacation destination, which meant enhancing the Southern Battle Sites Tour route while at the same time forging an image, if not a reality, of a Tourist Okinawa that went beyond battlefields and monuments. Three problems emerged from this situation: keeping so-called sacred ground sacred amid its crass commercialization; reconciling sharp juxtapositions between leisure sites and war-related sites; and handling the conspicuous U.S. military presence. These are problems that have persisted, in different manifestations, from the 1950s to the present.

A fourth practical problem also beleaguered Okinawa tourism, more so before Reversion than after: the issue of capital investment. One of the paradoxes of pre-Reversion tourism promotion is that while American authorities actively began to encourage tourism development in the 1960s to help solve Okinawa's economic woes, there was little done to encourage capital investment or offer much in the way of direct aid for tourism ventures outside occupation-related infrastructure development that coincidentally helped tourism. Okinawan investors were virtually nonexistent, American investors skeptical, and potential Japanese investors denied by American authorities. In this state of affairs, the enthusiastic visions for Tourist Okinawa that ran through USCAR, OTA, and GRI circles largely remained just that—visions. And yet an examination of these visions offers a view of basic political, cultural, and economic structures that shaped post-Reversion development and presaged its own set of issues.

In many respects, the 1960s—not the better-known early post-Reversion period—was the formative transitional period for the shaping of Tourist Okinawa. Consultants were hired, surveys taken, plans drawn up, committees formed, and some development undertaken—all centered around parlaying the interest in battle sites and war memorials into a broader definition of Okinawa as tourist destination. The broader definition that competed with the image of Okinawa as battleground was Okinawa as tropical haven, and both of these had to deal with the popular image of Okinawa as "foreign country" under U.S. military and cultural occupation. But before the widespread tropicalization of the island's image came the makeover of the stops along the Southern Battle Sites Tour. This chapter takes this makeover as its focus, bridging the pre- and post-Reversion touristification and transformation of war-related sacred ground before moving on in chapter 3 to the overall physical transformation of the landscape that went beyond battle sites and war ruins.

## THE SELLING (OUT) OF SACRED GROUND

Nothing captures the controversy over the touristification of sacred ground better or reveals relations of economic, political, and cultural power more succinctly than the simple issue of flower vendors—typically war widows trying to scratch out a living or young girls sent out by families to do the same—who accosted visitors in front of war memorials with flowers to make as offerings to the "glorious spirits" (*eirei*) of the war dead. While visitors complained about such commercial crassness being carried out on sacred ground (*reiiki, reichi*) and about the inadequacy of creature comforts at memorial sites, little did they know that the terms of U.S. control of Okinawa made difficult any direct Japanese support for the maintenance of monuments, ossuaries, and infrastructure, leaving locals with the burden and little means to recompense their efforts. Selling memorial flowers and souvenirs near these sites was, crassness aside, a modest way to help locals make ends meet. This situation embodies the conundrums that Okinawa tourism has faced from its beginnings—satisfying local needs and, at the same time, outsider demands.

The saga of the flower vendors in particular and of souvenir sellers in general appears in print as early as the February 1960 edition of *Kankō Okinawa,* but it likely had been going on for years previous. Sprinkled throughout that OTA-sponsored publication and the organization's own in-house history for the years 1960 to 1965 are repeated mentions of the "unpleasant" (*fuyukai*) "aggressive peddling" (*oshiuri*) of memorial flowers at the most popular war memorials, the Himeyuri-no-tō and Kenji-no-tō.[6] The rise of such complaints coincided with the surge of Japanese interest in participating more directly with war memorialization in Okinawa, with the political tensions this interest caused between Tokyo and USCAR, and with what was perceived as the beginning of a real boom in Okinawa tourism, which could potentially ride the coattails of a wider boom in domestic tourism that was then taking place in mainland Japan—the "Hokkaidō in summer; Okinawa in winter" catchphrase derives from this time.[7] What we see with this sudden and unexpected rise in the number of visitors in this early period is a frontier tourist trade among local inhabitants, which sprang up unregulated around pilgrimage-cum-tourism destinations. As such, this phenomenon provides insights not only into the structure and drive behind the touristification and commercialization of sacred ground but also into the political, social, and cultural relations among Okinawans, Japanese, and Americans.

In his February 1960 article "Kankō meguri no kansō" (Impressions of Sightseeing Tours), local observer Inamine Kunisaburō raises the question of sacred ground as tourist site, which at the time was tantamount to questioning the entire project of Okinawa tourism. He begins by flatly declaring that the southern region of Okinawa is a place for consoling the spirits of the war dead, not for sightseeing, although he admits that the fair weather and early blossoming of flowers in the winter does invite a "sightseeing mood." The flowers—dandelions, morning glories, silverleafs, and hibiscus-covered hedges—alleviate the sense of sadness and mourning even at the Himeyuri-no-tō and Kenji-no-tō until one realizes that these beautiful flowers are offerings to the spirits of the war dead, who are protected and consoled by them.[8] He then begins to criticize the flower vendors at the Himeyuri-no-tō in no uncertain terms:

> First, in front of the Himeyuri-no-tō, when you alight from your vehicle several unsightly girls with flowers in their hands dart over shouting and putting on the hard sell. As friends, they quarrel and compete against each other. It is, you'd agree, a despicable sight. No doubt because it's the tourism business one can't help but to focus on money making, but I thought that rather than being so lewd and conspicuous one would like to do it nowadays in a way that's a little more sensitive to public relations [*sukoshi PR-shiki ni yatte hoshii*].[9]

Similarly, five years later in the same publication in an opinion piece titled "Kankō Okinawa to wa iu keredo" ("You Call It Tourist Okinawa, but . . ."), Matsukawa Kunio presents, as the title suggests, his skeptical assessment of Okinawa as tourist destination. The first section of his critique focuses on the need for general cleanup and beautification of the place, especially the most tourist-exposed areas such as the airport and main transportation arteries. He then turns to the issue of selling things at battle sites by relating the impressions that members of the Hawaii Merchants' Association had of their recent visit to Okinawa. In contrast to those who questioned the appropriateness of developing the battle sites as tourist destinations, these visitors viewed the battle sites as wonderful tourist attractions, save for the pushy flower vendors, rickety refreshment stands, and unsightly souvenir sellers lined up at solemn memorial sites (the quality of appropriate souvenir items had been an ongoing issue). They suggested forbidding such activity directly at those sites and moving them to a more appropriate area. There was a certain irony in this criticism of selling souvenirs given separate complaints about inadequate local items for purchase as souvenirs (*o-miyage*) and, in contrast, Okinawa's growing appeal to mainlanders at this time as a place to purchase foreign goods (perfume, liquor, jewelry, golf clubs, etc.) at considerable discounts because of much lower import tariffs.[10]

Needing to see the selling out of sacred ground for himself, Matsukawa reports going down to Himeyuri-no-tō and Kenji-no-tō and indeed witnessing an unpleasant scene, one that contrasts with and, he says, spoils the efforts of the various mainland prefectures that have established handsome monuments along the southern battle sites route. The underlying message is clear—there is a lack of decorum surrounding the Okinawan-related memorials (Himeyuri and Kenji, the two most popular among tourists) that reflects poorly on Okinawans in general and reinforces mainland images of Okinawan backwardness. Matsukawa then urges better oversight of these memorials and alludes to discussions held at the OTA on that topic, but they have gotten nowhere because of the question of jurisdiction—should regulations be set by local municipal offices or by those who manage battle sites and sacred ground?[11] The answer was not clear, especially when much of the maintenance of Okinawa's monuments and ossuaries had, to this point, been carried out by local volunteers.

A counterpart to the well-received tour bus guides, rude flower vendors swooping on visitors at Himeyuri-no-tō quickly became fixed among the negative images of the Southern Battle Sites Tour, disseminated alike by locals (such as Inamine above) and by visitors from Hawaii and mainland Japan. Invariably added to criticisms of flower vendors were the poor quality of roads to memorial sites, the lack of adequate markers offering explanations to visitors, and the absence of comfortable rest areas. The OTA recognized the infrastructural issues as problems to address and did so piecemeal as their meager budgets allowed, but paving a road, planting shrubbery, and building a covered bench for relatively well-off visitors were—funds willing—easier to accomplish than managing destitute locals trying to make ends meet selling flowers, drinks, and trinkets at the big-draw war memorials. It was not until 1983 that there was finally an accommodation for flower vendors at

Himeyuri-no-tō that involved building a fixed vending booth at the access path to the memorial grounds but well away from the memorial complex itself.[12] Effectively corralling the flower sellers, this solution forced visitors to approach the vendors rather than the vendors approaching the visitors.

The trope of the rude flower vendor holds, however, more than the overt negative message of uncultivated Okinawans crudely capitalizing on the war dead. Read within the larger historical, cultural, political, and economic contexts structuring American-Okinawan-Japanese relations at the time, it encapsulates the crux of those relations. The most glaring aspect is of course the economic differential between Okinawa and the mainland: aggressive selling by widows and girls speaks more to economic desperation than to willing insensitivity toward visitors and the war dead. USCAR provided only indirect and incidental support to the development of the Southern Battle Sites Tour route by way of road building and repair that was coincident to U.S. military needs on the island. At the same time, for political reasons, U.S. policy aimed to restrict if not prohibit direct Japanese aid to Okinawan development for fear that Tokyo would be able to influence Okinawan opinion through such aid. In their attempts to chip away at U.S. restrictions, Japanese officials in the early 1960s turned to the rhetoric that Okinawans had for too long shouldered the economic burden of tending to Japanese monuments (and, despite outward shows of appreciation, they implied that Okinawans had not been able to maintain them with due dignity). Such economic support for war memorialization and for the ongoing recovery of war remains was largely incidental and self-serving for Japanese political ends rather than born of genuine concern for the economic plight of Okinawans. As we will see below in the case of Japanese tourism experts assessing Okinawa's potential for development, a historically long-standing sense of Japan's cultural sophistication and technical superiority over Okinawa could not help but color in tones of condescension any advice and aid coming from the mainland. Even when the critique of flower vendors and of the condition of memorial sites came from an Okinawan man such as Inamine Kunisaburō (gender here is significant), the indignation expressed might be better interpreted as subaltern embarrassment stemming from an internalized sense of cultural and technical inferiority vis-à-vis mainland Japan. Such embarrassment was plainly expressed, for example, by Toguchi Masao, one Okinawan man who recollected what he deemed a pitiful ensemble of female bus guides with shell leis and an accompanying brass band playing folk tunes when greeting mainland visitors on the tarmac of Naha Airport: "Without doubt, what was operating behind my feeling of embarrassment was a psychology that held in contempt an amateurish welcoming scene that smacked of provincialism."[13] This sense of embarrassment at Okinawa's provincialism shadows, as we will see, nearly every aspect of Okinawan tourism development at the time despite the earnestness of the effort. If many Okinawans in the prewar strove—some would say slavishly—to become good imperial subjects, many in the postwar now labored to become good hosts to Japanese tourists in a comparable structure of power relations.

## THE FLOWERING OF MONUMENTS

The mid-1960s "memorial boom" acted to throw into sharp relief the inherent tensions in turning sacred ground into full-fledged tourist sites. These tensions existed on two levels, political and cultural. Politically, increased direct mainland involvement in the building and maintenance of war monuments in Okinawa represented to U.S. authorities a blatant attempt on the part of the Japanese government to stake claims of sovereignty on land that it had effectively lost to the United States. And it was. As I have argued elsewhere, given the sensitivity and the mutual interests in proper treatment of war dead in general, Tokyo successfully forced a very reluctant USCAR to allow more mainland involvement with war memorialization in Okinawa.[14] In addition to funding a central ossuary for the relocation of bones in 1958, the Japanese government during this period negotiated for more direct involvement in the excavation of battle sites and refugee caves; for the retrieval and return of Japanese remains; and for more systematic construction of war monuments. By 1963, the floodgates were open to dozens of new monuments on symbolically charged Mabuni Hill, site of the suicides of Japanese Thirty-second Army generals Ushijima Mitsuru and Cho Isamu, the commanding officers in the defense of Okinawa. Over two dozen prefectures hurried plans to have monuments up on Okinawa in time for the twentieth anniversary of the end of war in 1965. Despite the new protocols hammered out in 1962, which intended to make new monument building more orderly, memorial plots still appeared to be carved out willy-nilly without a uniform sense of design or landscaping. While prefectures and other mainland organizations funded, in Matsukawa's words, "handsome monuments," the area around them and access roads to them fell under local care and jurisdiction as USCAR rebuffed Japanese efforts to provide engineers and direct funding for local improvements.

The politically driven economics of this situation spawned, in turn, culturally tinged complaints from Japanese about Okinawans' capacity to host monuments in a fashion befitting the dignity the war dead and the bereaved deserved. While Japanese officials, in their skirmishes with USCAR, publicly praised Okinawans' underfunded efforts (and offered to do more), a distinct sense of cultural superiority comes across in their assessments of Okinawa's situation. A similar tone is echoed in the assumptions and evaluations of tourism development professionals hired by the OTA and the GRI and in the visitor surveys they collected in the early 1960s. Rather than acknowledging the connections among politics, economics, and visitor accommodations, critical commentators were more apt to imply that shortcomings in tourist facilities and services—including things as simple as access paths, restrooms, and benches at war memorial sites—stemmed from a lack of cosmopolitanism and (modern) cultural sophistication among Okinawans. A 1962 survey of mainland student visitors, for example, listed "noticed the dull-wittedness [*noromasa*] of the Okinawan people" as one of the "things bad about Okinawa."[15] Aspiring Okinawans, such as Inamine and Toguchi cited above, also reinforced these criticisms of local culture and suggested that improvements in Tourist Okinawa could only flow from a more cultivated tourism consciousness among the local population.

Ironically, the first documented suggestions for areas of improvement to the early tourism developing throughout Okinawa Island's former battlegrounds came to the OTA from a group of twenty-seven Okinawan-Hawaiians who visited their homeland in April 1954. Their recommendation: along the Southern Battle Sites Tour, install restroom facilities and plant hibiscus as they do in Hawaii.[16] In the latter recommendation we have the seed of the general floral makeover—the tropicalization—of the Okinawa landscape that is the topic of the next chapter. Here, however, the hibiscus was tied specifically to the beautification of war memorial grounds, not to the generation of an image of a tropical getaway. And for this function, the particular hibiscus referred to—*Hibiscus rosa-sinensis*, or China rose hibiscus—was well qualified given its historical association with grave sites in Okinawa.

The China rose hibiscus has gone by several names in Okinawa. Before the Japanized English word *haibisukasu* became popularized, the local terms *akabanā* (アカバナー), *bussōge* (仏桑華 or 仏桑花, "Buddha's mulberry"), and *gusōbana* (afterlife flower) were the most common. *Bussōge*—the word used in the OTA account of the Okinawan-Hawaiians in 1954—and *gusōbana* reveal the flower's connection with Buddhist funerary practices. In South China, cut hibiscuses were often placed at tombs to signify life's transience as the brilliant blossoms quickly faded. The same practice spread to Okinawa, as Kabira Chōshin recalled:

> When I would have fun cutting sprigs of those *akabanā* and bringing them inside from the garden, my grandmother would say, "That flower is a *gusōbana*; it's a flower we offer to the Buddha." As a mere child at the time, I didn't know what a *gusōbana* or a *hotoke-sama* [Buddha] was. After having grown up some, I understood that a *gusōbana* was a flower that we place at mortuary tablets and offer at graves. That was my first encounter with this flower that in later years I called *bussōge* and knew as *haibisukasu*.[17]

The coincidence between hibiscus as grave flower and hibiscus as tropical icon was almost too perfect—planting hibiscus at war memorial sites would later become a fitting transition from battle site tours to beach resorts. Two hundred *bussōge* found their way onto Mabuni Hill in 1967, and they still exist there today in even greater numbers. At this earlier time, however, outside its everyday use in hedges and gardens, the hibiscus (as *bussōge* and *gusōbana*) signified "grave site offering." Planting them at established and newly constructed war monuments extended a local, everyday practice to a larger scale and to nonlocals (mainland Japanese soldiers). It also beautified the generally barren sites around the monuments sprouting up on and around Mabuni Hill and in Komesu.[18]

This modest beautification effort at war sites did not go unnoticed among increasing numbers of non-Okinawan visitors during the 1960s who frequented the increasing number of war monuments. However, most missed the funerary context for the flower and instead associated it directly with the tropical as it was understood by mainlanders from the north—that is, as "the southern islands" (*nangoku*). As one visitor put it in 1964, "When you tour around the southern part of the island and see the blooming red hibiscus [*bussōge*] scattered along the roadside, you do indeed feel that you've come to the southern islands [*nangoku*]."[19] The OTA and other tourism boosters capitalized on this double reading of the hibiscus; it had a natural place as grave flower for Okinawans but signalled exotic south sea islands to outsiders. In this dual role, the hibiscus could thus respect the solemnity of sites honoring the war dead at a time of an unprecedented war memorial boom while simultaneously imparting an atmosphere of tropical getaway when that idea was beginning to gain more serious consideration. Importantly, this second layer of symbolic meaning of the hibiscus and other tropicalesque flora in Okinawa was cultivated in large part through the intervention of outsiders, primarily mainland Japanese, whose view of Okinawa juxtaposed dominant images of the place as an exotic place of lush landscapes, coral reefs, and warm winters on the one hand and as a place of war ruins, memorial sites, and military bases on the other. Before we follow the full blossoming of tropical tropes in the next chapter, further analysis of how outsiders envisioned the display of Okinawa's wartime legacies is in order.

## THE VIEW FROM THE NORTH

Both the Tourism Section of the Government of the Ryukyu Islands (established within the GRI's Economy Division in August 1961) and the OTA were very interested in outside evaluations of the practice and prospects of tourism in Okinawa from the early 1960s. Some of this feedback came through solicited visitor questionnaires, some through impressions and casual commentary from tourism observers, and some through hired professional consultants. Among these, the most direct and systematic representation of the tourist gaze from mainland Japan came in the form a professional survey the OTA commissioned in 1962. It brought together much of the comments and criticisms floating in the media and among visitor surveys at the time, but it did so under the imprimatur of a mainland Japanese official who was a keen observer and enthusiastic supporter of both global and domestic tourism development. For eleven days and ten nights in February of that year, the OTA hosted Senge Tetsuma, the executive managing director of the Japanese National Park Association, for an island-wide tour of Okinawa's tourist sites and facilities. The results of Senge's survey were published by the OTA in November 1962 as a fifty-page booklet titled *Okinawa kankō shindansho* (A Diagnosis of Okinawa Tourism). Senge's report is wide-ranging and will also figure into later chapters; we will focus here mainly on the sections that address Okinawa's war history and the U.S. military presence in the context of general tourism before moving on to the overall Tourist Okinawa that Senge envisioned.

In the middle of his report, Senge summarizes the appeal of Okinawa for mainlanders (people from *hondo*, the term he uses when referring to non-Okinawan Japan). According to him, this appeal is based on an image of Okinawa as (1) islands south of Kyūshū full of beautiful southern (i.e., tropical) scenery; (2) having a subtropical to tropical climate and therefore warm even in winter; (3) being a green island full of subtropical to tropical foliage; (4) possessing a unique culture; (5) having visible war remains from the Battle of Okinawa; and (6) having a strategic U.S. military base.[20] Half of these points center on differences in climate and scenery relative to mainland Japan to the north. The key term here and throughout the report that marks this geographical and climatic difference is *nangoku,* literally "southern country" or simply "the South." In this context, "south sea islands," or simply "tropics," is a more accurate translation, for it is clear that when used adjectivally (*nangoku teki na*) to describe imagined or desired aspects of atmosphere and scenery in Okinawa, it is intended to connote the tropical or at least tropicalesque. Significantly, *nangoku* is a term that was not widespread in Okinawan discourse on Okinawa to this point, but it is one that became embraced and internalized by Okinawan tourism promoters once introduced by mainland observers.

Two of the other three mainland images of Okinawa that Senge offers are war related. The seeming juxtaposition of the image of would-be tropical paradise and of war-scarred landscape occupied by a foreign military does not seem to faze Senge. In fact, he enthusiastically recommends the development of both aspects of Okinawa in the creation of a more appealing tourist destination. Both, in his estimation, constitute the unusual and the exotic in the eyes of mainlanders. The juxtaposition of the two only furthers this allure. He treats the idea of Okinawa's "unique culture" (by which he means Okinawa's historical, not contemporary, culture) in the same way, as something worth displaying to mainland Japanese because it is not something they are able to encounter directly on the mainland. According to Senge, Okinawa's attractiveness and value as tourist destination for Japanese thus lies entirely in its difference from the northern norm, whether that difference is manifested in climate and scenery, war experience, or historical culture. The problem, as he diagnoses it, is that the reality of Okinawa scarcely lives up fully to the outsider's preconceived image. Unsurprisingly, his recommendations aim to align reality with image, especially with respect to enhancing Okinawa's *nangoku teki na kibun* (southern island feeling) through the planting of tropicalesque flora, a strategy that, as we will see in the following chapter, tourism developers took up with gusto from the mid-1960s to the present.

Given present-day ambivalence toward highlighting Okinawa's war history and militarized condition within its tourism, Senge's treatment of war legacies—both the remnants of war and the continuing U.S. military presence—strikes one as somewhat surprising. He acknowledges the existence of myriad war monuments and bus guide tours of battle sites but argues that these alone do not do justice to Okinawa's war experience and its important place in World War II history. Pointing out that actual traces of the Battle of Okinawa are largely gone, limited to memorial markers to the war dead (which in their haphazard construction have become, in his words, "a disgraceful eyesore"), he complains that there is no memorial museum to give a broader account of the battle and the tragic extent of the suffering among the people of Okinawa.[21] A nationalist sentiment rather than simply sympathy toward Okinawan victims seems to have been motivating Senge in this instance; earlier, when describing the degree of war damage evident in Okinawa, he submits that these "remains of the Battle of Okinawa are not the traces of a nightmare but rather manifestations of the patriotism of Okinawan troops and of the island people who fought to the death for the sake of the Japanese race."[22] One of his more urgent recommendations, the building of a proper Battle of Okinawa memorial museum (preferably in Naha near the Central Ossuary and at the beginning of any Southern Battle Sites Tour), was born of a desire to offer a particular explanation of the battle, one that conformed with mainstream Japanese ideas and ideals about it as an uncomplicated patriotic sacrifice on the part of Okinawans. The Okinawa Peace Memorial Museum that was finally opened at the foot of Mabuni Hill (not in Naha) as part of a growing peace memorial park in June 1975, three years after Okinawa's reversion to full Japanese sovereignty, did not exactly fulfill Senge's recommendations in that it took the war experience of ordinary Okinawans as its focus and was more circumspect about framing Okinawan loss of life and livelihood in terms of patriotic sacrifice for the homeland. It drew relatively large crowds in its inaugural year, the same year as the high-profile Marine Expo '75 was held on the northern and least war-affected part of Okinawa Island, but by that time the energy driving Okinawa tourism had already shifted from its early origins in pilgrimages to war memorials to an emphasis on Okinawa as a lesser (and cheaper) Hawaii for mainland Japanese, relegating the museum—and arguably Okinawa's war history—to a secondary status within newly revised visions of Tourist Okinawa. In this sense Tada Osamu is correct in pinpointing Marine Expo '75 as pivotal in the creation of the image of an ocean-oriented, beach resort Okinawa that glossed over recent war experience. I would refine his argument, however, by pushing the "birth of the [present-day] Okinawa image" further back in time and by crediting Okinawa's dark war history and legacies with providing the impetus to create this bright image in the first place.[23]

Senge's call in 1962 to preserve what actual war ruins still remained on Okinawa Island complemented his insistence on establishing a war memorial museum and on improving the organization and appearance of the burgeoning number of monuments. In particular, he suggests excavating, preserving, and making viewable for the public three specific cave complexes: the Himeyuri Student Nurses Cave, the Naval Headquarters Cave, and the caves on Mabuni Hill where Japanese forces made their last stand and Generals Ushijima and Cho committed suicide.[24] As Okinawa is an island interlaced with dozens and dozens of natural caves that were used by military personnel and civilian refugees alike, caves are especially iconic of the war experience on Okinawa and possess their own politics of representation.[25] A comprehensive survey of war-related sites in Okinawa conducted from 1998 to 2006 underscores this distinction; it notes that because of the extent of surface damage to the island during the war, 207 of the 254 sites surveyed (81 percent) are natural or manmade caves.[26] For many, "Battle of Okinawa" means tunneled-out defenses and natural caves, which in turn connote a tenacious war of attrition. In Senge's case, naming these three cave complexes as candidates for tourist sites conforms to the dominant Japanese view of the Battle of Okinawa. Each represents, in its own way, the ultimate sacrifice to country and an appropriately heroic tale with which to impress visitors; none represents civilian experience as equally notable but—until recently—ignored refugee caves where cases of Japanese military abuse and violence toward Okinawan noncombatants have been documented.[27] This unsavory side of certain refugee caves was not what mainland visitors expected and sought. To include it would be an offense to those (paying guests) accustomed to the dominant mainland Japanese view of the battle. It would take nearly forty more years and the activism of progressive Okinawan historians and of former governor Ōta Masahide in the 1990s to achieve any kind of truly critical depiction of the battle at a public museum.

## THE EXCAVATION OF MEANING

As mentioned in chapter 1, the Himeyuri story has held a special place in Japanese interpretations of the battle as the most poignant example of patriotic Okinawan sacrifice for the fatherland, and the Himeyuri-no-tō has since the 1950s been one of Okinawa's most visited sites. The physical marker for the memorial, originally a simple stone cenotaph later joined by a more elaborate wall listing the names of victims, was placed above one of several caves where many sought refuge and perished during the final days of the battle in mid-June 1945. "Himeyuri-no-tō" refers to the memorial marker—the monument—and to the cave itself. In other words, the cave is the memorial/monument in the same way, as we have seen, that the original ossuaries (*nōkotsu-dō*) in Okinawa are memorials (*irei-tō*). Bone collection at Himeyuri-related caves continued as late as the mid-1980s, underscoring the difficulty of thoroughly accessing and clearing them for any kind of public display.[28]

While Senge's suggestion of making the Himeyuri cave publicly viewable was not realized as he imagined, the Himeyuri Peace Memorial Museum, opened in 1989, contains a diorama of it. This life-sized replica of the cave, which places the viewer below a vine-strewn opening and next to the cave's floor where Himeyuri girls would have died, is located at the emotional heart of the museum—a room simply called Chinkon (鎮魂, "Repose of Souls"), three walls of which are lined with the large black-and-white photos of 206 of the faces of the Himeyuri girls captioned with their names and circumstances of death. At the center of the room are oversized reproductions of war-experience testimonies written by seventy-two surviving girls. The combination of stark, ghostly photos of the girls in their school blouses, the palpable words of survivors, and the realistic representation of the cave from the viewpoint of the refugees instills in the visitor an overwhelming sense of a tragic sacrifice of innocent schoolgirls who acted selflessly and dutifully for the nation. One cannot help but be moved by the display. Despite not being the real cave that Senge would have liked to display for tourists, the replica is arguably a more effective distillation and realization of its symbolic potential by the very fact of being contained and placed within the overall narrative of the museum as part of its climax in the Repose of Souls room. This museumification of the cave takes the real object out of its raw and natural setting and "cooks" it with a meaning—cave as tomb and soul-consoling monument (*irei-tō*). That it is not the actual cave does not diminish its effect; in fact, it is likely that some visitors do not even realize that it is a copy of the original, the mouth of which opens next to the memorial marker and wall of names of the students and their teachers to form together the Himeyuri-no-tō proper located outside the museum entrance (see figure 1.1).

The other two cave complexes that Senge singled out, the Navy Underground Headquarters and the caves of the final Japanese resistance in Mabuni, offer different facets of the same common mainland Japanese view of the Battle of Okinawa as nothing but a dutiful and glorious sacrifice for the fatherland. Little can trump the tragic appeal of the Himeyuri story as it is presented at the Himeyuri Peace Memorial Museum and adjoining Himeyuri-no-tō, where members of the Himeyuri Dōsōkai and tour bus guides narrate the drama on a daily basis. In contrast to the Himeyuri cave, some of those in Mabuni on the Kyan Peninsula are partially viewable and accessible, while the Navy Underground Headquarters was, in the spirit of Senge's recommendations, transformed into a very popular tourist site in 1970 and has remained a featured attraction ever since for those interested in Okinawa's war history. It is one of the few war-related sites—the Himeyuri-no-tō being one other—that has been prominently and consistently featured within general tourism promotional material from pre-Reversion days to the present.

On Mabuni Hill, beyond its crest where dozens of prefectural monuments had begun sprouting from around the time of Senge's visit, lies the cave where Generals Ushijima and Cho killed themselves in the predawn hours of June 23, 1945, bringing the final throes of organized Japanese resistance to an end.[29] Okinawa's Memorial Day (Irei no Hi) coincides with this event, a point that has been a source of some controversy for those who recognize the fighting—and deaths—that continued after this date.[30] As a dramatic closing scene to the Battle of Okinawa, the site of these suicides by the commanding officers is imbued with heightened symbolic appeal; it is a place that visitors interested in the battle would certainly want to see. To that end, makeshift grave markers were quickly erected at the site in June 1945, with an explanatory plaque set up by U.S. forces who henceforth referred to the spot as Suicide Cliff or Suicide Hill. The cave itself, however, has been shut off and today is not particularly conspicuous; one can see only a short way into the mouth behind a small gate cluttered with makeshift memorial plaques and offerings. What has served, rather, as the pilgrimage (and photo op) site for Ushijima and Cho's final act is the Reimei-no-tō memorial monument erected in their honor further up the path from the spot of their deaths. First dedicated in

June 1952 shortly after the end of the U.S. occupation of mainland Japan, the monument received a major renovation in October 1962 when it was redone in an abstract design symbolic of the blades the pair used to kill themselves (see figure 2.1). The redesign came on the cusp of Mabuni Hill's memorial-building boom and embodies the message of self-sacrifice for Japan's postwar peace and prosperity that emanates from the mass of prefectural monuments constructed soon afterward.[31] It stands in a dominating position on the edge of the cliff overlooking the Pacific Ocean at the end of the path one takes through the rows of prefectural monuments on Mabuni Hill. So positioned, it is the physical, symbolic, and narrative climax for one's pilgrimage to the final battleground on a Southern Battle Sites Tour and stands, in the dominant Japanese narrative of the battle, as a tribute to the glorious spirits of two selfless Japanese patriots.

If the place of Ushijima and Cho's demise and honor represents the climax of a trip to Mabuni, then heading down through jungly vegetation from the cliff to the Kenji-no-tō at the seaward base of the hill would constitute following the denouement. While lacking the gendered pathos of the plight of the Himeyuri schoolgirls, the schoolboys of the Imperial Blood and Iron Youth Corps have similarly been portrayed as self-sacrificing innocents cut down before their full flowering. As the male counterpart to the Himeyuri-no-tō,

**Figure 2.1.** Reimei-no-tō, memorial to the suicides of Generals Ushijima and Cho. *Source*: Gerald Figal.

the memorial to the 285 boys and 20 staff members of Okinawa Prefectural Teachers School who formed part of the Blood and Iron Youth Corps that followed in support of the Thirty-second Army Command was founded in March 1946 near caves and shoreline shelters where many of the students met their end. What is now immediately accessible of these caves resembles a rock shelter more than a cave proper. It lies just off and below the Kenji-no-tō cenotaph and is not identified as a particular site; one can, however, crouch down and walk around the shelter imagining what it might have been like hiding there from the enemy. It is this kind of empathetic experience of the battle at preserved war ruins—especially Okinawa's iconic caves—that Senge had in mind in his recommendations.

The eventual excavation and preservation accomplished at the Navy Underground Headquarters realized more fully Senge's vision for war ruins made into full-blown tourist attractions. The Okinawa Tourism Development Corporation (Okinawa Kankō Kaihatsu Kigyōdan), established in January 1968 under a newly legislated Okinawa Tourism Development Corporation Act, was in charge of carrying out the preparation of the cave as a new high-profile sightseeing spot on the well-established Southern Battle Sites Tour. Work took place throughout 1969, and in February of the following year, 275 meters of the original cave, with its maze of rooms and corridors, opened to the public.[32] Now administered by the Okinawa Convention & Visitors Bureau, while the content and tenor of the memorial is prominently influenced by navy veteran associations, it has been a heavy draw ever since for Japanese tourists and American war buffs alike. It has been called "a kind of Mecca for former naval personnel."[33] Previous to the opening of the cave itself, the impressive and unabashedly patriotic Kaigun Senbotsusha Irei-no-tō, the memorial to the naval war dead of the Battle of Okinawa, had since October 1958 towered from a spot directly above the cave located about three kilometers south of Naha on the Oroku Peninsula, where in early June 1945 Rear Admiral Ōta Minoru ordered his approximately four thousand men to a glorious death (*gyōkusai*) here rather than join the army's retreat to the south. Ongoing interservice rivalry likely played a role in his decision to hold his ground. Along with the nearby Oroku Naval Airfield, the dug-out and reinforced-concrete cave complex constituted the Japanese navy's base of operations during the battle. It was ultimately overrun by American forces in a ten-day assault on the peninsula beginning on June 4. As in the case of the cave where Ushijima and Cho killed themselves, a good deal of the fascination with this cave lies in the group suicide (*shūdan jiketsu*) of Ōta and five senior officers, reportedly lying in repose in their dress uniforms and with throats slit when U.S. forces found them. Dozens of other suicides were strewn throughout other rooms and corridors, in addition to the wounded whom medical staff had lethally injected under Ōta's last orders. Scars on the concrete walls from hand grenades used in suicides are still visible in some places and count among tourist highlights[34] (see figure 2.2).

Besides its intrinsically interesting physical presence and the morbid fascination of the suicides committed there, the Navy Underground Headquarters is also distinguished as the site where a week before his death Ōta dispatched a famous telegram to the Thirty-second Army Headquarters for conveyance to the vice admiral in Tokyo. Some, in fact, attribute the popularity of this cave to the existence of this telegram.[35] In it Ōta laments the loss of civilian life, speaks forthrightly about mistakes made, describes the forced conscription of Okinawans, praises in the highest terms the loyalty and sacrifice of the local population in the defense of the country, and asks that for their efforts the Okinawan people be given "special consideration."[36] Such a statement among Japanese military communications was unprecedented, thus its special interest. The pertinent text of the telegram is on display in the cave and is included as part of the recorded audio narration of facts related to the cave, which is pumped in through speakers within the complex. Ōta's telegram has, however, been a point of controversy; on the one hand it regrets Okinawan

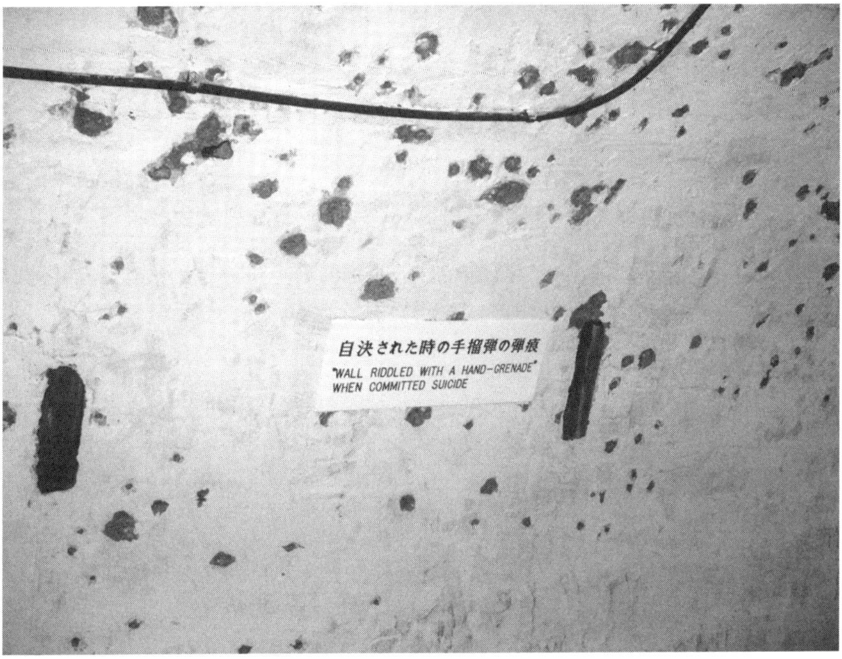


**Figure 2.2.** Shrapnel-riddled wall in the Navy Underground Headquarters Cave. *Source*: Gerald Figal.

civilian loss and contains evidence concerning harsh treatment of Okinawans by the military; on the other hand, this voice of sympathy and admiration for Okinawans is tied to glorification and aestheticization of war as well as to a questionable touristification of the site, which by nature arguably trivializes one's understanding of the war.[37] As historian Arasaki Moriteru and others point out, the original text of the telegram appeared printed in mainland newspapers on June 15, 1945, alongside an explication that framed it as an example of Okinawans' and the nation's unity of purpose and unwavering support for the Imperial Armed Forces in the defense of the homeland.[38] Unsurprisingly, controversy over the presentation of the cave in the wider context of the battle, questions about the appropriateness of turning the cave into a tourist site, and nuances in the meaning of Ōta's famous telegram do not make an appearance at the site, which I have toured on three occasions. From my observations and eavesdropping among tourists there, visitors are engrossed in the extraordinary experience of being in a real cave used during the war and are moved by the drama of the "glorious deaths" that took place there. Praise of Okinawans' war efforts is concatenated to that presentation so that theirs too were glorious deaths for the sake of the nation, made even more poignant as having come from the civilian population, especially its youths.

In contrast to the success of the Navy Underground Headquarters as a war-related tourist site, the main command center for the Japanese defense, the Thirty-second Army Headquarters, has frustrated efforts to develop it into a comparable attraction. Situated in a sprawling complex running about 390 meters north to south beneath the grounds of the former Shuri Castle, General Ushijima's headquarters was first surveyed for its sightseeing potential by Naha City in 1962, but it was found too dangerous and difficult to develop. The Okinawa Tourism Development Corporation conducted a similar survey in 1968 and reached the same conclusions despite drawing up detailed blueprints laying out tourist access.[39] In his report, Senge does not name the Thirty-second Army Underground Headquarters among his suggestions for war ruins to preserve and transform into tourist sites, probably assuming that the presence at the time of the University of the Ryukyus on the former castle grounds and the collapsed tunnels within the cave below made excavation and safe access impossible. Indeed, the lengthy cave, the majority of which ranges twenty to forty meters below the surface, has proven extremely difficult to clear out. Upon their retreat on May 27 from the command cave—flooded by the annual spring rains and threatened with imminent capture by American forces—General Ushijima's men imploded the entrances to the complex. Multiple attempts over the years to excavate the cave have made little progress because of the collapsed tunnels and inherent danger involved, but efforts have continued within the Peace Promotion Division of the Okinawa prefectural government to survey and clear the complex with the aim of perhaps offering some public access some day.[40] Published progress reports and my interview in June 2004 with representatives of the Peace Promotion Division (reorganized as the Peace and Gender Equality Promotion Division in April 2005) confirm the agency's dedication to the goal of putting the cave safely on public display and the slow progress to that end.[41] Most recently, the *Okinawa Times* reported in June 2009 on the progress to date in surveying and restoring the cave; prefectural assemblyman Toguchi Osamu examined it for himself and emphasized the importance of preserving these war ruins as a record for posterity: "Omitting the [Army Headquarters] cave, you can't relate the Battle of Okinawa. Even just partially opening it up to the public would be good."[42]

Unlike the Okinawa Tourism Development Corporation's original plans for this cave in 1968, which were in line with what was realized at the Navy Underground Headquarters as a successful general tourist attraction along the Southern Battle Sites Tour, what has been propelling the latest attempts to preserve and display such war ruins is Okinawa's burgeoning peace education (*heiwa kyōiku*) business. Serious education and peace activism, not casual sightseeing tours, constitute the new context and rationale behind salvaging the Army Underground Headquarters and developing others, most notably Itokazu Cave (Abuchiragama) and the Haebaru Army Field Hospital, a series of dug-out tunnels and caves. This peace education surged noticeably during Governor Ōta Masahide's administration (1990–1998) and included several new initiatives and projects. Plans were set in motion in the early 1990s for an impressive new memorial to the war dead of the Battle of Okinawa, the Cornerstone of Peace (Heiwa no Ishiji; see figure 2.3), which was dedicated on June 23, 1995, at the fiftieth anniversary of the end of the Battle of Okinawa. In its wake a volunteer network of "peace guides" (*heiwa gaido*) had hit the Southern Battle Sites Tour route, and Ōta's vision for a new Peace Memorial Museum, finally completed in 2000, began to take shape. Peace was being waged throughout the island.[43]

It was in this context that the first incarnation of the Peace Promotion Division was founded within the prefectural government in 1992. Among its activities has been the survey and excavation of the Army Underground Headquarters, work that it has continued since 1992. A short report published in 1996 by the Committee for the Study of the Preservation and Public Display of the Thirty-second Army Underground Headquarters lays out in plain terms the framework and goals of this group, making very clear that the primary intention for the preservation and public display of the cave is to further understanding of the "true face" of the defense of the mainland under the imperial government as part of a program to promote peace and peace education. It enumerates the historical and cultural value of its location under the castle in Shuri, the cultural cradle of Okinawa, and underscores the central importance of the cave as army headquarters during the Battle of Okinawa. In its role in relating "lessons for peace" for future generations through the display and direct experience of the cave, a restored Army Underground Headquarters is envisioned, in conjunction with the Cornerstone of Peace and a new Prefectural Peace Memorial Museum, as an anchor point for "Peace Beacon Okinawa" (*heiwa no hasshinchi Okinawa*).[44]

In this respect, a local—rather than an outsider—vision is now guiding how and why this cave should be put on public display. As if to counter the kind of patriotic touristification of the Navy Underground Headquarters—and what was similarly planned at the same time for the Army Underground Headquarters—peace promotion agencies within and outside the prefectural government seem determined to develop this cave as an antiwar, antitourism tourist site placed squarely within peace courses and discourses that have significantly advanced as part of public policy and private initiative since the

**Figure 2.3.** The Cornerstone of Peace emanates its message over the sea and across the island from the Peace Flame at the center of Peace Plaza. Mabuni Hill, with its rows of prefectural memorials honoring the Japanese war dead, looms in the background and fronts the Pacific Ocean. *Source*: Gerald Figal.

1980s. So, conceived within the terms of peace education (*heiwa kyōiku*) and as a site that is less glamorous than the Navy Underground Headquarters, the Army Underground Headquarters ends up having more in common with the civilian refugee caves that have also been explicitly developed for alternative sightseeing routes designed for a deeper and more critical understanding of Okinawa's wartime past and peacetime present. These alternative configurations of the physical and discursive terrain of war-related Okinawa take up much of the original Southern Battle Sites Tour, recontexualize it, add to it, and package it in maps and critical commentary as "the other Okinawa" that has been scarcely featured in mainstream tourism, both in its earliest days and now.

The Haebaru Army Field Hospital and mixed military and civilian refugee caves, most notably Itokazu Cave and Garabi Cave in the south, started to appear in published guides for alternative peace study routes (*heiwa gakushū kōsu*) in the 1980s after a decade of local rediscovery and independent research began to coalesce into working groups set on promoting these sites as part of a *senseki meguri* (battlefield tour).[45] At the same time, the facts about the compulsory group suicide (*shūdan jiketsu*) of eighty-two civilians (including forty-seven children) in Chibichiri Cave in Yomitan Village (at the heart of the American invasion landing on April 1, 1945) came to light through interviews local market owner Chibana Shōichi conducted in 1983 with survivors who had kept quiet about the incident until then.[46] The same year also saw the publication of the first edition of the jointly authored book *Kankō kōsu de nai Okinawa: Senseki, kichi, sangyō, bunka* (The Okinawa Not on the Tourist Route: Battlefields, Bases, Business, Culture). Reaching its fourth edition in 2008, this book takes these caves as anchor points for peace study tours designed to compensate for the unreflective touristification of Okinawa, especially of its war-related sites that too easily succumb to depictions of the Battle of Okinawa that cater to conservative mainland Japanese sensibilities. Alongside critical appraisals of the Navy Underground Headquarters, of the prefectural monuments on Mabuni Hill, and of what it calls the "Yasukunification" of certain other memorials to Japanese war dead on Okinawa, *Kankō kōsu de nai Okinawa* offers historical context, maps, photos, and sobering commentary on refugee and hospital caves that had previously not figured into the traditional Southern Battle Sites Tour or into the visions for tourism development that professional consultants like Senge Tetsuma had offered since the early 1960s.

This Okinawan-led (re)discovery of this other stratum of wartime experience—captured in a counterrepresentation of Okinawa's emblematic caves—has in effect prompted a rethinking of the form, content, and aims of the Southern Battle Sites Tour. Casual tourists still can and do take something approximating the original Southern Battle Sites Tour offered by one of the local bus lines, which includes as its marquee attractions the Navy Underground Headquarters, Himeyuri-no-tō, Konpaku-no-tō, and Mabuni Hill. Since 1995 these set tours have also encompassed the expansive Cornerstone of Peace at the foot of Mabuni Hill and, since its opening in April 2000, the adjacent Prefectural Peace Memorial Museum. Those visitors particularly interested in the war might seek out the off-the-beaten-path refugee caves, but not (yet) as part of mainstream packaged battlefield tours. On the other hand, one of Okinawa's most significant tourism segments—school field trips from the mainland—has notably expanded since the early 1980s to include the latest sites developed within the rubric of peace education. Having the direct experience of going down into a refugee cave is a highlight of such tours, for which a variety of learning materials have been published over the years. The 1986 edition of the self-proclaimed "loose-leaf format battlefield and bases guidebook" *Aruku, miru, kangaeru Okinawa* (Okinawa to Walk, Look At, and Think About), authored by members of the southern branch of the Okinawa High School Teachers' Union and the Peace Education Research Committee, exemplifies this form of alternative tour book. Published as a binder with removable card stock pages detailing forty-seven locations with maps, photos, descriptions, and analyses, it was designed specifically for field use on more in-depth war- and base-related study tours and on school "peace study field trips." It contains advice on the gear needed on such field trips (flashlights, gloves, hats, hiking or rain boots, towels, water bottles, walking sticks, etc.), contact info for transportation, bibliographic references for further study, and blank pages for note taking. It also offers several "model routes" organized according to focus of interest (battlefields and/or bases) and more specific themes (civilian refugees, Himeyuri student corps, Shiraume student corps, monument epitaphs, nuclear bases, communications bases, and antiwar landlords). Itokazu Cave and Garabi Cave are highlights of the battlefield routes. One of the principal contributors to this and revised editions of *Aruku, miru, kangaeru Okinawa* is Okinawa International University professor Ishihara Masaie, who has developed materials for cave visits in the wider context of field research he has conducted collecting wartime testimonials since 1970.[47] His research serves as the basis for the entries on Itokazu Cave and Garabi Cave, which he and his peace studies seminar have studied for many years.[48]

In recent years, tours of Garabi Cave have diminished because of dangerous conditions in the cave and its location on private property, while Itokazu Cave (Abuchiragama)[49] has emerged as the premier place to get a sense of how wounded soldiers and civilian refugees might have experienced the Battle of Okinawa. The Haebaru Army Field Hospital has similarly led the way as a model war-ruins site developed on local initiative for wider public display. Both have been developed extensively in recent years for regular touring. Itokazu Cave, a natural cave measuring about 270 meters long, was originally designed as an army cave encampment but was converted over at the end of April 1945 to serve as a hospital annex and then de facto refugee cave with the rapidly growing numbers of wounded after the Battle of Okinawa began. Equipped with medical rooms, food and milk storage, six pit stoves, a well, and military gear lockers, Itokazu Cave hosted nearly one thousand wounded who were treated by two doctors, five or six medics, and three regular nurses (see figure 2.4). Sixteen members of the Himeyuri Student Nurses Corps spent time tending the wounded there; seven of them ended up dying on the battlefield. The remains of one Korean "comfort woman" (*ianfu*) were also discovered inside. The interior of the cave has been thoroughly excavated, restored, and fitted with handrails, walking paths, signposts, and floodlights (although the only lighting used on tours comes from individual flashlights).

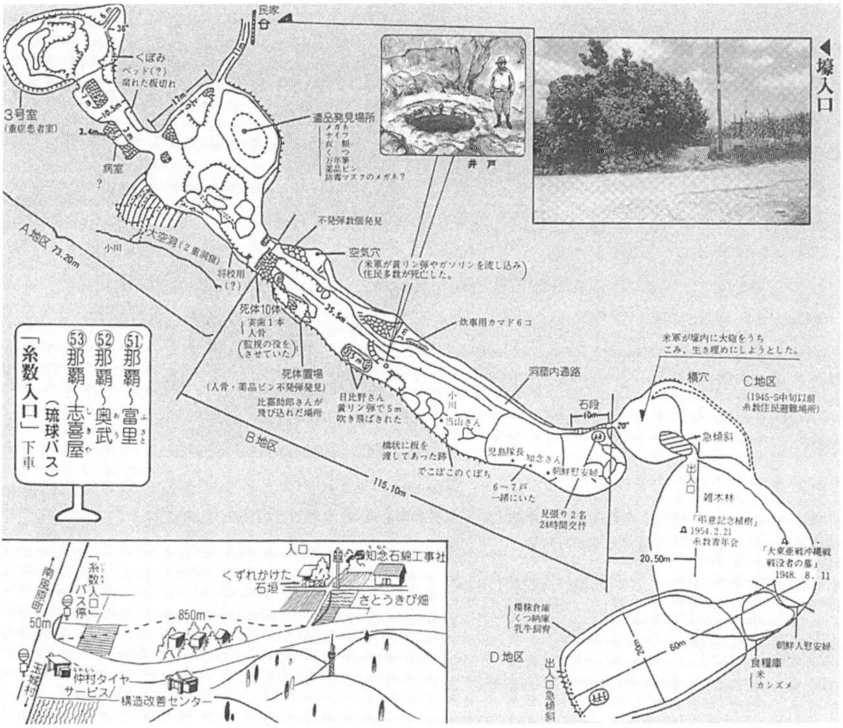


**Figure 2.4.** Map of Itokazu Cave (Abuchiragama). *Source*: *Aruku, miru, kangaeru Okinawa*, adapted courtesy of Okinawa Jiji Shuppan.

With the boom in Okinawa peace education tours and the emphasis within them on having a "cave experience" that features a few minutes in complete darkness, Itokazu Cave has gained wider popularity. In fact, the "complete blackout" with a *heiwa gaido* (peace guide) has become a well-known set piece, as exemplified in this reproduction:

> Guide: Shall we try turning off our flashlights and perking up our ears?
>
> Student: Huh!? Why? It's scary!
>
> Guide: Let's try to get close to how it was back then. I wonder what we can see, what we can hear. I wonder if we could imagine the feelings of the people who were here.[50]

To accommodate and to capitalize on the increased traffic to Itokazu Cave, Tamagusuku Village, where the cave is located, opened on May 25, 2002, a Southern Tourism Comprehensive Guide Center (Nanbu Kankō Sōgō Annai Sentā) that offers parking and general tourist information for Okinawa Prefecture and beyond but specializes in providing information on the nearby cave and offering (required) rental flashlights and helmets for a modest one hundred yen fee. A manned booth was also built at the mouth of the main entrance to the cave and signs posted prohibiting photographs and video from being taken within it, all of which indicates increased development and regulation of the cave as its popularity has grown.

My two solo descents into Itokazu Cave, the first in July 2001 and the second in November 2009, attest to the significant change in the public standing of the cave. The first instance involved finding my way through rural back roads, parking in a makeshift dirt parking lot, and following minimal signage through sugar cane fields to reach the unattended entrance to the cave. There were no indications of regulation of the cave; I had the run of the place for the twenty to twenty-five minutes it takes to go through the site. The interior of the majority of the cave had by then been cleared and stairs, pathways, and signs prepared for individual and school group tours, but by the time of my second visit, more of the cave had been cleared and paths more clearly marked. The new Guide Center parking lot can accommodate four buses and sixteen cars, and volunteer staff serve as guides for school groups. For spelunkers without guides, a yellow painted line leads from the Guide Center to the cave entrance about a three-minute walk away, and signs from the cave exit lead back to the Guide Center. In contrast to my first visit, Itokazu Cave has become a much better-developed and organized sightseeing spot—not one that earns profits but one that does process thousands of visitors, especially schoolchildren, per year in what appears to be a smoothly running operation designed to foster peace education.

This kind of local development and promotion of wartime ruins—caves in particular—as specialized tourist sites framed within the rhetoric and practice of peace education exemplifies current local trends that are still marginalized from the mainstream of big moneymaking beach-and-sky-oriented tourism. Without steady streams of school field trips from the mainland and throughout Okinawa Prefecture (on average over three hundred thousand students per year since 2000), they would be scarcely visited; the "cave experience" would begin and end at the Navy Underground Headquarters, coloring—or perhaps simply confirming—the mainland visitors' understanding of the on-the-ground (and under-the-ground) experience of the battle. These not-on-the-tourist-route tourist sites are, however, slowly gaining a wider audience through steady local promotion that reaches national channels. Significantly, these national channels have since the mid-1990s been reached not only through linkages with other "peace sites" such as Hiroshima and Nagasaki but also through an increasing awareness throughout Japan (and the world) of modern war ruins as important cultural properties. As the only place within Japan proper of a major World War II land battle, Okinawa has been spearheading this growing movement that was accelerated in Japan and worldwide by the fiftieth anniversary of the end of the war in 1995. And at the forefront of Okinawa's efforts stands the Haebaru Army Field Hospital (redesignated by its wartime name, Okinawa Army Field Hospital).

The Army Field Hospital was not originally intended to be in Haebaru, a town due east from the Navy Underground Headquarters and south along the path of retreat from the Army Underground Headquarters in Shuri to the Kyan Peninsula (see figure 1.2). After the original Okinawa Army Field Hospital was destroyed in the October 10, 1944, American air raid of Naha, it was moved from the city to rooms at the Haebaru National Elementary School, where it was staffed by 350 army doctors, nurses, and medics. Once that facility too was destroyed in a March 1945 air raid, just prior to the American landing on Okinawa, it was moved to a complex of about thirty caves and tunnels of varying length dug into the hillside of Kogane Forest (Koganemori, locally pronounced Kuganimui) in Haebaru, which American troops reached in early June during their final push to the south of the island. As the main Japanese field hospital during the battle, it figures prominently in the Himeyuri Student Nurses Corps saga. Here the schoolgirls treated the wounded, disposed of waste, transported water, and buried the dead. The field hospital was also the starting point of their perilous retreat to the Kyan Peninsula and has been featured in theatrical films about the Himeyuri.[51] Finally, according to a memorial marker originally placed there by Haebaru Town in 1953, it was "the suicide spot [*jiketsu no chi*] of over 2,000 of the gravely injured," a claim that speaks to the undoubtable tragedy that befell the hospital but is not consistent with the size of the facility or the remains recovered there afterward. The use of the term *jiketsu*—implying a voluntary act—has, as in other references to self-inflicted deaths of the war wounded and of civilians in caves, also been criticized for masking the compulsory nature of such acts ordered by the military.[52] In short, the Haebaru Army Field Hospital was a physically significant site during the battle, and through its association with the Himeyuri Student Nurses Corps and so-called *jiketsu* incidents, it has become a symbolically significant and contentious site in postwar battles over the memory and meaning of the place.

This wartime history and postwar use of the site have strengthened the rationale and efforts to preserve and display it as a local and national *cultural* property. It is this pursuit of official cultural recognition that distinguishes the Haebaru Army Field Hospital locally, nationally, and even internationally as a pioneer in the context of architectural and cultural appreciation of wartime ruins. Awareness of the value of modern war ruins as cultural assets spiked in Japan during the run-up to the fiftieth anniversary of the end of the Asia-Pacific War in 1995 and has in turn spurred the growth of nationwide war-ruins preservation movements and of battlefield archeology (*senseki kōkōgaku*) as a specialized subfield of archeology, one that has been notably featured in the work that has already been done in Okinawan caves and tunnels, particularly at the Haebaru Army Field Hospital. Before the term *senseki kōkōgaku* entered broad use, Okinawan archeologist and Okinawa International University professor Tōma Shiichi first broached the concept in his 1984 article "Recommendations for Battlefield Archeology" (*Sensō kōkōgaku no susume*) wherein he focused on postwar bone collection and the excavation of underground shelters in Okinawa.[53] Other scholars, such as Ikeda Ichirō and Itō Atsushi, further developed the field more broadly during the 1990s, the latter placing it within the ongoing discourse concerning the scope of important cultural properties.[54]

Riding on this national wave, battlefield archeology and war-ruins preservation in Okinawa have in recent years been invariably framed within and underwritten by peace education discourse that has emanated from the grass roots and grown into broader national networks. The Haebaru Army Field Hospital stands out as one of the best examples of this phenomenon and of the confluence of forces that make possible the realization of a local countervision of war-related sightseeing that stands in contrast to the Navy Underground Headquarters. The attention to the Army Field Hospital that has brought it wider recognition sprang from the most local of levels. In 1983, as part of a school exhibition titled "The Battle of Okinawa as Told by Haebaru," *Aruku, miru, kangaeru Okinawa* editor Yoshihama Shinobu organized 130 of his students at Haebaru High School to conduct door-to-door interviews of war survivors for a war damage survey of the Haebaru area. As expected, the Army Field Hospital figured frequently in interviewee accounts as being at the core of Haebaru's experience of the Battle of Okinawa. Yoshihama proceeded to oversee the publication of twelve volumes of local war-experience testimonies from 1983 to 1996 based on these kinds of local interviews, which have become a typical form of local oral history and personal history writing (*jibunshi*) in Okinawa.[55]

Recognizing that wartime ruins could not at the time be officially designated cultural assets under the guidelines of Japan's Cultural Properties Protection Law (*Bunkazai Hogohō*), Haebaru Town amended its own local guidelines to allow for such a designation. As a result, in June 1990, the Number One and Number Two Surgery Caves (the longest ones of the complex) were formally recognized by the town government as Municipal Cultural Properties. In this act Haebaru proved to be five years ahead of the rest of the country: in March 1995, in the heightened historical awareness surrounding the fiftieth anniversary of the end of the Asia-Pacific War, the Japanese Ministry of Education (Monbusho) revised its standards for the designation of important cultural properties to include wartime ruins. It then promptly bestowed—some would say in a distinctly political gesture—the designation on Hiroshima's A-Bomb Dome, paving the way for its inclusion on the UNESCO World Heritage List a year later against the protests of the United States and China.

In a parallel but related development, the National Network for the Protection of War-Related Sites (Sensō Iseki Hozon Zenkoku Nettowāku) was formed in July 1997 at its first symposium held at Matsushiro, a suburb of Nagano City where a massive underground bunker complex, intended as an alternative Imperial General Headquarters, was built during the last eight months of the war by an estimated seven to ten thousand Korean slave laborers. The controversial site stands at the center of battlefield archeology and war-ruins preservation on mainland Japan, with only about a five hundred meter length of tunnels of a total 5,856 square feet of space open to the public for sightseeing, operated by the Nagano City Bureau of Tourism since 1990.[56] The foundation of the National Network for the Protection of War-Related Sites initiated a period, still ongoing, of systematic surveys, educational outreach, and advocacy for war-ruins preservation across all of Japan's prefectures. For its part, the Okinawa Prefectural Board of Education undertook its own prefecture-wide comprehensive survey of all war-related sites for possible designation as cultural properties.[57] Total numbers vary widely depending on one's definition of "war-related sites" (*sensō iseki*), but this survey, conducted from 1998 to 2006, yielded 254 notable war remains throughout the islands of the prefecture, 131 (52 percent) of which are on Okinawa Island. More remarkable is the confirmation that natural and manmade caves and tunnels constitute the vast majority of war ruins in Okinawa. Of the 254 sites, 207 (81 percent) are underground, a testimony both to the severity of surface bombardment and destruction during the Battle of Okinawa and to the fundamental nature of Okinawa's geography and the defense strategy adapted to it—dug-in positions, often formed from natural caves, designed to slow the enemy as long as possible.

Following its inaugural symposium, the National Network for the Protection of War-Related Sites held its second symposium in 1998 in Haebaru Town. The choice of location signified the relatively advanced stage of battlefield archeology at the Army Field Hospital site and widened national awareness of it. By this time the Haebaru Board of Education had overseen four years of archeological surveys of the tunnels, producing detailed reports photographing, measuring, sketching, cataloguing, and describing with scientific precision the contours and contents of the complex. The March 2000 report was the third volume of the Haeburu Town Cultural Properties Survey Reports series, reinforcing the identification of these war ruins as cultural assets on par with more traditional ideas of what constituted valuable cultural items worthy of official study and protection.[58] Study and public display of recovered objects and photographs—from shards of bone and rusted tools to medicine jars and microscopes—had been organized at the nearby Haebaru Culture Center, a modest facility that was established in 1989 and underwent major renovations and expansion at a nearby site in 2009 in the wake of the public opening of Cave No. 20 on June 18, 2007. The center recruits and trains volunteer guides to take—by reservation only—small groups on a twenty-minute tour inside Cave No. 20 (see figure 2.5). Guides are well versed in the history of the Battle of Okinawa and in the details of the Army Field Hospital and its excavation. Ideally, a visitor is encouraged to tour the cave first at a reserved time and then linger over the exhibits housed in the impressive new museum facility, built entirely on initiative and funding from Haebaru Town. It features a permanent exhibit on the Battle of Okinawa from a Haebaru perspective, complemented by an exhibit of traditional local society and culture organized around the model of a typical life course from birth to burial. As curator Taira Tsugiko explains, "The idea is to present as a counterpart to the darkness of the war history a display of traditional life and customs that are gradually fading from local life."[59] Juxtaposing war history with traditional peacetime social and cultural practices is one way the Haebaru Culture Center attempts to distinguish itself from other war history exhibits. The center is also committed to broadening the scope of its displays through a series of temporary international cultural exhibitions that somehow relate to local culture, the first one featuring textiles from Southeast Asia. This effort to make connections and meaning beyond a circumscribed account of the Battle of Okinawa and beyond local cultural geography resembles writ small the efforts, prominent since the Ōta administration, to fashion Okinawa as a "beacon of peace" for the world while pointing to its history of peaceful multicultural connections as special qualification for this role. The difference is that at this local level in Haebaru, this kind of activity appears to spring less from idealistic rhetoric than from a sense of rooted commitment—a moral obligation even—to excavate meaning for the present out of physical remnants of the wartime past that lie before oneself. Haebaru has also appeared to be ahead of Okinawa Prefecture in engaging with the war and its legacies in the kind of depth and breadth that it has.

Since its founding, the Haebaru Culture Center—in addition to organizing material on the Army Field Hospital—has been a focal point for general exhibitions and conferences on issues of war and peace education in Okinawa. The 2007 opening of Cave No. 20 represented the culmination of over two decades of work, which, like that at Itokazu Cave and the Army Underground Headquarters, aimed to bring a hands-on experience to peace education field trips in particular and to offer another dimension to battlefield tourism in general. After a comprehensive bone-collection operation in 1985, the site's

**Figure 2.5.** Touring Field Hospital Cave No. 20. *Source*: Photo taken for author (second from left) by another tour group member.

designation as a Municipal Cultural Property in 1990, the organization of the Committee for the Survey, Use, and Protection of the Haebaru Army Field Hospital in 1993, a symposium on the hospital caves in 1995, and hosting the Second Annual National War Ruins Preservation Symposium in 1998, the work to survey and develop sections of the complex accelerated in hopes of a public opening by 2006. A brief examination of planning documents and public statements surrounding the eventual 2007 opening of Cave No. 20 allows a glimpse at the layers of individual initiative, institutional frameworks, social trends, and political considerations that shape the development of a war ruin into an arguably successful sightseeing spot—albeit an alternative one—in contemporary Okinawa.

The Committee for the Survey, Use, and Protection of the Haebaru Army Field Hospital (hereafter Survey Committee)—composed of historians, archeologists, geologists, civil engineers, and individuals related to the field hospital—was originally charged in 1993 with (1) conducting a survey of the present condition of the caves and interviewing persons related to them, (2) surveying war-related sites within Okinawa Prefecture, and (3) researching surveys of war-related sites outside Okinawa Prefecture, especially the Matsushiro Imperial General Headquarters Caves in Nagano. After three years of work, the Survey Committee reported its results and recommendations to the Haebaru municipal government.[60] This initial report and the implementation proposal presented a year later by a wider committee of city officials, educators, urban planners, the chair of the cultural properties protection committee, and representatives from the Survey Committee exemplify how war ruins—"sacred ground" to many—can be defined and conceptualized as objects for public viewing, as tourist sights. The Survey Committee's first report characterizes its "basic conception" of the field hospital caves as possessing "value as a cultural property," harboring "legacies of the Battle of Okinawa for future generations" and encouraging "peace memorialization and consolation for the war dead." Within this conception, the Survey Committee recommended the opening of Caves Nos. 20 and 24 for public entrance and viewing under the rubric of "place of learning, place of prayer, place of repose." The subsequent implementation committee followed this lead in its report in 2003 but changed "place of prayer" to "place of prayer and peace foundation." It also specified the need to preserve the central caves, to establish a "Battlefield Zone," and to link the site to a new Haebaru Culture Center. It also reflected debates over how best to put the caves on display: clear out observation areas at the mouth of the caves or allow access deeper into them. The former was decided upon as the safest and most feasible for both caves, but after arguments were put forth for the "educative power" of experiencing firsthand the interior of a wartime underground shelter, the recommendation was later changed to allow for visitor observation inside Cave No. 20. Haebaru Town appropriated 72 million yen (about $700,000 at the time) for fiscal year 2004 to realize the project and held a public forum in 2005 to gather opinions on the plan to make Cave No. 20 accessible to visitors. With wide public approval, work began in 2006 according to the guidelines of the implementation committee.

The ribbon-cutting ceremony for this latest war/peace tourism site in Okinawa was held on June 17, 2007, and received a fair amount of media attention. Yoshihama Shinobu, Okinawa University professor and chair of the Haebaru Cultural Preservation Committee, invoked the site's importance for peace education but went beyond the usual such pronouncements that dominate Okinawa public discourse on war memory and memorialization. He characterized the site itself as a storyteller (*kataribe*) taking the place of survivors who would otherwise relate the ordeal of being in the field hospital during the battle.[61] This conceit of the artifact that "speaks" the past, of earthen walls that bear witness to the events, to the "truth" that took place within them, is an old one. Here it signals the anxiety of losing the last witnesses to the event and masks the passing of the authority to speak the past from the survivor to the historian and the archeologist, the ventriloquists who make the site speak. But, symbiotically, the site is also important as a physical prop facilitating the historian's and the archeologist's accounts and drawing in their audience. This practical function is perhaps the real significance of transforming this war ruin into a destination for war/peace tourism. The physical place prompts the scholars and captures the audience as it offers visitors a simulation of a war experience valued for the peace that it is assumed to instill.

In contrast to narratives of patriotic sacrifice and unproblematic pilgrimages that predominated in the Southern Battle Sites Tours of the 1950s and 1960s, post-Reversion additions such as the Okinawa Army Field Hospital and Itokazu Cave are actively pedagogical and physically engaged and aim to foster critical reflection while respecting a sense of sanctity for the war dead and the bereaved. In this function they differ from simply saying a prayer and laying flowers at a memorial marker or listening to a tour bus guide's dramatic interpretation of the last desperate days on the Kyan Peninsula, although those activities are also often built into the "experience" that these latest sites feature. As has been common at battlefield memorials throughout the world, a rhetoric of peace and education envelops the rationale given to preserve these war ruins as cultural assets and to develop courses (both in the sense of study and in the sense of tours) around them. In comparison to early postwar tourism to war memorials, however, the most current Okinawan efforts display greater refinement of this basic peace message and greater sense of urgency for the need to preserve war ruins as "living witnesses" to replace the dwindling number of living war survivors. Most notably, these newly styled Southern Battle Sites Tours strive to get beyond ritual practices and passive consumption of places and artifacts even as they develop new tropes and rituals such as the blackout experience within a refugee cave. This is the context in which so-called peace guides (*heiwa gaido*) have been trained and deployed from the mid-1990s, forming a network of counterparts to traditional tour bus guides whose presentations of war-related sites they have influenced.[62] Both the Okinawa Peace Network and Naha City have taken the lead in recruiting young adults to serve as peace guides, emphasizing that such peace education goes beyond mere statistics on the war dead. The opening of the Okinawa Field Hospital Cave necessitated the founding of its own Haebaru Peace Guide Association (Haebaru Heiwa Gaido no Kai) and monthly newsletter.[63] When leading groups at memorial sites and into wartime caves, these peace guides are, in effect, proxies for tour bus guides and for war survivors whose aim is to draw the student and the general tourist nearer to the historical experience of the war, to impart through unfiltered facts and compelling narratives—especially about civilian refugees—which ideally moves one to forms of peace activism. The trajectory of the touristification of sacred ground in postwar Okinawa has thus moved downward in two ways: more attention is now focused on the common civilian experience, and to do that one has, more often than not, to head underground and get one's hands dirty rather than simply purchase a bouquet of flowers to lay at a memorial. This is a far cry from the Tropical Okinawa that tourism promoters have sought to cultivate on the surface of that sacred (under)ground since the 1960s.

## NOTES

1. Hayashi, "Ireitō shinsetsu okotowari," *Asahi Shimbun*, January 26, 1962, 7.
2. Akamine Namaki, "Irei no Hi ni omou," in Okinawa-ken Izoku Rengō Kai Seisōnen-bu, ed., *Wakatake sōshūhen: Sōritsu 25 shūnen kinenshi* (Naha: Okinawa-ken Izoku Rengō Kai Seisōnen-bu, 1966), 257.
3. Naha Nihon Seifu Nanpō Renraku Jimushochō, "Ireitō (hi) no konryū nado ni tsuite," January 31, 1962, OPA R00084010B.
4. For further details, see Gerald Figal, "Bones of Contention: The Geopolitics of 'Sacred Ground' in Postwar Okinawa," *Diplomatic History* 31, no. 1 (January 2007): 96–99.
5. Kitamura devotes a chapter to the material transformation of Mabuni Hill during the postwar period, focusing specifically on the 1960s *irei-no-tō* boom. See Kitamura Tsuyoshi, *Sensha-tachi no sengoshi: Okinawa senseki o megure hitobito to no kioku* (Tokyo: Ochanomizu Shobo, 2009), ch. 5.

6. For example, the aggressive selling of flowers became a topic of discussion among OTA members during their 1961 meetings, as recorded in the organization's history, Okinawa Kankō Kyōkai, *Okinawa kankō jū shūnen shi* (Naha: Okinawa Kankō Kyōkai, 1964), 59. The topic shows up again at their April 10, 1965, meeting, ibid., 133.

7. *Kankō Okinawa*, no. 35 (June 1960): 4–6.

8. Inamine Kunisaburō, "Kankō meguri no kansō," *Kankō Okinawa*, no. 31 (February 1960): 2.

9. Inamine Kunisaburō, "Kankō meguri no kansō."

10. The struggle to establish an attractive set of *meibutsu* (local specialties) as *o-miyage* is documented throughout the yearly reports of the OTA. Senge Tetsuma, in his report on Okinawa tourism discussed below, does cite local lacquerware, pottery, hats, dolls, and *awamori* (a whiskey-like spirit) as good *o-miyage*, an important aspect of Japanese tourism. He also acknowledges the deals to be had on foreign goods, providing a comparison chart of typical items that carried much (25 to 40 percent) lower import tariffs in Okinawa. See Senge Tetsuma, *Okinawa kankō shindansho* [A Diagnosis of Okinawa Tourism] (Naha: Okinawa Kankō Kyōkai, 1962), 40–41.

11. Matsukawa Kunio, "Kankō to iu keredo," *Kankō Okinawa*, no. 91 (February 1965): 4.

12. Anonymous, "Hanauri henjō," *Okinawa Times*, April 2, 1983.

13. Toguchi Masao, "Kankō ishiki no kōjō to watashi," in Okinawa-ken Kankō Renmei, ed., *25-nen no ayumi* (Naha: Okinawa-ken Kankō Renmei, 1979), 37.

14. Figal, "Bones of Contention," 81–109.

15. Ryūkyū Seifu Keizai-kyoku Kankō-ka, "Hondo gakusei no Okinawa ryokō jikken chōsahyō," OPA R00070382B.

16. Okinawa Kankō Kyōkai, *Okinawa kankō jū shūnen shi*, 20.

17. Kabira Chōshin, *Midori to seikatsu* 1, no. 6 (n.d.): 33.

18. Another conspicuous use of flowers on war ruins exists in the 1966 Ryukyu postage stamp commemorating the designation of June 23 as Irei no Hi (Memorial Day), although with a more particular referent—it shows a bombed cityscape superimposed with white lilies (symbol of the Himeyuri Student Nurses Corps) cascading over it as if falling from the heavens.

19. Anonymous, "Kankōdan no mita Okinawa," *Kankō Okinawa*, no. 41 (December 1964): 5.

20. Senge, *Okinawa kankō shindansho*, 24.

21. Senge, *Okinawa kankō shindansho,* 25.

22. Senge, *Okinawa kankō shindansho,* 18.

23. On the effect of Marine Expo '75 on the formation of contemporary images of Okinawa, see Tada Osamu, *Okinawa imēji o tabisuru—Yanagita Kunio kara ijū būmu made* (Tokyo: Chūō Kōron Shinsha, 2008), especially ch. 2.

24. Senge, *Okinawa kankō shindansho,* 43.

25. A map displaying the distribution of ninety-one *gama* (caves) in southern Okinawa Island appears in Ishihara Masaie, *Okinawa no tabi: Abuchiragama to Todoroki no gō* (Tokyo: Shūeisha Shinsho, 2000), 6–7.

26. Shimizu Hajime and Murakami Akiyoshi, "Sensō iseki shōsai chōsa to kindaika isan sōgō chōsa ni miru Okinawa-ken no sensō iseki no haaku jōkyō," *Nihon kenchiku gakkai gijutsu hōkoku shū* 13, no. 25 (June 2007): 311–12.

27. On two of the most famous refugee caves, Abuchiragama and Todoroki no gō, which have been excavated and, in the case of the former, open for guided tours organized by peace studies groups, see Ishihara, *Okinawa no tabi*.

28. For a detailed account of the founding of the Himeyuri-no-tō and an analysis of the mainland Japanese reception and use of the Himeyuri story, see Kitamura, *Sensha-tachi no sengoshi*, 2009, ch. 2.

29. For a detailed account in English of these final days and hours of the Thirty-second Army Command, see Yahara Hiromichi, *The Battle for Okinawa*, trans. Roger Pineau and Masatoshi Uehara (New York: John Wiley & Sons, 1995), 135–56. (Colonel) Yahara was among the staff officers with Ushijima and Cho until the end.

30. See Gerald Figal, "Historical Sense and Commemorative Sensibility at Okinawa's Cornerstone of Peace," *Positions: East Asia Cultures Critique* 5, no. 3 (Winter 1997): 751–52, for a discussion of this point.

31. The redemptive message of self-sacrifice in wartime as foundation for Japan's postwar peace and prosperity is one that Kitamura documents among the epitaphs inscribed on the prefectural monuments. See Kitamura, *Sensha-tachi no sengoshi*, 297–302.

32. A schematic map of the Naval Headquarters Cave and a succinct presentation of it from a peace activist's point of view appears in Okinawa Heiwa Nettowāku, ed., *Shin aruku, miru, kangearu Okinawa* (Naha: Okinawa Jiji Shuppan, 2000), 42–43.

33. Arasaki Moriteru, *Kankō kōsu de nai Okinawa: Senseki, kichi, sangyō, bunka* (Tokyo: Kōbunken, 1998), 98.

34. For one account of the assault on the Oroku Peninsula and the scene within the Naval Headquarters Cave, see George Feifer, *Tennozan: The Battle of Okinawa and the Atomic Bomb* (New York: Ticknor & Fields, 1992), 441–43.

35. Arasaki, *Kankō kōsu de nai Okinawa*, 98–99.

36. The main part of the telegram is reprinted in Japanese in Ōta, *Okinawa senbotsusha o matsuru irei-no-tō*, 142–43.

37. Such criticism is alluded to in Okinawa Heiwa Nettowāku, *Shin aruku, miru, kangearu Okinawa*, 42.

38. Arasaki, *Kankō kōsu de nai Okinawa*, 100–2.

39. Yoshihama Shinobu, "Okinawa-ken no okeru sensō iseki no hozon katsuyō: Sensō iseki no bunkazai shitei o shiten," *Okinawa Kokusai Daigaku shakai bunka kenkyū* 11, no. 1 (June 2008): 44.

40. Efforts in this regard were accelerated under the governorship of Ōta Masahide during the 1990s by the Peace Promotion Division he established in 1992 within the prefectural government. Since Ōta's 1998 gubernatorial defeat, his successors, Inamine Keiichi (1998–2006) and Nakaima Hirokazu (2006–), have consolidated the work of peace promotion and gender equality into the present Peace and Gender Equality Promotion Division (Heiwa • Danjo Kyōdō Sansaku Ka).

41. Dai-32 Gunshireibugō Hozon • Kōkai Kentō Iinkai, *Dai-32 gunshireibugō no hozon • kōkai ni tsuite* (Naha: Dai-32 Gunshireibugō Hozon • Kōkai Kentō Iinkai, 1996). Interview with Peace Promotion Division representatives, June 26, 2004.

42. "32 Gunshireigō hozon motomeru/kengira ga naibu o shisai," *Okinawa Taimusu* Online, June 4, 2009, http://www.okinawatimes.co.jp/news/2009-06-04-M_1-025-1_002.html (accessed July 14, 2009). Assemblyman Toguchi's own account of his June 3 survey of the cave and photos he took while inside are posted at http://www13.plala.or.jp/osamusan-t (accessed July 14, 2009).

43. See Gerald Figal, "Waging Peace on Okinawa," in Laura Hein and Mark Selden, eds., *Islands of Discontent: Okinawan Responses to Japanese and American Power* (Lanham, MD: Rowman & Littlefield, 2003), 45–98. See also Kitamura, *Sensha-tachi no sengoshi,* 313–45, for another overview and analysis of the Cornerstone of Peace memorial.

44. Dai-32 Gunshireibugō Hozon • Kōkai Kentō Iinkai, *Dai-32 gunshireibugō no hozon • kōkai ni tsuite*, 2–3.

45. Yoshihama Shinobu distinguishes the kind of *senseki meguri* developing on local initiative in the 1970s from the earlier "Nanbu Senseki Meguri" promoted from the 1950s as the initial draw of postwar visitors to Okinawa. Yoshihama, "Okinawa-ken no okeru sensō iseki no hozon katsuyō," 45.

46. Norma Field, *In the Realm of the Dying Emperor: Japan at Century's End* (New York: Vintage, 1991); Shimojima Tetsurō, *Chibichirigama no shūdan jiketsu: Kami no kuni no hate ni* (Tokyo: Gaijūsha, 2000). See also Chibana Shoichi, *Burning the Rising Sun: From Yomitan Village, Okinawa: Islands of U.S. Bases* (Kyoto: South Wind, 1992).

47. Ishihara discusses the history of his field research in "Watashi no sensō taiken chōsa to daigakusei to no kakari" [My Field Research Collecting Testimonials of the Battle of Okinawa and Its Impact on University Students], *Okinawa Kokusai Daigaku shakai bunka kenkyū* 7, no. 1 (March 2004): 77–78.

48. Heiwa kyōiku kenkyū iinkai, ed., *Aruku, miru, kangaeru Okinawa* (Naha: Okinawa Jiji Shuppan, 1986), sects. 9 and 10. Ishihara has written the most extensive account of the history of Itokazu Cave in *Okinawa no tabi: Abuchiragama to Todoroki no gō* (Tokyo: Shūeisha Shinsho, 2000).

49. "Itokazu" refers to the name of the district of Tamagusuku Village where the cave is located, while "Abuchiragama" is the local Okinawan name for the cave. Both are used interchangeably, but more recently scholars have taken to concatenating the two names into one.

50. This typical scene is reproduced in Sensō Iseki Hozon Zenkoku Nettowaaku, ed., *Sensō iseki kara manabu* (Tokyo: Iwanami Jyunia Shinsho, 2004), 101.

51. Arasaki, *Kankō kōsu de nai Okinawa,* 81–82. Kitamura, *Sensha-tachi no sengoshi,* 146–50, treats the first of the Himeyuri films, the 1953 *Himeyuri-no-tō*, which had a large impact in shaping mainland Japanese images of the Battle of Okinawa.

52. Okinawa Heiwa Nettowaaku, *Shin aruku, miru, kangearu Okinawa*, 44–45. On the controversy surrounding this term in the context of Chibichirigama, see Field, *In the Realm of the Dying Emperor*, 56–67.

53. Toma Shiichi, "Senseki kōkōgaku no susume," *Nantō kōkōgaku dayori*, no. 30 (1994).

54. See, for example, Ikeda Ichirō, "Sensō iseki • ibutsu, sensō kōkōgaku ni tsuite," *Kōkōgaku kenkyū* 41, no. 3 (1994), and Itō Yushi, "Make no bunkazai—sensō iseki

no jūyōsei," in Bunkazaigaku ronshū kankiōkai, ed., *Bunkazaigaku ronshū* (Nara: Bunkazaigaku ronshū kankiōkai, 1994).

55. The bulk of Ishihara Masaie's work involves the collection of war testimonies. On the broader *jibunshi* movement that coincided with the death of the Shōwa emperor, see Gerald Figal, "How to Jibunshi: Making and Marketing Self-Histories of Shōwa among the Masses in Postwar Japan," *Journal of Asian Studies* 55, no. 4 (November 1996): 902–33.

56. For more details, see Sensō Iseki Hozon Zenkoku Nettowāku, *Sensō iseki kara manabu*, 28–33; Sensō Iseki Hozon Zenkoku Nettowāku, ed., *Nihon no sensō iseki* (Tokyo: Heibonsha Shinsho, 2004), 174–79.

57. Sensō Iseki Hozon Zenkoku Nettowāku, *Sensō iseki kara manabu*, 98.

58. See, for example, Okinawa-ken Haebaru-cho Kyōiku Iinkai, ed., *Haebaru rikigun byōin gōgun I* (Haebaru: Okinawa-ken Haebaru-cho Kyōiku Iinkai, 2000).

59. Interview with Taira Tsugiko at Haebaru Bunka Sentā, November 13, 2009.

60. Yoshihama, "Okinawa-ken no okeru sensō iseki no hozon katsuyō," 49–50.

61. *Ryūkyū Shimpō*, June 18, 2007, http://ryukyushimpo.jp/news/storyid-24716-storytopic-1.html.

62. Former Okinawa bus guide and now bus guide trainer Shiroma Sachiko relates the impact that the war testimonial work of Ishihara Masaie in particular and the presence of peace guides in general have had on contemporary bus guide narratives. The in-house scripts she allowed me to read (but not copy) displayed more forthrightness in presenting controversial aspects of the Battle of Okinawa and adopted a more critical tone in discussing U.S. bases. Interview at Okinawa Bus Company offices, Naha, June 2001.

63. The Haebaru Heiwa Gaido no Kai's newsletters, published from April 2008, are all available for download as PDF files at http://goo.gl/resM9. A map with photos of the cave is available at http://goo.gl/6fYcW.

# Part II

# CREATIONS AND RECREATIONS

# 3

# "Tropical Image Up"

## *Landscape under (Tourist) Occupation*

One cannot stroll nowadays through Naha International Airport, down Naha's main shopping drag Kokusai Dōri (International Street), or into the lobby of Okinawa's tourist hotels without encountering a tropical motif, often with a visual reference to the Ryukyu Kingdom nearby, if not actually incorporated with it. From the hibiscus-spangled baggage area sign mentioned in this book's prologue to shell leis hanging in souvenir shops to live coconut palms dangling their fruit above busy thoroughfares, universalized icons of an imagined South Pacific island getaway—a place of vibrant exotic flora, clear blue-green waters, coral reefs, yearlong warmth, and white-sand beaches with stands of windswept palms—have provided since the 1960s the foundation for Okinawa's identity as tourist destination even as other tourism concepts (neo-Ryukyu Kingdom, eco-haven, health mecca) have been deployed alongside it. The tropical theme is so ubiquitous that it is practically taken for granted, and younger generations assume it to have always been this way. Despite its frequently crass commodification, its nonnative elements, and even an awareness of its artificiality, it has been largely naturalized by locals and visitors. In other words, its history goes unrecognized.

While it might seem paradoxical to speak of an artificially themed environment as naturalized, it follows from my adoption of Erve Chambers's approach to the idea of the "authentic" and the "traditional" within modern tourism. Chambers eschews identifying the traditionally "real" and "authentic" as always and only things of the past one strives to reproduce faithfully under conditions of modernity. Rather, he places authenticity in the degree of agency that a community has in deciding to change (or not change) its social settings.[1] If, for example, a representative Okinawan municipal body or a private community of local Okinawans actively decided and executed the demolition of crumbling premodern castle ruins to clear the way for a tropical paradise theme park for tourists, it would be acting more authentically than if it were prohibited by central Japanese government authorities from doing so and instead forced to preserve the castle ruins against its will. From this perspective, a local initiative to effect, as one Okinawa Prefecture tourism planning document puts it, "an image enhancement [*imēji appu*, "image up"] of 'Tropical Okinawa'" could be seen as an authentic act even if it required the removal of indigenous plants to accomplish. On the other hand, enacting such a plan on the prefectural level over the resistance of local neighborhoods and/or as part of a business deal with Tokyo-based travel and tourism companies would throw into doubt the authenticity of the act. The upshot here is that ongoing cycles of creations and recreations of cultural products—material objects of local everyday use, souvenirs for tourists, themed parks and cityscapes, regional cuisine, "folk" dance performances, rebuilt castles—involve multiple levels of often contested negotiation among actors, and their authenticity should not simply be measured by matching them with samples from the past. If one insists on speaking about authenticity among the cultural productions a place and a people have to offer, it would seem more productive that authenticity be situated in the present and indexed to the agency involved, not to how well something from the past is preserved or replicated. There is much in the physical and symbolic landscape of postwar Okinawa—in what has arguably become recognizable parts of Okinawa's identity to outsiders and locals alike—that shares little or nothing with its prewar or its premodern "traditional" past, and yet to deem such elements out of hand as "fake" or un-Okinawan is as misguided as uncritically accepting everything that is promoted and sold to tourists as "traditional" and "authentic." In the end, I see little value in getting hung up on these designations, except perhaps in analyses of their political and ideological effects for the present.

In this chapter I give (Tourist) Okinawa's present-day tropicalesque façade a history without worrying about its authenticity despite legitimate concerns about some of its cultural appropriateness and environmental impact. My approach is to think about this history first in the broader context of postwar revitalization (of devastated land, economy, and culture) and then as a key part of local branding for tourism development. In this aspect Okinawa's case is comparable to other war-torn regions faced with reconstruction and having aspirations for tourism. Post–World War II Hawaii and to a lesser extent South Pacific islands were Okinawa's immediate models for tourism development, while Okinawa's experience precedes that of places like Vietnam, Bosnia, and most recently Sri Lanka, where tropical resort tourism is being reestablished after decades of civil war.[2] The range of strategies and patterns of postwar tourism development across such diverse places is no doubt wide, but all share the two dimensions of transformation that I take up here in unearthing the layers of Okinawa's postwar tropical makeover: the physical and the discursive. First and foremost, in the immediate aftermath of the Battle of Okinawa, surviving residents were faced with an utterly ruined physical landscape in the southern half of Okinawa Island. The American landing on the west-facing beaches of Yomitan and Kadena at the island's midpoint on April 1, 1945, and the grinding push to the southern tip of the Kyan Peninsula over the following eighty days leveled foliage, pockmarked the ground, and left debris and bodies in its wake. As covered in chapter 1, the clearing of debris and the collection of human remains were among the very first tasks of reconstruction after the war and during the American occupation. The replanting and cultivation of flora in general followed in island-wide reforestation programs. It was within these programs and smaller American initiatives around U.S. bases that tropical plants were first cultivated on a large, public scale in Okinawa, a practice that has continued to the present. Intertwined with this physical tropicalization there developed throughout various media a discursive reinvention of Okinawa as a "tropical paradise" regardless of U.S. military presence and what support Mother Nature did or did not lend to this notion. A historical excavation of both dimensions will lend some depth and understanding to that stroll through the tropical tropes that bedeck Okinawa's tourist areas today.

The years 1961 and 1962 mark a signal period in the history of Okinawa's tropical transformation. A convergence of tourism-related activity from several sides produced a tangible buzz that something serious could be developed in Okinawa with proper planning and financing. In addition to soliciting Senge Tetsuma's diagnosis of Okinawa's tourism prospects (introduced in chapter 2), the Okinawa Tourism Association (OTA) sought further guidance from mainland Japanese tourism experts in 1962. Meanwhile, the United States Civil Administration of the Ryukyu Islands (USCAR) set up the Joint Ryukyu Tourism Development Board in November 1961 and the following month commissioned University of Hawaii professor and Hawaii Visitors Bureau assistant general manager Frank T. Inouye (1920–1995) to write a separate report on the topic of developing Okinawa tourism. Plans were subsequently made to have more representatives from the Hawaii Visitors Bureau visit Okinawa in January and February 1962, but this was ultimately postponed because of other pressing business. USCAR deemed its efforts to cooperate with local officials to foster tourism important enough for public relations to issue press releases to local newspapers announcing the deliberations of the Tourism Development Board and the "deep interest" that both USCAR high commissioner Paul Caraway and Government of the Ryukyu Islands (GRI) chief executive Ōta Seisaku had in developing Okinawa tourism.[3] This activity followed the GRI's reorganization of its Tourism Section under its Economic Division in August 1961, a sign that it too was responding to a perceived opportunity. A rush of business inquiries from private travel and tourism firms flowed from abroad to USCAR at this time, feeding this perception. In the meantime, much was made in the press about a pending boom in tourism to Okinawa that would go beyond battlefield pilgrimages and shopping tours for inexpensive foreign luxury items not subject to the same high tariffs in the U.S.-administered Ryukyu Islands as they were in mainland Japan. Perennial budget issues kept the real boom from happening until after Reversion when mainland Japanese investment could freely flow into Okinawa, but from 1961 to 1971 tourist traffic steadily increased, from about 25,000 to about 150,000 visitors per year. Thirty years later it would surpass 5 million visitors, over 95 percent of whom were from mainland Japan. Those 5 million came to Okinawa with media-fed preconceptions and expectations of the place that were remarkably similar to those Senge cited in his 1962 account: Okinawa possesses lush greenery, coral-ringed beaches, and a "south island [i.e., tropical] feel" (*nangoku teki na kibun*); it boasts cultural elements historically distinct from mainland Japan; and it exists in the long shadow of the battle once fought there and in the immediate shadow of the military now based there. The difference between then and now is that the substantial gap between the image and the reality of the natural and cultural landscapes of Okinawa has narrowed (but not disappeared), and the treatment of war legacies—from the Battle of Okinawa to the U.S. military presence ever since—has become more complicated. The historical transformation of the cultural landscape is the topic of the next chapter while the position of U.S. bases alongside beach resorts takes up the final part of this study. Here we will unpack the history of "tropical image up" beginning with the larger and earlier context of postwar greenification (*ryokka*) programs of the 1950s, which later encompassed more specialized and targeted efforts to groom a tropical landscape that would attract tourists and meet their expectations. Contrary to the common view that the image of Okinawa's land- and seascape was born from the 1975 International Marine Exposition—the event that certainly solidified Okinawa's place in the mainland Japanese tourist imagination and jump-started growth in Okinawa tourism in general—its roots go back to the 1950s and spread in the 1960s when the first concerted efforts to tropicalize Okinawa took place.[4]

## POSTWAR GREENIFICATION IN PRE-REVERSION OKINAWA

Among Okinawa's many nicknames and evocative associations (from "Land of Courtesy" to "Keystone in the Pacific"), *midori no shima* (island of greenery) and *hana no shima* (island of flowers) have some basis in both tourist imagination and material reality. They also have an interesting history since the war. In the postwar efforts to recultivate the island, practical concerns (preventing erosion, creating windbreaks, reestablishing agriculture and timber reserves) and ornamental concerns (beautification of public spaces and tourist areas) became increasingly interrelated to the extent that cultivation that we might view as only ornamental—that is, nonessential and noneconomic—established a very real and practical role in the everyday life and economy of Okinawa. The commitment to fostering a local version of the tropical brand to attract tourists set the transformation of landscape in general and afforestation (*ryokka*, literally "greenification") in particular on a peculiar path. Even when the tropical has not been explicitly emphasized in tourism promotion, the image of an island lush with foliage in a way distinct from anything on the mainland has been a conspicuous centerpiece of an outwardly advertised and locally embraced identity.

In the aftermath of war, however, the label *midori no shima* represented little but nostalgia for the past and desire for the future. While the northern half of Okinawa Island was spared devastation during the war, one of the common tropes in any description of immediate postwar Okinawa is that of a landscape flattened by bombardment and stripped bare of its foliage. As a result, the recovery of that greenery—like the later rebuilding of Shuri Castle detailed in the next chapter—represented an overcoming of war devastation. As Okinawan historian Miyagi Eishō put it writing from Yokohama University in 1959, "Rediscovering an Okinawa wrapped with verdure so lush it hurt your eyes would liberate Okinawans from painful memories of war."[5] In that same year, the first three-year All-Ryukyu Greenification Promotion Campaign (Zen-Ryū Ryokka Suishin Undō) began under GRI chief executive Ōta Seisaku (November 1959 to October 1964), who also served as the director of the main branch of the campaign and was a key player in the fledgling Okinawa Tourism Association. In his memoirs, Ōta relates the great need to restore the natural beauty of Okinawa's foliage from war damage and the sense of mission he felt to accomplish the task. He initiated preparations for the first Greenification Promotion Campaign in August 1958, emphasizing from the beginning the necessity for this effort to take the form of a large-scale citizens' movement complete with slogans, songs, and dances.[6] The first issue of the greenification promotion journal *Midori* (Greenery), which Ōta helped establish and wrote the introduction for in January 1960, carried a caricature of him as *Ryokka Otoko* (Greenification Guy), who thought about plants so much that they sprouted from his head. Ōta confirms this nickname in his memoirs, proudly adding to it *Ryokka no Oni* (Greenification Demon).[7]

In his introduction to this inaugural issue, Ōta recites the havoc the war wreaked on the island's once lush foliage and enumerates the reasons reestablishing it is important for human life and livelihood: agriculture and timber production, protection against typhoons, and the positive psychological effects of a beautiful natural environment. He then segues from the benefits of flora for an individual's psychic health and for healthy civic life to an appeal for all Okinawans to cooperate in beautifying Okinawa for the benefit of developing the tourism industry. Citing the example of other countries, his appeal turns on the notion that a flourishing tourism industry follows from cultural progress and leads to economic progress:

> As their culture progresses, countries have planned and realized tourist industries. A tourist industry also cannot flourish without green landscapes. It's said that tourists to the Ryukyus complain that there are no trees, no greenery. A tourist industry that neglects the revitalization of the ruined forests and fields of the Ryukyus will not flourish. By linking general forestation in parallel with the tourism industry, trees along roads and thoroughfares, foliage at sightseeing spots, estate forests and so on will quickly be cultivated. I think that in order to improve both our living environment and our acquisition of foreign currency, the recreation of greenery is absolutely necessary.[8]

During his tenure as chief executive and head of the just-established (in October 1959) conservative Okinawa Liberal Democratic Party, Ōta worked hard to promote economic development through stronger ties with and eventual reversion to mainland Japan while at the same time maintaining a pro-American stance. His visits to Tokyo in July and August 1960 led to agreements from the government of Japan to negotiate with the U.S. government a liberalization of Ryukyu-Japan economic relations. These were agreed to during Prime Minister Ikeda Hayato's conference with President John F. Kennedy in June 1961 but were never fully realized because of Ryukyu Islands High Commissioner Paul Caraway's famously staunch opposition to any Japanese involvement in Okinawa.[9] As a consequence, Caraway's intransigence thwarted a convergence of interests that might very well have led to some serious growth in Okinawa tourism. Still, Ōta—a lawyer by profession and businessman at heart—proceeded with whatever initiatives could be funded or accomplished through volunteerism.[10]

The labor behind the greenification efforts Ōta spearheaded would prove to be the largest island-wide volunteer campaigns after the previous decade's bone-collection activities. School and other youth groups, PTAs, women's associations, the Boy Scouts, the 4H Club, the Lion's Club and other associations, and "beautification clubs" participated. A fund-raising arm, Midori no Hane (Green Wings), was established in February 1962, and greenification campaign signs, slogans, and songs such as "Midori kōshinkyoku" (The Greenery March) and "Midori ondo" (The Greenery Work Song) were composed and disseminated in the media and schools. Practically all special events included sponsorship by greenification organizations and the planting of memorial trees by dignitaries—there are plenty of press photos of the chief executive and sometimes even USCAR representatives with spade in hand. The journals *Midori* (1960–1992; originally published by the GRI Forestry Section and then the Okinawa Prefecture Greenification Promotion Committee) and *Okinawa midori to seikatsu* (1981–1991)—part news, part gardening guide, part boosterism—generated in their pages an image of ceaseless and widespread greening projects joined by the entire populace throughout Okinawa. To some degree, reality matched it. An entire generation of Okinawans has some memory of planting trees and shrubs raised in Okinawan-run nurseries and purchased through GRI, USCAR, and private donations before Reversion. The Ryukyu Government Postal Service even issued three postage stamps commemorating the All-Ryukyu Greenification Promotion Campaigns in 1959, 1961, and 1963.

From 1959 to 1970, a total of four All-Ryukyu Greenification Promotion Campaigns were conducted in addition to ongoing GRI and private afforestation efforts: 1959–1961, 1962–1964, 1965–1967, and 1968–1970. The first All-Ryukyu Greenification Promotion Campaign easily exceeded its first-year goal of 3 million plantings across all of the Ryukyus with 1.8 million on Okinawa Island alone, a total that bespeaks both the extent of the wartime damage and the enthusiastic scope of this regreening of the island.[11] These grassroots efforts by Okinawans planted trees and flowers in nine general categories: economic, protective, roads and thoroughfares, schools, parks and tourism sites, public facilities, employment sites, residences, and other. In the first campaign the number of plantings in the first two categories—economic and protective—predominated (6,063,912 plantings, or 72 percent), while parks and tourist sites lagged (49,703 plantings, or 0.6 percent), out of a three-year total of 8,470,638 plantings of all types.[12] Among trees for both economic and protective use, the nonnative *mokumaou* (casuarina, or beefwood), imported mostly from Taiwanese nurseries, stood out as a mainstay over the three years, numbering 5,903,357 (70 percent of all plantings). Native to Australia, Southeast Asia, and western Pacific islands, the conifer-like casuarina are commonly cultivated in tropical and subtropical areas where they are prized as windbreaks, as has been their function in Okinawa. Ryukyu pines—Okinawa's official tree since 1966—also figured in both categories (284,029 total).[13] In comparison, outside some native *kuba* (fan palm; *birou* in Japanese), a type of palm that its advocates claimed would create a sense of "Okinawaness" for tourists, there were relatively few examples of overtly iconic tropical flora planted early on. Significantly, stereotypical tall palm trees—coconut palms, Washington palms, Canary palms—are not indicated in some records to have been planted at all during the first greenification campaign, while other statistics show up to twenty-two thousand plantings of palm varieties have taken place.[14]

The vast majority of any tropicalesque flora intended for visitor display fell within the categories of "parks and tourist sites" and "roads and thoroughfares" and did not make a publicly prominent appearance until 1962 and thereafter. As tourism consciousness rose in Okinawa throughout the 1960s, numbers of plantings in general and of tropical flora in particular increased in these so-called tourist-exposed areas. This change is evident throughout records of the GRI Forestry Section, the statistics maintained by the Greenification Promotion Campaign Committee, the general media at the time, and the pages of the journals *Midori* and *Okinawa midori to seikatsu.* The GRI Forestry Section, for example, notes in 1962 a sudden increase of 114 percent over the previous year in the number of plantings at tourist sites and parks. The same year saw the first appreciable appearance of palm trees—a total of 14,380 were planted among all areas. The years 1963 to 1966 witnessed a similar average planted per year.[15] Content and images from *Midori* during 1962 and 1963 corroborate the increased attention given to palm trees, including their model use in Taiwan, whence many of Okinawa's transplants arrived.[16] Planning documents from the third All-Ryukyu Greenification Promotion Campaign (1965–1967) also clearly indicate that much more concerted attention was being given to enhancing the flora image—specifically the tropical image—of tourist spots and routes. Plantings targeting tourist areas increased on average three- to fourfold and featured palms, hibiscus, bougainvillea, azalea, Indian oleander, and, in the north, cherry trees (particular to northern Okinawa Island).[17] The same patterns continued, although at a leveled-off pace, during the fourth Greenification Promotion Campaign (1968–1970). USCAR even made modest donations of a similar range of trees and shrubs during this time.[18] Although they constituted a very small percentage of all plantings, palms, hibiscus, and other tropicalesque flora were conspicuously placed and consciously designed to improve what Senge Tetsuma, in his 1962 report on Okinawa's tourism prospects, called Okinawa's "image problem." A return to that report, introduced in chapter 2, is relevant here to provide further context and explanation for this tropical twist in the postwar greenification of pre-Reversion Okinawa.

The appearance of more palms and hibiscus within greenification campaigns after the publication of Senge's report suggests a causal connection, although in recommending the tropicalization of Okinawa's landscape to make it feel more *nangoku teki,* he primarily advocated the use of native plants—particularly the *adan* (*Pandanus odoratissimus*, or screw pine) and *sotetsu* (*Cycas revolute*, or sago cycad, often referred to as a sago palm)—that had already created a tropical sensation among mainland Japanese. These, he maintained, represented a hardy, practical choice that also doubled as tropical signifier: "Rooted aerially in the sand on the seashore, *adan* flourishes. Gazing at a vivid ocean with the *adan* and *sotetsu* lining the shore possesses a brightness and warmth that you can't taste on the mainland."[19] In fact, the OTA had been promoting this use and association of *sotetsu* and *adan* at least since its founding in 1954, as witnessed by the cover of its first tourist pamphlet, which featured a drawing of *sotetsu* and *adan* by the seashore. Senge then immediately notes the difficulty of planting tall palm trees because of the threat of typhoon damage, but ultimately he would like to see more. He positively cites the use of *bussōge* (Buddha's mulberry, i.e., hibiscus) as hedges, seen particularly in private gardens and along the road from the airport to downtown Naha.

Throughout this appraisal of Okinawa's flora, Senge has the model of Hawaii in mind as he urges the spread of "tropical-like" flora such as hibiscus (one of the few native Hawaiian varieties of which, *Hibiscus brackenridgei*, is Hawaii's state flower). He also notes that one of Okinawa's distinctive sites (*meisho*) is "a pineapple landscape like Hawaii's" and that plans to increase the cultivation of banana plants, although not fully realized, would contribute to a more South Seas atmosphere.[20] This kind of tropical makeover of landscape—with *adan* and *sotetsu* standing in for proper palm trees—is key, he argues, to the success of tourism in Okinawa. That and the development of "beach resort zones" have the potential to transform Okinawa into "Japan's Hawaii."[21] That Okinawa would be mainland Japan's Hawaii in the same sense that Hawaii had already become mainland America's Hawaii is significant. The transformation of both came under a "tourist gaze" that seeks objects and experiences different from the everyday. John Urry, who first proposed the concept of the tourist gaze, emphasizes that a search for authenticity alone does not sustain the appeal of tourist objects. Rather, it is fundamental to tourism that "potential objects of the tourist gaze must be different in some way or another. They must be out of the ordinary. People must experience particularly distinct pleasures which involve different senses or are on a different scale from those typically encountered in everyday life."[22] Despite its historical Polynesian roots in streams of migration of people and plants from the South Pacific, Hawaii itself had undergone its own tropical South Seas image enhancement to preserve, manufacture, and stage those aspects of the place that had existed in a Caucasian tourist gaze in Hawaii's rise as an exotic tourist destination from pre- to post-World War II.[23] For Okinawa then, Hawaii possessed a model product—a tourist destination to emulate on some level—and a model process by which to achieve that product under the gaze of non-Okinawan mainland Japanese. Senge's view of Okinawa tourism is very much a distillation of a mainland Japanese gaze. His repeated use of the key descriptive *nangoku* qua tropical situates his mainland "northern" position with respect to Okinawa (as part of the Nansei Shoto, or southwest archipelago) and even carries with it echoes of the South Pacific islands under Japanese control during the war. These are southern islands existing for mainland Japanese consumption and should thus be cultivated as mainland Japanese desire.

In his summary of recommendations on how to respond to the (mainland) tourist gaze, Senge hammers home the need to tropicalize Okinawa, to make it look like something unlike mainland Japan. What tropical and subtropical flora Okinawa already had must be preserved, and what it lacked should be planted. He acknowledges the Greenification Promotion Campaign that was in process during his visit but says its scope should be vigorously expanded.[24] Here he focuses on cultivating a more tropical atmosphere through the use of such plants as *kuba* (fan palms), various palm trees, and *deigo* (Indian coral bean, Okinawa's official plant from 1966) at least along tourist arteries, at sightseeing spots, in tourist towns (by which he means Naha, Nago, and the base town of Koza), and, as we saw in the previous chapter, at well-visited battle sites. *Adan* and *sotetsu*, seemingly more appropriate for beaches and shorelines, are not singled out this time as the practical native alternative. The sense in reading Senge's text is that by the end of it, he is stating more bluntly what he, as representative of mainland Japanese, wants to see in Okinawa, be it native or not, authentic or not: beach resorts that conjure up the South Seas as Hawaii does; better presentation of war history, battle sites, and memorials (preferably beautified with tropicalesque plants); and more parks and gardens. Tropics-tinged greenification is the heavy emphasis among the physical improvements. Better food, hotels, and transportation will make repeaters out of first-time visitors, but a sustained image of an exotic south sea island within Japan's geographic, cultural, and linguistic orbits is what will draw them there in the first place. That this would-be tropical paradise hosted tens of thousands of foreign military personnel, was under a dollar economy, and had as many signs in English as Japanese did not detract from this image; it merely contributed to the sense of the exotic.

This emphasis on re-creating Okinawa in the image that mainlanders had of what an island in the Nansei Shoto should look like and what they wanted it to look and feel like received further reinforcement when, under Chief Executive Ōta's initiative, representatives from the GRI, the Okinawa Tourism Association, the city of Naha, and the local business council traveled to Tokyo in late May 1963 to seek advice from tourism industry experts. A detailed summary of the feedback that the OTA gained from this consultation appears in its in-house history. Like Senge, these Tokyo-based experts seized upon Okinawa's image problem. After complaints about the passport requirements and extra layers of documentation needed to enter the U.S.-controlled Ryukyu Islands, these observers were blunt in their assessments of Okinawa's scenery (*keikan*). While the color of the sea and coral reefs surrounding Okinawa Island was attractive, the scenery of the island itself left a lot to be desired: "The floral landscape is bad; cultivate tropical [*nangoku teki na*] plants and bring into view Japan's Hawaii. . . . A greenification campaign is flourishing, but it should be conceived so as to impart a taste of the tropical [*nangoku jōsho ga ajieru yō ni kangaeru beki da*]." They advised that "natural tropical plants" be visible to sightseers along roads and thoroughfares. And in what must have been felt as adding insult to injury to the Okinawan representatives, the floral pride of downtown Naha's self-proclaimed "Miracle Mile," Kokusai Dōri (International Street), was belittled: "Ginza willows are planted on Kokusai Dōri; it would be better to plant flora characteristic of tropical southern islands [*nangoku tokuyū no shokubutsu*]."[25]

This latter comment is a telling example of how Okinawa's aspirations of parity with the mainland could clash with mainland desires for an exotic yet accessible tourist destination. It also demonstrates the symbolic power the central capital had upon Japan's most peripheral and least developed regional city. Tokyo's Ginza—historically the city's showcase boulevard of modern, cosmopolitan consumer culture—was famous for the fabulous willow trees lining its sidewalks until they were replaced by ginkgo trees in 1921 to make way for increased vehicular traffic. So missed by Tokyoites, they were replanted in 1931, only to be destroyed in the firebombing of Tokyo in March 1945. The last surviving trees were finally removed in 1968, although nostalgia for the Ginza's willows has spawned a movement to bring them back.[26]

Naha's willows appeared in the late 1950s and evoked the ill-fated icons of the Ginza's prewar past, providing a sign for what city officials wanted Naha's "Miracle Mile" to be—a modern, sophisticated shopping and entertainment strip that would counter unflattering images of Okinawa as culturally backward and imply a commonality with mainland urban centers.[27] But it was precisely cultural difference—even primitiveness—that formed the main source of Okinawa's tourist appeal in the view of mainland observers, so long as that difference and primitiveness were comfortably packaged. This is what Frank T. Inouye called in his Okinawa tourism report to USCAR "back-to-nature-but-with-American-plumbing" in order to meet "the need for capturing and retaining a 'native' flavor in hostelries, while providing adequate facilities to house an increasing number of tourists" in the Pacific region.[28] The dynamic at work here is not unlike that between first-world tourists to third-world destinations across the globe: pressure from the former to keep the latter in a real or imagined premodern "traditional" (and therefore exotic) state for tourist consumption. These mainland observers are clear about the need to enhance Okinawa's exotic appeal: "The number of people hoping to go to Hawaii and Hong Kong has increased while Okinawa tourism has dropped. It has no exotic mood [*ekizochizumu no mūdo*]."[29] The tension between the primitive, exotic "back-to-nature" and the modern, familiar "American plumbing" is evident throughout the outside advice that the OTA recorded: modernize hotels and infrastructure, but do not obliterate local color; feature more "local flavor" in tourist cuisine, but adapt Okinawan food (generally thought of as unappealing) to mainland palates; advertise the convenience and appeal of linguistic familiarity in a quasi-foreign environment, but have locals use as much dialect as possible around tourists; replace the native greenery lost in the war, but do it with nonnative tropical plants.[30]

Improving Okinawa's natural infrastructure—the trees, shrubs, and flowers that compose and accent its scenery—had both real and symbolic effects. For Okinawans who initiated the Greenification Promotion Campaigns, physical effects mattered first, the symbolism of overcoming the war through reforestation notwithstanding. For local and mainland tourism promoters and expert advisers, the symbolic effects were primary. As Urry reminds us, "The [tourist] gaze is constructed through signs, and tourism involves the collection of signs."[31] The tourist is thus put into the position of sign reader, as seeker and decoder of symbols. As Jonathan Culler formulates it, "The tourist is interested in everything as a sign of itself. . . . All over the world the unsung armies of semioticians, the tourists, are fanning out in search of signs of Frenchness, typical Italian behaviour, exemplary Oriental scenes, typical American thruways, traditional English pubs."[32] In the case of Okinawa, the typical tropical island and, secondarily, traditional Ryukyu culture—and the exoticism they both represented—formed the pitch for tourism in the 1960s and continue to do so to a large degree today. The foreign military presence was arguably another exotic draw, despite its absence in mainstream public tourism promotion. It and a rediscovery of Ryukyu history and culture will be taken up in subsequent chapters. Here we will continue our examination of how pre-Reversion interventions of a tourist gaze played out in Okinawa's physical landscape and symbolic identity up to and through the 1972 reversion to Japanese sovereignty. What began as a straightforward program to replant a war-torn landscape for practical ends had, by the late 1960s, taken on a component conspicuously focused on a particular kind of greenification, the material reality of which was subordinate to its symbolic function as sign of an exotic tropics.

## TROPICAL TROPES

Despite the difficulties and potential dangers they presented, thousands of nonnative palm trees counted among the specimens planted in parks, at sightseeing spots, and along major thoroughfares during the 1960s. Paired with the palm as the most direct signifiers of the tropical in general and Hawaiian tourism in particular was the China rose hibiscus (*Hibiscus rosa-sinensis*), which, as we saw in the previous chapter, was originally associated with grave sites in Okinawa. By 1975, the year Okinawa hosted the International Marine Exposition, Shibusawa Tatsuhiko was able to assert in the January issue of the travel magazine *Tabi* that the local *akabanā* had become globalized *haibisukasu* by dint of the current Okinawa tourism boom.[33] Disseminated as flora and overdetermined as tropical tropes to appeal to non-Okinawan visitors, the hibiscus and the palm tree became nativized within the physical and symbolic landscape of Okinawa in a way they had never been before and that has persisted to this day despite other layers of identity produced for local and tourist consumption.

The increasing consciousness to brand Okinawa as "tropical"—and the ease with which mainlanders displayed such consciousness compared to residents of Okinawa—is evident in comparisons of assessments for tourism from the early 1960s and early 1970s. A 1963 GRI Tourism Section document titled "Recommendations to Municipalities for Advancing the Tourist Industry" is preoccupied with explaining the most basic infrastructure needed for a successful tourist industry: food, laundry, accommodations, transportation, and entertainment. It shows little thought with regard to defining, branding, and marketing Okinawa. Only a general reference is made about the "attractiveness of nature" as something that draws tourist interest. The closest the document comes to suggesting how to groom the natural scenery is when it explains that tourists desire to see and experience things other than that which they see and experience at home.[34] In other words, there is recognition of the need to exoticize the landscape but no clear idea of how to go about it.

In contrast, nine years later in a Japan Travel Association (JTA) conceptual plan for the development of Okinawa tourism published just two months before Reversion, there is a very clear vision of what the place should be as a tourist destination and very clear ideas about how to achieve it. In this report hibiscus and other "tropicalesque [*nangoku teki*] plants" blossom and palm trees soar, at least in the tropical imagination. Discussing the natural assets of Okinawa, the JTA praises its sun, sky, sea, coral reefs, white-sand beaches, and "scenery particular to southern countries" while regretting that there is hardly any touristic development of them. More regrets—generated by unfulfilled desires and expectations—come when it details the state of Okinawa's flora: "Among the flora too, subtropical plants that are hardly found in mainland Japan, such as *sotetsu*, *adan*, fan palm trees, and bougainvillea, hibiscus, bromeria, and so on lie neglected. However, looking at Okinawa as a whole, pineapple fields can be seen in parts, but in general fields are mostly sugar cane, and it's a pity that because of typhoons, tropicalesque trees such as palms and bananas are hardly spotted."[35] The report acknowledges that war made a mockery of the island's reputation as *midori no shima* and insists that "afforestation is increasingly urgent business for the creation of a tourism image of tropical Okinawa [*nangoku Okinawa*]."[36] It is a testament to the extent of the war's devastation of Okinawa's landscape that this disappointed appraisal comes after over 20 million specimens had already been planted during greenification programs since 1959, the most recent of which did strive to impart a South Seas atmosphere in tourist-exposed areas. It is also a testament to the extent of northern expectations for Okinawa and of stereotypes of the tropics. Once Okinawa returned to Japanese sovereignty, tourism promoters, prefectural officials, and afforestation advocates embraced these stereotypes to the point that they were practically assumed to have always been an active and natural part of Okinawa's projected identity. At the Reversion Memorial Tree Planting Ceremony held on November 26, 1972, for example, it was announced that the first principle of greenification campaigns henceforth would be "to strive for greenification of the environment consonant with actively protecting Okinawa Prefecture's distinctive tropicalesque [*nettai teki*] natural scenery."[37] This kind of local articulation of Okinawa's public face was possible only after hearing it from mainland observers for over a decade.

Blue sky, blue ocean, coral reefs, and mild winter temperatures provided a basis for a more *nangoku* image in Okinawa, but the landscape scenery itself was the prime focus for generating the tropical atmosphere that outsiders demanded and that locals slowly set about cultivating. Despite the Japan Tourism Association's 1972 assessment, by the time of the third All-Ryukyu Greenification Promotion Campaign (1965–1967), the impact of the advice that the Okinawa Tourism Association, the Government of the Ryukyu Islands, and USCAR had gathered from mainland Japanese and Hawaiian consultants was tangible. Not only had *nangoku* become part of the tourism lexicon in Okinawa—the OTA awarded first prize in its 1963 promotional "catchphrase" contest to "For a south country mood, Okinawa" (*Nangoku mūdo wa, Okinawa*)[38]—but tropical flora also became a conspicuous part of afforestation programs. Planning documents published in *Midori* for the third and fourth Greenification Promotion Campaigns highlight the targeted planting of thousands of Washington, Canary, and coconut palms along key roads and indicate increased interest in planting palms, hibiscus (*bussōge*), bougainvillea, azaleas, and the like at tourist sites. The plans for the fourth campaign (1968–1970) in particular—coinciding with "International Travel Year" (1968)—shifted much more focus of resources (about 30 percent of total plantings) to tourist sites and foregrounded "development of tourism resources through greenification" among three explicit goals. The same set of tropicalesque plants—now including Okinawa's newly designated official flower, the *deigo*—and the usual palm trees were allocated for sightseeing spots, parks, and thoroughfares.[39]

The floral tropicalization of Okinawa Island in the midst of general afforestation programs and through outsider interventions raises thorny issues concerning Okinawan identity. In short, we can conceptualize tourism-induced tropicalesque afforestation as an effect of the tourist gaze, the act of tourists visualizing a destination before, during, and after a trip to it, which shapes what they see and how they see it. The power of the tourist gaze is also actively implicated in a dialectic between native and visitor in the production, packaging, and promotion of the product, the "sightseeing spot." This is where issues of local identity surface. It would be easy to assume a view that there is, on the one hand, a *tatemae* (outward, superficial) identity projected solely for tourist consumption that is somehow inauthentic and, on the other hand, a *honne* (inward, true) identity that is somehow authentic and preciously guarded in the community. But I reject such simple binaries because on the level of everyday practice—where I believe any meaningful identity must be actuated—there are not only plural sites of identities that one can take on at given times; there is also the undeniable phenomenon of the so-called superficial and the so-called true operating in tandem to make up the identity of a place and of the people who inhabit it. To put it bluntly, in the context of afforestation and tourism in postwar Okinawa, an artificially created landscape is, on its own, no more or no less "authentic" than a natural one, and the power directing its creation may or may not flow from within Okinawa. Again, here is where Chambers's focus on the source of agency behind a cultural production is a better measure of its authenticity—to the extent, I would argue, that authenticity as such loses much of its usefulness as a descriptive or analytical tool.

One way of looking at this problem is to ask at what point icons of identity—here the tropical tropes of the hibiscus and palm trees—become so rooted after transplantation that natives treat them as native, or at least willingly and actively embrace them in a significant way so that their "foreign" origin (in the sense of nonnative species being cultivated to fulfill nonnative tourist expectations) is not a significant issue. This is not to suggest that *all* Okinawans are pleased with or embrace hibiscus and palm trees as emblems of Okinawan identity; no doubt many see these plants, especially the problematic palm tree, as "phony," even dangerous. Still, they are there, and they figure significantly in self- and other-created portrayals of Okinawa.

The transformation of the meaning of the hibiscus in Okinawa, from Buddhist symbol of an ephemeral world into ubiquitous unofficial official flower of "Japan's Hawaii," parallels the path of postwar Okinawa tourism from its early focus on war memorials and battle sites—places of death—to its present focus on conjuring a carefree and revitalizing tropical beach resort for stressed-out Japanese from the north. Thus, in the case of the hibiscus, it was not its physical presence that Okinawans had to accommodate and become familiar with; rather, it was the symbolic meaning and emotional resonance of the flower that needed reinscription on local minds and hearts in order to understand tourist expectations. Visitors from mainland Japan carried no such burden; in fact, they faced the opposite problem of accommodating a physical presence that did not fulfill what for them signified a proper south island atmosphere. Tropicalesque flora went a long way to generating this atmosphere. That the hibiscus had already existed in Okinawa for at least three centuries as an escape (that is, a privately cultivated species that "escaped" and established itself in the wild) was convenient. It was naturalized, albeit in a different context.[40] The use of hibiscus in tropical branding thus involved increasing and grooming their presence at strategic locations and recontextualizing their symbolic meaning through promotional media, ornamentation, and souvenirs that pushed the Hawaiian tropical resort association. Today, the ubiquity of the hibiscus—from the airport baggage claim and parking lot to Kokusai Dōri souvenir shops and hotel lobbies to the hedges decorating war memorials on Mabuni Hill to popular songs and films—would lead one to believe that the prefectural flower was the hibiscus, not the *deigo*.

In contrast, palm trees present a different and more complex story. Having only a very tenuous claim to native status through varieties of small palms and palmlike shrubs—Yaeyama palms farther south in the Ryukyu Island chain are the only prominent exception within the entire prefecture—palm trees on Okinawa Island are the result of planned landscaping designed to achieve a tropical look; they exist for no other purpose. In fact, I would argue that a palm tree on Okinawa Island, although an actual palm tree, is not a palm tree as such. Rather, it exists as a pure icon, as a signifier of the tropics. This is probably true to some extent in any place where palm trees have been transplanted, but the iconic status of a palm tree in Okinawa is particularly intense and overdetermined once one realizes the amount of time, labor, expense, and patience that is expended to cultivate and maintain a tree that many Okinawans consider a wasteful nuisance. That palms have proliferated on Okinawa in spite of practical concerns attests to their power as tropical icon and to the willingness of tourism developers as well as prefectural and municipal governments to invest in tapping that power to meet the tourist gaze. Even as the recent direction of prefectural forestry authorities and tourism promoters has shifted away from officially highlighting palm trees and instead focused more on indigenous species as the natural backdrop to indigenous cultural productions, the palms are firmly rooted in the Okinawan landscape, and their status as tropical trope persists on key thoroughfares, at botanical gardens and theme parks, and in much of the visual media in tourist-exposed areas. As a crowning example of the palm tree's triumph, in 2008 Naha City finally installed a southern Ryukyu variety of palm trees down the length of both sides of Kokusai Dōri, a request that mainland advisers had been making for several decades (see figure 3.1).

The story of palm trees in Okinawa has a history of empire as its backdrop. Outside of the *sotetsu* and ocassional palm tree in ornamental gardens in far southern Japan, Japanese did not encounter palm trees and other tropical and subtropical flora in large numbers until Japan's imperial expansion beginning in the late nineteenth century and ending with its wartime push into South China, Southeast Asia, and the South Pacific during the Asia-Pacific War. The "disposition of the Ryukyu Kingdom" (*Ryūkyū shobun*) and the formation of Okinawa Prefecture under Japan's sovereignty in 1879 comprised the first step in this southern colonial expansion that brought Japanese into closer contact with a real, physical *nangoku*.[41] Taiwan,

**Figure 3.1.** Palm-lined Kokusai Dōri, Naha (November 2009). *Source*: Gerald Figal.

acquired by Japan as its first official colony after the First Sino-Japanese War (1894–1895), lay at the southwest end of the Ryukyu Island chain and is more firmly tropical in climate as it is bisected by the Tropic of Cancer. Here the Japanese colonial government established in Taipei (Taihoku) the Tropical Medicine Research Institute (Nettai Igaku Kenkyūjō) in 1939 within Taihoku Imperial University, which also housed a College of Science and Agriculture where the study of regional flora and fauna took place. This colonial connection was crucial for Okinawa's reforestation in general and its tropicalization in particular. Not only was there significant immigration of people from Taiwan to Okinawa before and after the war, plants too moved from Taiwan up the Ryukyus. Nurseries in Taiwan supplied various seedlings for transplantation to Okinawa, and palm-lined roads and *mokumao*-lined windbreaks in Taipei supplied models for GRI study tours of Taiwan's use of flora in various contexts. Taiwan appeared frequently in the pages of *Midori* during the 1960s. Issue 13 (May 1962), for example, features cultivated palms in Taiwan on its front cover, while Issue 17 (May 1963) opens with a report on a GRI Forestry Section observation tour of Taiwanese landscapes and cultivation practices. Despite acknowledgments of the danger tall palms presented in typhoon season, appreciable numbers of palm trees—seedlings and more mature specimens—had found their way from Taiwanese sources through nurseries on Okinawa Island and into the ranks of more practical plantings during the third and fourth All-Ryukyu Greenification Promotion Campaigns by the late 1960s. Others were gifted to the GRI by organizations such as the International Lions Club for lining parks and roadways, and many were featured in memorial and celebratory plantings by dignitaries.[42]

The Taiwan connection to the popularization of nonnative palm trees as part of Okinawa's tourist identity is most explicit in the history of one of the island's longest-standing and successful homegrown tourist attractions, the Southeast Botanical Gardens, founded by Chinese-Taiwanese immigrant Obayashi Masamune. Born and raised in colonial Taiwan (thus the assimilated Japanese name), Obayashi studied horticulture and botany at the National University of Taiwan (former Taihoku Imperial University) under the well-known Japanese botanist Tamari Kojirō. His training led to a successful plant-exporting business with the Taipei Tropical Plants Trading Company in the late 1950s and early 1960s, while he occasionally served as a consultant for botanical gardens on mainland Japan. Sensing opportunity in the Ryukyus, Obayashi sold his Taiwan operation in 1965 and parlayed his profits and life savings to purchase seven hundred thousand square meters of land on Iriomote Island in the far southwest Ryukyus, where he set up a tropical fruit plantation. His plan, however, failed for an inadequate number of workers and the lack of convenient transportation for his product from the remote and sparsely populated Iriomote. Broke, he joined friends on Okinawa Island who rented him thirty-four thousand square meters of land in Chibana Town, near Kadena Air Base, where he began work in March 1968 to build a new nursery. Besides tropical fruit, Obayashi specialized in the cultivation and transportation of full-grown palm trees, a difficult procedure that often ended in failure. For this operation he developed methods that increased success rates, and he eventually found himself taking orders for palm trees throughout the western Pacific. To sell palm trees and other exotic plants, Obayashi maintained beautiful display specimens—most prominently full-grown palm trees—on the premises of his nursery, which friends suggested he might, for a small entrance fee, open for public viewing. The appeal of seeing rare, lush tropical plants and picturesque palms proved itself as visitors flocked to the nursery, encouraging Obayashi to reconsider his original plan for a simple tree-export business. This was the humble beginning of the Southeast Botanical Gardens, so named in February 1970 when it was officially opened to the public as a tourist attraction.

Curiously—and tellingly—Obayashi's vision for the gardens was to create "a paradise of species unseen elsewhere in Asia," while at the same time making "a more Okinawa-like site" (*motto Okinawarashii basho*). In fact, the original name of the gardens was going to be "Southeast Paradise," a name retained within the Japanese version of the park's name, *Tōnan Shokubutsu Rakuen* (literally, "Southeast Botanical Paradise").[43] The (il)logic of an unprecedented Southeast Asian tropical garden that expressed Okinawaness speaks to the heart of turning Okinawa the place into Okinawa the tourist destination—it must have unique exotic appeal as "tropical paradise" but simultaneously be representative of Okinawa, which was decidedly not a tropical paradise of the tourist imagination in the late 1960s and early 1970s (nor is it even now). Aspiring to create the "Okinawa-like" *meisho* in this way is a declaration of what Okinawan identity will be, not a plan to preserve and display what it has been. It is an attempt to shape, not to reflect. Obayashi's approach to the physical siting of the then fifty-acre gardens also embraced this tension between actively manufacturing and simply expressing Okinawaness. He insisted on maintaining all existing natural topography (hills, slopes, cliffs, ponds) while clearing the surface of the land to replant with selected tropical and tropicalesque flowers (hibiscus were highlighted), shrubs, and of course palm trees. The majority of these plants were nonnative imports.

Obayashi's tropicalization of this plot of land in Chibana Town represented an intense, small-scale, and specialized greenification project in the wider context of general campaigns designed to reforest a landscape stripped of vegetation by war. As such, the Southeast Botanical Gardens distilled in one tourist spot an overdetermined and self-consciously fantastical staging of Okinawa as tropical paradise. It made no pretense to displaying natively Okinawan plants (many were labeled with an indication of foreign origins) and yet claimed to produce Okinawaness. While other tourist ventures came and went, the Southeast Botanical Gardens secured the title of Okinawa *meisho* and could back its claims to Okinawaness. Even Emperor Hirohito recognized the value and appeal of the Southeast Botanical Gardens, meeting with Obayashi at His Majesty's Spring Garden Party in May 1978 (Obayashi responded by gifting a bottle palm to the emperor). Two years later the Okinawa Prefectural Education Commission granted "museum equivalent" status to the gardens, which were frequently featured on the itineraries of visiting dignitaries until finally closing operations on December 29, 2010, after a public announcement on October 18, 2010, that expressed appreciation for a successful forty-year run without detailing reasons for the closure. One can speculate that it simply became too difficult for this old-school attraction to keep up-to-date and attractive in a more competitve, sophisticated, and fast-paced tourism environment.[44]

The Southeast Botanical Gardens serves as a good example for considering claims of authenticity according to the condition, means, and agency of production of a tourist item rather than according to the product, although its status in this regard must take into consideration that it was a private facility owned by a foreign immigrant who former Southeast Botanical Gardens president Vicky Obayashi, daughter of Masamune, claims had not gotten the same level of recognition and credit as Okinawans have for his efforts at bringing palm trees to Okinawa. She also claims that competing botanical gardens following in the wake of the Southeast Botanical Gardens, such as Nago Paradise and Bios no Oka (Bios on the Hill), received more free publicity and preferential treatment from authorities, suggesting that the gardens were put at an unfair disadvantage that helped bring on their eventual demise. She clearly implied in an interview with me that there had been ethnic-based discrimination against the owners of the gardens.[45] Regardless of the validity of such charges, Southeast Botanical Gardens exemplifies the process of nativizing the foreign by permeating exotic flora with familiar Okinawan motifs. Okinawa-themed gift shop items, Okinawan folk music, and other Okinawan connections in promotional material insinuated themselves within what was otherwise visually themed "Polynesian," in much the same way Hawaiian resorts and of course Hawaii's famous Polynesian Culture Center are staged (minus the luaus and hula dancers). For example, the Southeast Botanical Gardens visitor guides begin by stating that one of Okinawa's trademarks is a warm subtropical climate that allows for a variety of plants and flowers to flourish year-round, which is true enough. However, following that statement is the claim that the Southeast Botanical Gardens contains "fifty species of palm trees and four hundred species of tropical plants and flowers."

The rhetorical effect is to suggest that these plants are natural if not native to Okinawa without actually claiming that they are. Among the U.S. military personnel, there are those who indeed considered the gardens as capturing "the essence of Okinawa" and assumed that the flora on display were all native.[46] Many Japanese visitors probably assumed the same given that what was presented at the gardens conformed to stereotypical images of "tropical paradise" used for decades as one facet of Okinawa tourism promotion, which was first urged by mainland Japanese observers in the early 1960s.

This kind of reception of the Southeast Botanical Gardens demonstrates the viability of the Okinawa-as-tropical-paradise theme and the role of properly cultivated flora in achieving it. With the advent of the International Marine Exposition (Expo '75), which would draw over 1.5 million visitors to Okinawa, Obayashi also seized upon the opportunity to bring the expo's water theme into his manufactured tropics by adding aquatic gardens that featured a huge koi and lily pond dredged from marshland. This addition too was tropicalized via flora. Rather than resembling a typical Japanese koi pond, the resulting body of water adhered to the tropical theme of the botanical gardens. Bordered by palms, hibiscus hedges, and other water plants, this man-made pond became known as Polynesian Lake (see figure 3.2). Along

**Figure 3.2.** "Polynesian Lake" at the Southeast Botanical Gardens. *Source*: Gerald Figal.

with two other natural ponds on the premises, the aquatic gardens completed the park—about hundred acres total—in its final form as a serene tropical oasis amid the most militarized areas of Okinawa Island. Only the occasional jet at nearby Kadena Air Base could remind one of the surrounding reality.

Judgments about the naturalness and authenticity of the tropical at the Southeast Botanical Gardens aside, the realization of Obayashi's vision represents the first successful, full-fledged tropical paradise attraction in Okinawa, one that relied on a concentrated and coordinated arrangement of live tropical material to create a rich environment in which visitors could immerse themselves. Despite the manufactured and manicured nature of that environment, it had a certain integrity, cohesion, and concreteness, even as themed environment. While still symbolizing Okinawa-as-tropical, the gardens' iconic palm trees seem to have had a right to be there as trees rather than simply symbols or theme park attractions. Here is where they stand in contradistinction to the island-wide tropical-themed tourism landscaping that had its modest beginnings in the mid-1960s and took off in earnest in the years after Expo '75, which contributed especially to the "blue sky, blue ocean" aspect of a tropical image for Okinawa.[47] It took a long time, however, for the actual physical landscape to merit the same attention as Okinawa's sky and sea. An anonymous observer in 1982 commented that "in the airport no one is heard praising Okinawa's beauty [on land]. They will comment on the wonderful color of the sea and sky, but nothing about the landscape."[48] Surveys by tourism consultants, planning documents by prefectural authorities, and promotional material by industry agencies all tend to abstract the palm tree and other tropical flora into pure and isolated symbols functioning to signal the tropical from within an urbanized or otherwise built environment. This is when a palm tree is no longer a palm tree but rather functions solely as tropical signifier and arguably the most efficient one in a chain of tropical tropes deployed in the path of tourists to Okinawa.

## GOING NONNATIVE

Picking up where Senge Tetsuma's 1962 diagnosis of Okinawa tourism left off and pointing to where post-Reversion tourism development begins, the 1972 Japan Travel Association assessment report cited in the last section exemplifies the reduction of palm trees and other plants to tropical trope. Whereas Senge, as a director of national parks, acknowledged the hazards of adding nonnative palm trees to the native *adan* and *sotetsu,* while ultimately desiring them to enhance a *nangoku* atmosphere, the JTA showed no such regard in pressing for a proliferation of palm trees for tourist appeal throughout urban areas and along roadways.[49] Obayashi—whose newly opened Southeast Botanical Gardens the JTA does not note even as it urged the construction of "large-scale tropical botanical gardens"—was well aware of the threat that typhoons presented. He thus installed rigorous and costly safety precautions to protect the trees and the people and assets around them in times of dangerous storms, the same techniques prefectural forestry officials would later adopt.[50] The JTA's disregard for environmental appropriateness extended to its desire to see mango, papaya, and banana trees added to Okinawa's modest pineapple plantations, not as an extension of its fruit industry but merely for the "appeal as both touristic and tropical scenery [of] tropical fruit that is impossible to produce in mainland Japan."[51] Any meaningful expansion of fruit cultivation would have, in any case, exacerbated the agricultural runoff problems that plague Okinawa Island's coastlines today.

One cannot overstate the overriding power and abiding impact of this dimension of the tourist gaze looking to tropicalize Okinawa's scenery with exotic plants that are often unsuitable if not harmful. Simmering since the early 1960s and sporadically acted upon by Okinawan tourism promoters to the extent possible until Reversion, the push to shape Okinawa's landscape in the image of a second Hawaii or an echo of Tahiti intensified after Reversion. With much larger mainland investments flowing into Okinawa Prefecture for Expo '75 and beyond, it was difficult for prefectural and municipal governments as well as local resort developers and tourist-site operators not to adopt—if only for business—the vision for their native landscape that nonnatives possessed. Embracing to some degree the physical cultivation of a tropical image—through landscaping, gift items, and names and logos—was dominant in tourism development until tempered by the "Okinawa boom" of the late 1980s and early 1990s, which heightened interest in "native" Okinawan (Ryukyuan) culture, the topic of the next chapter.

In many respects, advice Okinawans received before Reversion was uncritically accepted in the post-Reversion rush to tourism-related development that Expo '75 jump-started for better or for worse.[52] With Okinawa on the Japanese tourist map after Expo '75, prefectural tourism development policy, including its approach to the physical makeover of Okinawa, became better coordinated and comprehensive. Afforestation tuned for tourism took center stage, rather than remaining an adjunct to general greenification programs as had been the case before Reversion. In turn, this renewed effort at large-scale landscaping intensified the focus on tropicalization. The hibiscus-strewn 1980 *Summary of the Okinawa Prefectural Plan for Tourism Landscaping and Afforestation* is blunt about its vision and aims: "We should emphasize that the great appeal of tourism, symbolized by

'Tropical Okinawa,' is the natural scenery of our nation's only subtropical zone, but the state of our prefecture's flora does not sufficiently merit it the moniker 'Southern Islands Wrapped in Flowers and Greenery.' In response to this condition, the present plan aims to enhance the image [*imēji appu*, literally 'image up'] of 'Tropical Okinawa' through planned landscaping and afforestation."[53] To achieve this goal in a systematic and scientific-seeming way, the plan breaks down the Ryukyu Islands at large and Okinawa Island in particular into natural zones. Detailed grids and maps divide Okinawa Island and the smaller outlying Ryukyu Islands into various zones according to topography and climate: mountain, plains, hills, seashore, and natural forests. Each zone is identified with a characteristic native plant or tree, respectively: *shii* (Japanese chinquapin), *gajumaru* (banyan), *Ryūkyū matsu* (Ryukyu pine), *adan* (screw pine or screw palm), and mangrove marshes and Japanese chinquapin forests.[54] While many different species are discussed for different zones throughout Okinawa Island, palms—specifically coconut palms whenever possible—figure significantly in "tourist-exposed areas," especially at beaches and parks. Palms, however, do not belong to any of the basic categories explicated at the onset of the report; rather, they belong to the special category of "tropical-type" (*toropikaru-kei*).

"Tropical-type" is notably absent from this list of categories and is treated separately because the plan acknowledges that it is an unscientific category derived from the context of tourism:

> The word "tropical-type" [*toropikaru-kei*] means "tropical-like" [*nettaiteki na*]. Okinawa belongs to a subtropical zone, and it's best to think of the Sakishima chain [i.e., Miyako, Yaeyama, and Senkaku Islands to the southwest] as semi-tropical. For this reason, from the viewpoint of someone visiting from the mainland, they expect the plant life to all appear tropical [*toropikaru*]. However, in general the image they have of plants that correspond to this word are represented by "palm trees and tropical [*nettai no*] flowers" that signal the tropical [*nettai*]. Moreover, because people in tourism-related businesses choose catchphrases that make you think of natural scenes full of blooming flowers and swaying palms in order to create images of Okinawa, they happily use this word. As a result, the majority of tourists come expecting the landscapes of Hawaii and Tahiti to open out before them. For this reason, we have decided on "tropical-type" for landscaping that is represented by "palm trees and tropical flowers" and intentionally plan on zones where the "tropical-type," distinct from "native-type" [*fūdo-kei*], is deployed.[55]

In short, "tropical-type"—using the Japanized English word *toropikaru* rather than the proper term *nettai*—is a term coined from popular usage and media images. It is a practical concession to tenacious connotations embedded in the minds of would-be visitors to Okinawa, in no small part the result of Hawaii's successful Polynesian-themed beach resort tourism, itself a simulacrum of Tahiti and the South Pacific.

The plan specifically targets the seaport and the airport areas, Kokusai Dōri, Routes 58 and 332 in Naha, the public and tourist beaches in Onna Village, and other "tourist-exposed areas" for "tropical-type" flora such as palm trees and hibiscus plants. In a sense, prefectural authorities sought to seed the island strategically with the kind of plants cultivated in the Southeast Botanical Gardens, although no mention of the gardens appears in the plan's overview of the present state of tropicalization on Okinawa Island. The most overdetermined seeding appears in the vision planners had for the road from the airport to downtown Naha, "Okinawa's *genkan* [entryway]." Airports are significant in casting the first impression of a place to visitors, but if such branding ends abruptly at the airport's exit, its artificiality is thrown into relief, and any effectiveness it might have in establishing an identity for the destination is diminished. The case of Naha's airport is particularly interesting because planners also had to contend with the unavoidable presence of the U.S. and Japan Self-defense Forces military base that shares part of the airport complex. Since the 1960s hibiscus (*bussōge*) hedges and Washington palms existed as the primary plantings along the road skirting the base from the airport to the Kakinohana intersection just across Meiji Bridge that leads into downtown. Coconut and king palms and *adan* had been placed here and there for interest. By 1980, however, the hibiscus and palms were in poor shape according to the prefecture's survey of the current condition of flora: "Hibiscus [*bussōge*] are planted between the Washington palms, but the damage due to the salty air to those trees exposed to strong winds is exceptional." The king palms at the end of this stretch were not faring much better: "Because of considerable environmental stresses (salt air, poor soil), the growing conditions for the king palms at the Kakinohana intersection are not good." And then there was the problem of the base: "The base's fencing extends on both sides of the road. The interior of the base that is visible beyond the fence, with its rows of buildings, tanks, and other facilities, hurts the scenery."[56] In these assessments we begin to see one of the major problems of tropicalizing Okinawa—sometimes nature does not cooperate when nonnative plants are forced upon the landscape or when native and naturalized varieties are forcibly planted in ill-suited areas. Another problem displayed here is how to reconcile the image of serene tropical paradise with the material reality of military facilities and equipment that are in plain sight. Possible responses to the first problem include switching to native and more adaptable plants or finding ways to alter or neutralize nature's objections. Responses to the second include directing the tourist eye elsewhere or camouflaging the eyesore. Tourist landscape development in Okinawa has tried all of these approaches.

In this particular instance of flagging hibiscus and ill-suited king palms on Okinawa's doorstep, the response was to swap out the king palms with more coconut palms, making them the primary plant; to add some *adan*, banyan, *deigo* (the prefectural flower), and *ōhamabō* (Okinawan *yūnaa*, or beach hibiscus, *Hibiscus tiliaceus*) as secondary specimens; and to retain some Washington palms and red hibiscus for interest despite their damage. The emphasis on coconut palms and the addition of beach hibiscus are significant as attempts to better match plants to the surrounding soil and air while implanting a more tropical look; both admirably withstand salty breezes and brackish water. As South Pacific mainstays, they fulfilled stereotypes of the tropics. The goal for this area of replanting was to "strengthen the impression of Tropical Okinawa by spreading a planted scenery that puts coconut palms and *adan* at the center." As for the ugliness of the bases, camouflaging them with the same plants along the inside and outside the fences was recommended.[57] This technique to beautify, if not actually camouflage, base perimeters is in widespread use today although the appearance of the actual plants recommended here is infrequent. The *kyōchikutō* (Indian oleander)—being easily maintained and tolerant of drought, poor soil, and exhaust fumes—is the preferred *kichi no hana,* or "base flower," as it is known by the locals.[58] This prefectural planning guide gives similar considerations for the most appropriate plants in particular microclimates and contexts (urban, highway, rural, military, coastal, mountainous) for other tourist-exposed roads in and around Naha and up the west coast to the beaches of Onna Village and beyond. The stretch from the northern outskirts of Naha City to Kadena Town, site of Kadena Air Base, also embraces the idea of coconut palms as its signature roadside plant. Eventually hundreds of palm trees of several varieties—but relatively few actual coconut palms—were planted along this route and exist today as distractions from the U.S. base facilities. As one follows the map of the plan farther north to the Nago area where topography and foliage are noticeably different—less naturally "tropical"—there is more suggested use of *deigo*, Ryukyu pines, Japanese chinquapin, and other trees and shrubs with and without overt tropical associations.

Signs that this strategy of afforestation and landscaping might achieve its intended effect if carried out systematically—but at the same time might be difficult to achieve—reside in the comments of one mainland Japanese visitor to Okinawa in 1980. Iwata Eisuke related entering the lobby of Naha International Airport and "feeling enveloped by the warm air characteristic of the tropics [*nangoku*]" and "being reminded of my visit to the South Pacific. . . . The sensation of having come to the tropics welled up." Upon leaving the airport for Naha, however, he recalls that "the Washington palms and hibiscus lining the road pleased my eyes, but as I approached the city, this sensation disappeared."[59] Iwata was alluding here to the growing "concrete jungle" (his term) that unchecked post-Reversion urban sprawl was spawning on the compact and crowded main island, making the illusion of a relaxing and lush tropical getaway impossible to maintain. The sprawl of U.S. bases that took about one-sixth of the island's real estate, including some prime beachfront property, only made the situation worse. Attractive tourism development, plagued by a war-devastated landscape and lack of adequate investment before Reversion, had to contend in post-Reversion with the very thing that many had hoped Reversion would bring: better infrastructure, modernized urban areas, more paved roads, more jobs. The persistence of the South Seas sensation that Iwata initially felt upon entering Okinawa for the first time was what comprehensive landscaping and well-placed tropicalization aimed to achieve so that people like him would want to come back a second and third time.

In government and private efforts to "image up" Tropical Okinawa, however, the "tropical" and "Okinawa" did not always come together and stay together easily. Outlining the concept of Tropical Okinawa and the logic behind it was easy; so too was producing media images that cast Okinawa as tropical paradise. The difficult task lay in realizing concepts and images in tangible and sustainable ways. Okinawa Prefecture's Second Development Plan (1981), for example, repeated the mantra of needing to enhance the prefecture's "abundant subtropics" to draw tourists. Greenification-promotion publications in the wake of that general plan, like *Midori* and *Midori to seikatsu,* continued to stress the need to tropicalize the landscape for tourism while pointing out the gap between tropical image and tropical reality. Significantly, much of the focus was on the first impressions obtained at the airport and on the road into downtown Naha. The observations and advice of Kinjō Yukimitsu, then vice president of the Okinawa Tourist Hotel and Inn Association Union and owner of the Moon Beach Hotel, was typical: "The flora in the areas around the airport parking lot is poor. There is absolutely no tropical mood [*nangoku no mūdo*], no OKINAWA mood. It's imperative that we offer as the first impression to visitors the aroma, the flowers, the greenery of OKINAWA (we completely lose out in comparison to greenification of tourist sites in Hawaii). I want there to be abundant flora like at the Honolulu and Singapore airports and a building up of an even more enjoyable atmosphere of flowers and greenery than they have."[60] "Tropical mood" and "OKINAWA mood" are written in parallel, as if to suggest that they are interchangeable synonyms—Okinawa *is* tropical and tropical *is* Okinawa. In this passage "OKINAWA" is written in the katakana script used primarily for foreign words as a way to offer emphasis and to exoticize the place/name (Hawaii and Singapore, as foreign places, are naturally in katakana), a technique common in Japanese marketing where there can be much graphic play with text. But Kinjō's use of "OKINAWA" in katakana is selective and goes beyond the usual use in advertising; he switches to it when referring to the tourist product that is consciously manufactured at places like the airport lobby and parking lot, the road into town, hotel lobbies, and guest room interiors. In the transformation that is supposed to take place in the airport, Okinawa (沖縄) becomes OKINAWA (オキナワ). The same is intended when a tourist takes a cab from the airport along Route 332 to Meiji Bridge in Naha and when he or she walks into a guest room at a tourist hotel. The airport is the entry point not only to the place called Okinawa but to the illusion, the destination "OKINAWA" of the visitor's dream. Verandas and interiors of guest rooms—like those at his Moon Beach Hotel, Kinjō is quick to point out—should be amply planted with flowers and greenery so that they can "lend a taste of the tropical mood [*nangoku no mūdo*] to tourists."[61] "Mood" (*mūdo*, in katakana) is glossed earlier in this passage as "dream," referring to an earlier discussion in the essay about fulfilling the visitor's dream of Okinawa. In short, Kinjō is responding to and is complicit with the tourist gaze, creating a Tourist Okinawa between reality and image of the place. He took his own pioneering Moon Beach Hotel—established in the 1950s as Okinawa's first real beach resort—as a model of Tropical Okinawa mood, offering photos of its lobby's interior garden and flower-filled verandas. Unsurprisingly, his essay is also accompanied by two photos of palm trees planted around the airport parking lot and along the road leading to town, which attempt to conjure up for the just arrived the tropical dream mood that is OKINAWA, the destination they have been anticipating. The current (as of October 2011) Welcome Hall of Naha International Airport represents the logical evolution of Kinjō's concept; as the airport's homepage explains, "Palm trees tower in the expansive space, allowing you to fully enjoy the atmosphere of tropical [*nangoku*] Okinawa."[62] Of course, the visitor is experiencing this tropical atmosphere within a modern climate-controlled building, but that's the point—to create a *comfortable* and *accessible* sense and sensation of tropical beauty, free of hellish humidity and annoying pests.

The beach resort boom that began later in the 1980s was guided by many of the concepts Kinjō and others had articulated, reinforcing the push to cast Okinawa in a more tropical light. This trend did not necessarily mean, however, that it was any easier to align image and reality. As it had in 1979 with its *Prefectural Plan for Tourism Landscaping and Afforestation,* Okinawa Prefecture endorsed branding Okinawa as tropical playground in its high-profile 1990 publication *Resort Okinawa Master Plan: Aiming for the Formation of a World-Class "Tropical Resort Okinawa."* The ambitious plan—which I take up in more detail in chapter 6 when discussing resort tourism—envisioned the prefecture as one big playground for tourists, zoned into different sectors specializing in different attractions. Beach resorts along the coast of Onna Village anchor this "Tropical Resort Okinawa" (*Toropikaru Rizōto Okinawa*), which in turn is defined as one point of a "Golden Triangle" formed with Hawaii and Australia's Gold Coast. Together the three demarcate a "Tropical Resort Zone" that effectively embraces the Pacific islands Japan held at the greatest extent of its wartime empire, from the Northern Marianas to Guadalcanal. Photos of accommodations in Hawaii and the main boulevard in Waikiki present exemplary tropical resort and street environments created by palm trees and tropical flowers. Other photos chosen to evoke scenes from residential and research parks are given the tropical treatment with ample numbers of palm trees and an unrelated, gratuitous close-up of a China rose hibiscus labeled "one of Okinawa's representative flowers—the hibiscus." Now completely distanced from its past use as grave offering, bereft of a context that did identify it with Okinawa, this photo of a hibiscus—presumably from Okinawa but there is no guarantee of that—functions in the master plan as generic signifier of the tropical that superficially confers tropical credentials on Okinawa, the would-be "Tropical Resort Okinawa." Opposite this hibiscus photo, under the "Research Park Image Photos" page, is another gratuitous shot, a stock photo of windswept coconut palms on a white-sand beach with translucent blue-green ocean. Captioned "facing the nearby emerald green ocean," it gives no location, but it is definitely not Okinawa. It is placed there to suggest the kind of atmosphere, the kind of idea—not an actual physical space—that would be desirable for a research park in Tropical Okinawa.

The insistence on nonnative coconut palm trees as the tropical trope par excellence is the best example of reality being bent to concept, often at considerable risk and great expense. On several counts, tall palm trees are wholly unsuited to the densely populated areas of Okinawa Island; there are good reasons why they are not native. Not only can they be damaged in typhoons, they can cause damage in urban areas, crushing roofs and blocking roads. Coconut palms also present the additional hazard of falling fruit. Despite complaints from residents about the ill-suited nature of palm trees on their island, they have not been removed. On the contrary, once palm trees were planted along roads and highways more or less according to the recommendations of the *Prefectural Plan for Tourism Landscaping and Afforestation*, they were there to stay, requiring the Forestry Section of the prefectural government to develop elaborate measures to maintain their presence to ensure their symbolic function. The principal defense against falling palms and other tall trees in urban areas is buttressing (see figure 3.3). The palm trees appearing in the photos of Kinjō's article, for example, displayed typical buttressing. Indeed, palm trees in urban areas are typically supported by wooden frames requiring

**Figure 3.3.** Buttressed palm trees versus telephone poles. *Source*: Gerald Figal.

extra material and labor costs. In the case of coconut palms, special crews tediously hand-tie green netting around the coconuts to catch any falling fruit. There is no better testament to the purely symbolic status of palm trees in Okinawa than a buttressed coconut palm with its coconuts wrapped in green nylon netting. These trees provide no fruit, no shade, no timber while sapping considerable time and resources. Even their physical form becomes compromised with bulky buttressing, detracting from the atmosphere they are pressed into service to evoke—they are nothing like the windswept palms of travel posters. Their sole value lies in the intangible *nangokuteki na kibun,* that tropical feel they and postcard-perfect hibiscus generate. The calculation here is that the effort and expense put into their maintenance is worth the economic benefits derived from fulfilling the expectations of tourists whose visions of a south island atmosphere are lined with rows of palm trees punctuated by colorful exotic flowers.

## TROPICAL BRANDING AND THE REDISCOVERY OF THE NATIVE

The tropicalization of Okinawa's landscape—real and imagined—within the broader context of practical afforestation campaigns from the 1950s provided the foundations for a broader tropical branding of Okinawa's tourist identity. It was not the most original identity to cultivate at the time, but it was the one perceived most marketable to mainland Japanese who could not afford Hawaii or the South Pacific. Hibiscus and palm trees, which had already been thoroughly turned into global logos signifying "tropical escape," were appropriated for that same function in postwar Okinawa, although through differing trajectories. During that process, native plants previously identified with the place were cast into supporting roles or had their referents redefined.

In the case of palm trees, the imposition of dramatic and stereotypical nonnative varieties appears blunt, even crude, given the lengths that must be taken to sustain them. Majestic—but problematic—Washington, king, and coconut palms create an overdetermined "southern island feel," which sometimes overflows into tourist sites where it is historically or emotionally inappropriate. For example, at the rebuilt Shureimon that welcomes visitors on the way to the rebuilt Shuri Castle (the central topic of the following chapter), the painstaking detail given to historical authenticity visually competes with palm trees that were never part of the castle complex (see figure 3.4). Dating past photos of Shureimon suggests that the palms there appeared in the early 1980s. In other words, even Shuri Castle Park, now the single most-visited tourist site in Okinawa, has not been beyond the reach of the tropical touch amid efforts to create "Tropical Resort Okinawa." Similarly, probably

**Figure 3.4.** Shureimon, tropicalized. *Source*: Gerald Figal.

Okinawa's second most-visited tourist site, the famous Himeyuri Memorial discussed in chapters 1 and 2, has seen its own dramatic floral transformation since 1947. What was once a quite barren site is now very lush and flanked by palms that are actually difficult to grow in the type of soil common in the southern part of the island. The emotional dissonance between tropical trees and tragic war tale is heightened by barkers crassly peddling colorful hibiscus-and-palm-spangled T-shirts and handbags just across the street from the memorial's entrance, replacing the pushy flower sellers of the past who have been corralled into a designated vending booth opposite the souvenir shops (see figure 3.5).

Although also part of tropical branding, the hibiscus is not without its own roots in Okinawa. Strictly speaking it is not indigenous but naturalized as it became an escape that developed its own local, organic meanings. Referring to *bussōge* in Okinawan as *akabanā* somehow nativizes it as well, taking it beyond its associations with Buddhism and grave sites, turning it into a more neutral emblem of *furusato* (home town) Okinawa. The word *haibisukasu* (ハイビスカス), on the other hand, drains *bussōge* and *akabanā* of previous local associations except perhaps among elderly Okinawans. Mainland tourists typically see only Hawaii, not *hotoke-sama*, in that hibiscus. Absent that original meaning, hibiscus can be reduced to tropical icons and representative

**Figure 3.5.** Himeyuri-no-tō and commercial tropicalia. *Source*: Gerald Figal.

logos for Tourist Okinawa. They can be deployed alongside equally iconic palms on the welcome sign in the airport baggage claim area, used to designate the second floor of the Naha International Airport parking lot, and liberally dispersed on the covers and pages of tour guides promoting resort tourism. They find their ultimate dispersal as mass-reproduced images on mass-produced souvenirs or, better yet, as a label on a mass-produced shopping bag for mass-produced souvenirs. In this instance, hibiscus and palms are truly functioning as identifiers for a generic tropical brand that has only tenuous native roots.

While we could dismiss this tropical branding as just marketing, and thus somehow only superficial to Okinawan identity, it raises issues concerning the impact of that branding on local identity. After all, branding involves creating a convincing and marketable identity for consumers, in this case predominantly mainland Japanese tourists who, looking past U.S. bases, see "south sea island." It follows that the more successful the branding, the more deeply the brand's associations are going to be attached to the public character (identity) of the place. We must consider then to what extent tourism has transformed the scenery of staged environments so that those palm trees no longer seem staged to guests and hosts alike. In practical terms, how narrow is the gap between "Okinawa" and "Tourist Okinawa," especially given that

Okinawa has aspired since Reversion to be Japan's "Tourism Prefecture"? This is another way of asking how blurred the place and the representation of the place become, the extent to which reality imitates image. Should a souvenir photo of a tropicalized Shureimon be captioned, a là Magritte, "This is not Okinawa"? Or is it? (See figure 3.6.) Given the consciously planned high-level presence of tourism in Okinawa by the 1990s, I am inclined to accept this mash-up of "Tropical Ryukyu" as a significant facet of everyday Okinawa despite the protest to the contrary by cultural purists.

While the tropical brand, enhanced by palms and tropical plants against a backdrop of blue sea and sky and white-sand beaches, may have arguably been the most obvious and the most "natural" for Okinawa tourism developers and promoters to pursue, it is not without its limitations. If one goal for tourism development is to offer something distinctive that cannot be experienced—or experienced as well—elsewhere, then Okinawa as tropical paradise would always be at a qualitative disadvantage versus its more advanced models, particularly Hawaii. It could, however, compete in price and in geographic and cultural proximity. For a new, aspiring middle-class family that could not afford or was intimidated by a real overseas vacation, there was an appeal to a quasi-overseas trip to a quasi-foreign, quasi-tropical Okinawa

**Figure 3.6.** Souveniring Shureimon. *Source*: Gerald Figal.

where Japanese was spoken, the travel time was relatively short, and overall costs were reasonable. If one were willing to overlook the rough spots and the strained attempts to assert a landscape that existed only partially at best in nature there, then one could leave thinking it was a good deal and expectations were adequately met. With enough primping and pruning, Okinawa could reasonably pass for the image it reflected in the tourist gaze.

And yet, a desire for a better conjunction between image and reality and for a homegrown—rather than transplanted—destination identity has been percolating lately among prefectural authorities. The 2002 general landscaping plan for Okinawa Prefecture is noticeably less ebullient about creating "Tropical Okinawa" than the 1979 tourism landscaping plan, even when discussing tourist zones. Rather, it offers more practical landscapes that make effective use of appropriate indigenous and naturalized flora, with primary attention given to historical and cultural value. While the idea of palm trees and hibiscus in tourist resort zones has not been abandoned—indeed, the newly planted palms along Kokusai Dōri are testament to their staying power—the broad categories governing the classification and content of different geographical areas now include specific reference to historically and culturally appropriate species.[63] Accordingly, *akagi, fukubi, gajumaru, deigo, momotamana, monpanoki, bussōge,* and other native and established species figure as representative types whose origins, distribution, and attributes are duly noted. In the case of *bussōge/akabanā*, details of its probable arrival in the Ryukyus in the sixteenth century and its longtime local appearance in hedges and gardens are offered, as if to make a case for its use dissociated from tropical resort tourism. Significantly, palm trees make an appearance only in street plans for Ishigaki City on Ishigaki Island in the southwestern Yaeyama chain, and only the native Yaeyama palms are used. This rediscovery of native flora in the wake of widespread tropicalization of Okinawa's landscape is best seen in the context of the foregrounding of traditional Ryukyu culture that came with the re-creation of Shuri Castle in the early 1990s. A 1998 exhibit in Okinawa of botanical specimens from the Ryukyu Kingdom—based on recently discovered specimens taken by botanists with Commodore Matthew C. Perry's expeditions in 1853 and 1854—has, for example, inspired new directions in planting and landscaping within the Prefectural Greenery Promotion Section.[64] Despite the palm trees flanking Shureimon at the approach to the castle, concern for historical accuracy—or at least the appearance of historicalness—in the architecture and material culture at Shuri Castle Park and other Ryukyu-themed tourist attractions has prompted more careful consideration of the historical, cultural, and natural contexts in the flora for greenification projects. "Ryukyu" offers another dimension to Okinawa's destination identity, even if it is sometimes imaginatively blended with the tropical. It is that dimension to which we now turn.

## NOTES

1. Erve Chambers, *Native Tours: The Anthropology of Travel and Tourism* (Prospect Heights, IL: Waveland Press, 2000), 98–99.

2. For Vietnam's case, see Scott Laderman, *Tours of Vietnam: War, Travel Guides, and Memory* (Durham, NC: Duke University Press, 2009).

3. Okinawa Prefectural Archives, RG 260, Box 78 of HCRI-AO, Folder No. 8.

4. See, for example, Tada Osamu's important study *Okinawa imēji no tanjō—aoi umi no karuchuraru sutadeizu*, which focuses on Marine Expo '75 as the site for the generation of what becomes the Okinawa brand. I largely agree with Tada's astute analysis of the cultural impact of the expo; he is historically shortsighted, however, in identifying it as the ground zero for the "Okinawa image."

5. Miyagi Eishō, "Ryokka undō—watashi no mita Okinawa," *Midori*, no. 1 (January 1960): 27.

6. Ōta Seisaku, *Omoide o zuikitsu ni nosete* (Naha: Kitajima Kenzō, 1970), 246–49.

7. Ōta Seisaku, *Omoide o zuikitsu ni nosete*, 253.

8. Ōta Seisaku, "Ryokka undō ni kyōryoku o," *Midori*, no. 1 (January 1960): 1–2.

9. On the friction between High Commissioner Caraway and Chief Executive Ōta and between Caraway and U.S. ambassador to Japan Edwin O. Reischauer under the Kennedy administration's attempt to liberalize policy in Okinawa, see Nicholas Evan Sarantakes, *Keystone: The American Occupation of Okinawa and U.S.-Japanese Relations* (College Station: Texas A&M University Press, 2000), 112–27.

10. For Ōta's own perspective on Okinawa under U.S. occupation and a sense of his thought and character, see his memoir, *Omoide o zuihitsu ni nosete*.

11. Forestry Office, GRI, "Ryūkyū no ringyō gaikyō" [General Situation of Ryukyu Forestry] in *Midori*, no. 2:19.

12. Forestry Office, GRI, "Okinawa no ringyō" [General Situation of Okinawa Forestry] in *Midori*, no. 18:11.

13. Agriculture and Forestry Department, GRI, *Ringyō shiryō 7: Ryūkyū no ringyō* (Naha: GRI, 1966), 40.

14. The GRI Agriculture and Forestry Department's 1966 publication *Ringyō shiryō 7: Ryūkyū no ringyōi* leaves blanks in the palm category for the years 1959 to 1961, while a later 1970 GRI publication has generally higher figures for all categories and total plantings, including about twenty-two thousand palm trees. One problem with GRI figures is that at times it is not clear whether they are reporting just the figures for the Greenification Campaigns or for all greenification efforts combined.

15. Agriculture and Forestry Department, GRI, *Ringyō shiryō 7*, 40.

16. The cover of *Midori* no. 13 (May 1962) featured a photo of a palm-lined road in Taiwan. Articles from this and other issues around this time included discussions of the cultivation of certain trees and shrubs in Taiwan for use in Okinawa as well as uses in Taiwan that might be applied to Okinawa.

17. Zen-Ryū Ryokka Suishin Undō Honbu, "Dai-san-ji Zen-Ryū Ryokka Shinshin Undō jisshi yōkō," undated, OPA R00059561B (Ryokka undō ni kansuru shorui).

18. Memorandum on the subject of allocation of tree seedlings, from USCAR Forester to Lieutenant Sprict, 824th Civil Engineer, Kadena Air Base, February 5, 1968, OPA R00059561B.

19. Senge Tetsuma, *Okinawa kankō shindansho* [A Diagnosis of Okinawa Tourism] (Naha: Okinawa Kankō Kyōkai, 1962), 4.
20. Senge, *Okinawa kankō shindansho,* 5.
21. Senge, *Okinawa kankō shindansho,* 45–46.
22. John Urry, *The Tourist Gaze: Leisure and Travel in Contemporary Societies,* 2nd ed. (London: Sage, 1990; 2nd ed., 2002), 12.
23. See Jane C. Desmond, *Staging Tourism: Bodies on Display from Waikiki to Sea World* (Chicago: University of Chicago Press, 1999). Desmond is most concerned with the development of the "hula girl" image and Polynesian cultural display in Hawaiian tourism, taking the cultivation of tropical flora and landscape for granted.
24. Senge, *Okinawa kankō shindansho,* 44.
25. Okinawa Kankō Kyōkai, *Okinawa kankō jū shūnen shi* (Naha: Okinawa Kankō Kyōkai, 1964), 75.
26. See Old Photos of Japan website at http://oldphotosjapan.com/photos/759/ginza-streetcar (accessed September 6, 2011).
27. For a casual history of Kokusai Dōri, see Ōhama Sō, *Okinawa Kokusai-dōri monogatari: "Kiseki" to yobareta ichi mairu* (Gushikawa, Okinawa Prefecture: Yui Shuppan, 1998).
28. Frank T. Inouye, "Requirements for Successful Development of Tourism in the Ryukyus," USCAR Tourism Committee, 1962, RG 260, Box 78 of HCRI-AO, Folder No. 8, U.S. National Archives.
29. Okinawa Kankō Kyōkai, *Okinawa kankō jū shūnen shi,* 76.
30. Okinawa Kankō Kyōkai, *Okinawa kankō jū shūnen shi,* 75–76.
31. Urry, *The Tourist Gaze,* 3.
32. Jonathan Culler, "Semiotics of Tourism," *American Journal of Semiotics* 1, no. 1/2 (1981): 127.
33. Quoted in Tada Osamu, *Okinawa imēji o tabisuru—Yanagita Kunio kara ijū būmu made* (Tokyo: Chūō Kōron Shinsha, 2008), 140.
34. GRI, Tourism Section, "Shi-chō-son ni kankō jigyō o susumeru sho," 11. OPA R00070385B.
35. Nihon Kankō Kyōkai Okinawa Chiiki Kankō Sōgō Chōsa Ii-in Kai, *Okinawa chiiki kankō kaihatsu no kansō keikaku* (Tokyo: Nihon Kankō Kyōkai, 1972), 16.
36. Nihon Kankō Kyōkai Okinawa Chiiki Kankō Sōgō Chōsa Ii-in Kai, *Okinawa chiiki kankō kaihatsu no kansō keikaku,* 79.
37. Shinohara Takeo, *Anettai chiiki no Okinawa ringyō no ayumi* (Naha: Ryūkyū Ringyō Kyōkai, 1984), 104. *Nettai* is the technical climate term for "tropical," while *anettai,* which is what is usually used to describe Okinawa, means "subtropical."
38. Okinawa Kankō Kyōkai, *Okinawa kankō jū shūnen shi,* 91.
39. "Dai-3-ji zen-Ryū ryokka suishin undō jikkai yōryō," *Midori,* no. 23 (November 1964): 6–8; "Dai-4-ji zen-Ryū ryokka suishin undō jikkai yōryō," *Midori,* no. 35 (November 1967): 6–8.
40. It is unclear exactly when hibiscus arrived in Okinawa, but first records of it there date from the early seventeenth century and it most probably came from Fujian, China, where it was associated with Buddhism, temple gardens, and elite residences. By 1800, about six different varieties were recorded in Okinawa. "Haibisukasu no subete (jō): Sono rekishi to haikei," *Midori to seikatsu* 1 no. 4 (August 1982): 4–5.

41. For a summary of the Ryukyus' forcible transformation into a Japanese prefecture, see Gregory Smits, *Visions of Ryukyu: Identity and Ideology in Early-Modern Thought and Politics* (Honolulu: University of Hawaii Press, 1999), 143–62. Also see Gregory Smits, "The *Ryūkyū Shobun* in East Asian and World History," in Josef Kreiner, ed., *Ryūkyū in World History* (Bonn: Bier'sche Verlagsanstalt, 2001), 279–304.

42. *Midori*, no. 16:16–17.

43. "Tōnan Shokubutsu Rakuen no ayumi," Southeast Botanical Gardens, http://www.sebg.co.jp/about/ayumi.html (accessed September 6, 2011). Also see Gordi Breyette, "A History of the Southeast Botanical Gardens and Himeyuri Cactus Park" (unpublished internal document, n.d.).

44. A copy of the closure announcement is available at https://www.sebg.co.jp/sebginfo.pdf.

45. Interview with Vicky Obayashi at the offices of the Southeast Botanical Gardens, June 2001.

46. Travis V. Easter, "Step into an Enchanted Forest," *Okinawa Marine*, May 12, 2006, 10–11; Robert C. Frenke, "Okinawa Paradise," *Okinawa Marine*, February 29, 2008, 13.

47. This is essentially the thesis of Tada Osamu's study, *Okinawa imēji no tanjō*, that Expo '75 launched the "blue ocean" image of (tourist) Okinawa.

48. "Haibisukasu no subete (jō): Sono rekishi to haikei," 6.

49. Nihon Kankō Kyōkai Okinawa Chiiki Kankō Sōgō Chōsa Ii-in Kai, *Okinawa chiiki kankō kaihatsu no kansō keikaku*, 79.

50. Breyette, "A History of the Southeast Botanical Gardens and Himeyuri Cactus Park," 8.

51. Nihon Kankō Kyōkai Okinawa Chiiki Kankō Sōgō Chōsa Ii-in Kai, *Okinawa chiiki kankō kaihatsu no kansō keikaku*, 79.

52. The value Expo '75 had for the local economy is still debated. Part of the promise of Reversion was integration into the Japanese economy, which had been booming in the 1960s until the "oil shocks" and general slowdown of the 1970s. Expo-related construction and the business the event would draw were supposed to be an unmitigated good for Okinawa when in actuality the results were much more mixed—the lion's share of profits went to Tokyo-based companies and overbuilding left many new hotels unfilled in the aftermath, not to mention questionable changes to the local landscape. On the other hand, Okinawa acquired more viable facilities, accommodations, and a destination identity that attracted over 1 million visitors, a number that—except for a sharp decline in 1976 and after the 9/11 terrorist attacks and a slight dip in 2000 when Okinawa hosted the G8 Summit—has steadily increased ever since. In 2007, the number of visitors reached 5.89 million. The year 2008 saw the first drop (0.1 percent to 5,697,300) in Japanese tourists to Okinawa since 9/11, but at the same time it had a record number of foreign visitors (up 25.5 percent to 237,000), which pushed totals to 5.93 million, but short of Okinawa Prefecture's target of 6.2 million (*Ryūkyū Shimpō*, April 29, 2009; available online at http://ryukyushimpo.jp/news/storyid-143883-storytopic-4.html). The prefecture projected 7.2 million visitors by 2011, but Okinawa's leading scholar of small island economy, Kakazu Hiroshi, is care-

ful to frame current tourism growth in terms of Okinawa's "carrying capacity"—that is, the natural limits on resources that any small island hosting a tourism industry must face (Kakazu Hiroshi, "Sustainable Island Tourism: The Case of Okinawa," http://www.yashinomi.to/pacific/pdf/Kakazu_02.pdf. See also his *Island Sustainability: Challenges and Opportunities for Okinawa and Other Pacific Islands in a Globalized World* (Bloomington, IN: Trafford Publishing, 2009).

53. Okinawa Prefecture, *Okinawa-ken kankō shūkei ryokka keikaku* (Naha: Okinawa Prefecture, 1979), 1. This is a summary of the prefecture's 1979 *Okinawa-ken kankō shūkei ryokka keikaku chōsa hōkokusho*.

54. Okinawa Prefecture, *Okinawa-ken kankō shūkei ryokka keikaku*, 5.

55. Okinawa Prefecture, *Okinawa-ken kankō shūkei ryokka keikaku*, 14–15.

56. Okinawa Prefecture, *Okinawa-ken kankō shūkei ryokka keikaku*, 37.

57. Okinawa Prefecture, *Okinawa-ken kankō shūkei ryokka keikaku*, 37.

58. Oleander is the same shrub used extensively in landscaping freeway medians in California.

59. Iwata Eisuke, *Midori*, no. 24 (March 1980): 3.

60. Kinjō Yukikitsu, "Kankō ritsuken wa ryokka kara: Naha Kūkō kara shigaichi o hana to midori ni," *Midori to seikatsu* 4, no. 3 (July 1982): 31.

61. Kinjō, "Kankō ritsuken wa ryokka kara," 32.

62. "Naha kūkō kokunaisen ryokyaku taaminaru biru: Ibento gyararii" [Naha Airport Domestic Travelers Terminal Building: Event Gallery], Naha International Airport, http://www.naha-airport.co.jp/event (accessed September 6, 2011). The arrangement of palm trees in the Welcome Hall, however, was different when I was there in November 2009. Before then there had been the two tall palms as pictured on the website, along with a few smaller ones; at the time of my visit, those two tallest specimens had been replaced by smaller ones. The web page photo was not updated to reflect this change.

63. Okinawa Prefecture, *Okinawa-ken shūkei ryokka jissai keikakusho* (Naha: Okinawa Prefecture, 2002), 1–2, 17–24.

64. Interview with staff from the Greenery Promotion Section of the Department of Agriculture, Forestry, and Water, Okinawa Prefectural Office, Naha, June 2004. For details of the exhibit, see the exhibit catalog, Ryūkyū Ōkoku jidai no shokubutsu hyōhon tenjikai jikkō iinkai, ed., *Ryūkyū Ōkoku jidai no shokubutsu hyōhon: Perī ga mochikaetta shokubutsu-tachi* (Urasoe City, Okinawa: Chitose Publishing, 1998).

# 4

# Ryukyu Restoration

## *Shuri Castle and* Furusato *Okinawa*

A 1997 report on major Japanese theme parks conducted by the Japanese government's Okinawa General Bureau revealed that Okinawa Prefecture possessed markedly more theme parks that fell into the categories of "history/traditional culture" or "tourist farm/botanical garden" (77.7 percent) rather than "foreign town" or "entertainment" (11.1 percent). In comparison, the former two categories made up only 31.3 percent of the representative mainland theme parks, and the latter two totaled 44.6 percent.[1] While the report authors used these data to pitch concepts for an entertainment-centered water amusement park and for what they dubbed an "outdoor aquarium village" featuring eco-edutainment attractions, I would use it to point out the dominant trends in the postwar commercialization and branding of Okinawa relative to other Japanese prefectures: it is a place of unique (= exotic) botanicals and of unique (= exotic) culture, even to the point of suggesting a different world and ethnicity, albeit one that is ultimately made familiar enough for mainland Japanese to be at ease within the exotic. Every prefecture and many towns may boast their own regional *meibutsu* (specialty products), flora, geographical features, and particular cultural practices, but these are defined within a larger Japanese culture-nature matrix as variations of fundamentally familiar items despite how different they might initially appear on the surface—the *eki-ben* (train station box lunch) might have different contents at different locations, but it is still a culturally familiar *bentō* lunch (and probably will have rice in it).[2] A relatively large proportion of tourist attractions featuring local history, culture, and flora exists in Okinawa because they can; that is to say, they always already fulfill the primary requisite for attracting tourists seeking something out of the ordinary—they are defined largely outside the familiar everyday experience of mainland (especially urban) Japanese. In this sense, for the mainland tourist, all of Okinawa might be categorized as a "foreign-town-type" theme park containing "history/traditional culture" and "botanical garden" theme parks that are convenient concentrations of what is presented to and perceived by visitors as Okinawa-like Okinawa (*Okinawarashii Okinawa*). "Okinawa-like Okinawa" and "Okinawaness" (*Okinawarashisa*) are common phrases in tourist-directed descriptions of Okinawa. Sometimes Okinawan as a different ethnic group is emphasized by using the Okinawan word for the place, *Uchinā* (*Uchinārashii Okinawa*) or, as we will see, recasting Okinawa as "Ryukyu." While details might vary, "Okinawa-like" in tourism marketing most commonly refers to the post–International Marine Exposition "blue sky, blue ocean" image that Tada Osamu has delineated, the (sub)tropical look and feel of the landscape discussed in the previous chapter, and to revived displays of traditional Okinawa as derived from the history and culture of the premodern Ryukyu Kingdom (1429–1879), the focus of this chapter.

Notwithstanding the U.S.-enforced use of the term "Ryukyu Islands" over "Okinawa" during its occupation from 1945 to 1972, "Ryukyu" is Okinawa in heritage mode. In tandem with particular traits of Okinawa's natural (even if cultivated) environment, cultural items attributed to the Ryukyu Kingdom period constitute the foundation for "*Furusato* Okinawa," which in turn can be easily integrated into Tourist Okinawa. Literally meaning "old village" and signifying a nostalgic hometown, *furusato*, as a key concept in the Japanese state's cultural policy since 1984, often informs so-called *machi-* or *mura-zukuri* (city- or village-making) initiatives designed to build local identity and civic spirit as much as they are to improve infrastructure and public spaces. Many such initiatives are simply called *furusato-zukuri*, what Jennifer Robertson has identified as "a political project through which popular memory is shaped and socially reproduced. The dominant representation of *furusato* is infused with nostalgia, a dissatisfaction with the present on the grounds of a remembered or imagined past plenitude." The Ryukyu Kingdom during its golden age is imagined as Okinawa's past plenitude. Robertson emphasizes that as "nostalgic praxis" "*furusato* is shaped by, just as it shapes, a 'living historical' past."[3] The most prominent precursor to this cultural policy initiative was arguably the "Discover Japan" campaign that advertising giant Dentsū created for Japan National Railways (JNR) in the 1970s.[4] Government encouragement for local *furusato-zukuri* projects that are ultimately articulated within *Furusato* Japan are still tangible and ongoing into the twenty-first century—in the 2008 tax year a "*furusato* tax payment system" (*furusato nōzei seido*) was introduced whereby taxpayers receive deductions for contributing to approved prefectural or municipal *furusato-zukuri* projects conducted by their hometown or any other area they happen to like.[5] Agricultural initiatives; zoos, gardens, and museums; traditional arts, crafts, and performances; annual *matsuri* (festivals); tradition-themed public areas; manufacturing particular to a region, and the like are common types of *furusato-zukuri* projects.

Okinawa Prefecture currently promotes *furusato* tax payments at both the prefectural and the municipal levels, providing online guidelines, contributor application forms, mission statements, and project synopses.[6] Municipal *furusato* initiatives invariably include categories for the enhancement of natural and built environments and the promotion of cultural activities (traditional and contemporary) and often make statements for the promotion of peace and education. Areas containing particular historical sites might emphasize historical preservation and exhibit building. For example, Nakijin Village in northern Okinawa, site of the historically significant Nakijin Castle ruins, has adopted as its *furusato-zukuri* slogan "Village alive and rich in nature, history, and romance" (*Shizen to rekishi to roman ni michiyakudō suru mura*) and explicitly ties *furusato-zukuri* with *kankōchi-zukuri* (tourist-site making), promotion of local industry, protection of the natural environment, children's education, historical sites and cultural activities, and residents' health and welfare.[7] Yomitan Village—site of the American invasion on April 1, 1945, the ruins of Zakimi Castle, a beautiful coastline, a vibrant pottery community, the studio set for the 1993 TV drama *Ryūkyū no kaze* (Winds of the Ryukyus, discussed below), and a history of postwar peace activism—highlights among its goals for *furusato* tax donations the advancement of local self-governance and peace education, the protection of the environment and nature particular to Yomitan, and the advancement of local businesses, products, and handmade arts and crafts. Its municipal mission statement recognizes the importance of the tourist industry but does not single it out for special treatment within *furusato-zukuri* projects.[8] While typically cast in broad terms that take "natural environment" and "human culture" as together composing a fundamental totality, such small-town visions of hometown making are usually rather specific to local conditions and concrete needs, whether tourism related or not.

Turning to Okinawa's largest city, Naha, one sees statements of *furusato-zukuri* more directly aligned with the contours of general tourism promotion. In the preamble to its online guide for *furusato* tax donations—taken in part from its *machi-zukuri* policy statement found in the Fourth Naha General Plan (Dai-4-ji Naha sōgō keikaku, March 2008)—Naha City announces,

> Being in a subtropical maritime climate and located in an important spot within East Asia, Naha, as the seat of the Ryukyu Kingdom and as a mercantile city, has a long history of trade and relations, first with China and then with various Asian countries.

> Bringing to life the spirit of [Okinawan] *yuimāru* (close-knit relations) cultivated from the midst of such nature, history, and culture, and taking heed of the slogan "I love Naha! Let's build it together, a city where children's smiling faces sparkle!" that sustains the idea of *machi-zukuri*, the citizens and city administration have cooperatively recommended *machi-zukuri* projects that place a premium on the sense of happiness and degree of satisfaction of those who visit the city and its citizens.[9]

The first paragraph is oft-repeated boilerplate seen in many government and tourist industry publications designed to introduce and define in broad strokes basic identifying aspects of Okinawa. The combination of subtropical environment and a premodern history of peaceful relations with neighbors as the Ryukyu Kingdom—what I refer to collectively as "Tropical Ryukyu"—echoes common tropes of Okinawa's tourist identity while leaving out much that could legitimately be included as an introduction to things Okinawan. The nature-history-culture trio attributed to fostering a local spirit of cooperation (*yuimāru,* in Okinawan) corresponds to the images of tropical paradise and Ryukyu heritage dominant in Okinawa tourism promotion. Finally, the sensitivity paid to the enjoyment of visitors to the city in conceiving of *furusato-zukuri* projects for Naha betrays the extent to which the tourist gaze influences the shape of "hometown Naha." The city then lists six broad goals for which *furusato* tax donations are earmarked: the creation of a self-governing, cooperative peace city; a city of health; an environmentally harmonious city that is gentle on people, nature, and the earth; a city of rich learning and culture brimming with smiling children (Ryukyu history and culture are invoked here); a city of "beautiful island" (*churashima*) tourism relations (Ryukyu cultural items and Shuri Castle are mentioned here); and a subtropical garden city of comfort and safety.[10]

Okinawa Prefecture's six bullet points for its realization of "a proud hometown, an attractive hometown" (*akogareru furusato, miryoku aru furusato*) parallel Naha's while offering a little more detail. The "abundant nature of the subtropical climate" is first praised, noting a "beautiful sea surrounded by coral reefs" and "treasurable flora and fauna of [Japan's only] island prefecture." The Ryukyu Kingdom period is then invoked as source of "Okinawa's own unique tradition" of arts, crafts, trade, and culture that *furusato-zukuri* aims to protect and promote. "Music tourism" (*ongaku kankō*) is singled out in particular for support. Youth development within a "future *Uchinā* [ethnic Okinawan] network" that "*Furusato* 'Okinawa'" will build is third on the list, followed by a nod to the promotion of the outlying islands of the prefecture. The fifth point underscores a commitment to public safety and crime prevention. The list ends with a relatively long statement on the "creation and transmission of peace" that springs from the "heart of peace" that has been cultivated in "Okinawa's history, culture and climate [*fūdo*]." The prefecture's peace initiatives as manifested by the Cornerstone of Peace monument and its principle of memorializing the war dead from the Battle of Okinawa without regard for nationality or civilian status are restated here, as are the peace activities and projects sponsored by the nearby Peace Memorial Museum. *Furusato* Okinawa as envisioned in this statement weaves together war history, peace promotion, and tourism development within a now familiar two-pronged trope of an inviting (sub)tropical environment and a (peaceful) Ryukyu Kingdom past. As a result, the difference between *Furusato* Okinawa and Tourist Okinawa becomes blurred; the themed character of *Furusato* Okinawa becomes apparent.

Several large-scale tourist attractions and countless smaller themed public spaces, souvenir shops, goods, and services in Okinawa reference the Ryukyu Kingdom past as the source of authentic Okinawan heritage, of *Furusato* Okinawa. Okinawa's oldest "living history" theme park—among those cited in the 1997 theme park report—is the very successful Ryukyu Mura (Ryukyu Village, originally Takoyama Park). Having been built around ten traditional Okinawan houses that were moved from various sites throughout Okinawa, Ryukyu Mura excels at live performance (music, dance, karate), live demonstrations of folk arts and crafts (dyeing, *bingata*, pottery), and hands-on learning designed to give the visitor a direct sense of the Ryukyu past—the tagline for the place is *tsukuru, kataru, manabu* (making, narrating, learning) (see figure 4.1). It has been advertised with such slogans as "History comes

**Figure 4.1.** Ryukyu Mura as old village Okinawa. *Source*: Gerald Figal.

alive," "Slip back in time to Ancient Okinawa," and "An Okinawa of long past that we'd like to bequeath to the future." The Okinawa Convention & Visitors Bureau highlights it as a showcase of "all the culture and traditions of the Ryukyu Kingdom" as it "revives the Okinawa of old times." The identification of Ryukyu as the source of Okinawan heritage is clear; it (or a believable facsimile of it) is celebrated and on display in an idealized microcosm that aspires to entertain, teach, and in some small way preserve and pass on this heritage to others. The conceit of "living history" runs throughout Ryukyu Mura and the other Ryukyu-themed parks included in the 1997 theme park survey: Okinawa World (formerly Gyokusendo Ōkoku Mura, or Gyokusendo Kingdom Village) and Murasaki Mura (formerly Nankai Ōkoku Ryūkyū no Kaze, or South Sea Kingdom Winds of the Ryukyus, the set for the 1993 Japan Broadcasting Corporation's [NHK] drama *Ryūkyū no kaze* converted into a cultural/historical tourist park, discussed below). All of these sites include re-creations of Ryukyu Kingdom–period houses, live folk song and dance performances and/or traditional craft and industry demonstrations, local delicacies, and hands-on participation with aspects of *Furusato* Okinawa.

While adhering to many of the same general ideas for *furusato-zukuri* as its mainland counterparts, *Furusato* Okinawa stands apart in its emphasis—from village to prefecture—on its uniqueness of climate and culture within Japan; the tropical and the Ryukyuan do not (at least naturally) exist on mainland Japan.[11] *Furusato* qua traditional in Okinawa also appears temporally more distanced than might typically be the case for other areas of Japan and their respective relationships to what they define as the "traditional past" that informs nostalgic visions of *furusato*. *Furusato* Okinawa invokes a real time and place but evokes an idealized image of a peaceful and prosperous Okinawan past under the rule of the kings enthroned at Shuri Castle, the seat of Chūzan, one of three principalities that vied for power on Okinawa Island in the fourteenth and early fifteenth centuries and eventually emerged victorious. Characterized as flourishing politically, economically, and culturally in a golden age of relations with Ming China and through an extended network of trade across Southeast Asia during the fifteenth and sixteenth centuries, the Ryukyu Kingdom is seen in this context as having developed a rich and glorious heritage that it maintained even as it subsequently suffered economic hardship and lost its political independence under the subordination of the Satsuma domain after its invasion in 1609. Caught between Tokugawa Japan and Qing China and standing at a flash point of international tensions after Commodore Perry's arrival in 1853, the Ryukyu kings ruled in name only until the throne was dissolved and the last monarch, Shō Tai, was forced to abdicate in 1879 and leave Shuri Castle for Tokyo, where the former royal family was officially assimilated into the new Japanese peerage system of the

Meiji government. Ryukyu as kingdom thus ended when Okinawa became Japan's forty-seventh prefecture, but Ryukyu as Okinawa's *furusato* was just beginning. An identification that among many Japanese connoted premodern backwardness, "Ryukyu" would take on a restored meaning by the end of the twentieth century to designate a heritage to be valued—and put on display for tourists.

Shuri Castle itself, the embodiment of that Ryukyu heritage, was, upon the dissolution of the kingdom, transformed into barracks for a detachment from the Kumamoto Garrison until its disbandment after the conclusion of the First Sino-Japanese War in 1896. Its buildings then served variously as classrooms for the Shuri City Women's Crafts School, the Okinawa Prefectural School for Industrial Apprenticeships, and the Shuri Number One Elementary School while falling into disrepair throughout the first half of the twentieth century. Slated for demolition in the mid-1920s, its cultural and architectural importance was recognized by Kamakura Yoshitarō and, in particular, famed Japanese architect Itō Chūta, who petitioned the Ministry of Education for its preservation as a National Treasure and for its simultaneous conversion into the worshippers' hall of Okinawa Shrine. Itō thereby singlehandedly "saved" Shuri Castle from certain ruin by giving it value within the modern Japanese cultural properties system and institutional state Shintō.[12] Designated a National Treasure in 1925, the Seiden (Main Hall) subsequently underwent a major restoration in 1933, only to be completely razed by American bombardment during the Battle of Okinawa. Despite the slow demise of the Ryukyu Kingdom and the ultimate wartime destruction of its seat of government, to evoke "Ryukyu" in postwar Okinawa is to identify with a vigorous and refined cultural heritage cultivated throughout the premodern period and symbolized in the figure of Shuri Castle, particularly the Seiden.[13] This symbolic investment in Shuri Castle is what drove the campaign for its postwar rebuilding as the centerpiece of *Furusato* Okinawa and Ryukyu-themed heritage tourism on Okinawa Island.

## "OKINAWA'S POSTWAR WILL NOT END UNLESS SHURI CASTLE IS REBUILT"

If there were ever a case of wartime loss transmuting into postwar gain, the pulverization of Shuri Castle during the Battle of Okinawa and its subsequent rebuilding as Okinawa Prefecture's premier heritage tourism site would be it. After its opening in 1992, Shuri Castle Park[14] quickly became Okinawa's most visited tourist site as the restoration of the complex continued. It drew over 2 million visitors in 2000, the year Shuri Castle and eight other historical sites were registered as "Gusuku [Castle] Sites and Related Properties of the Kingdom of Ryukyu" on UNESCO's World Heritage Sites list.[15] Ten years later annual attendance surpassed 4 million. What UNESCO did not recognize and what goes unnoticed by most tourists is the extent to which Shuri Castle owes its present existence and its symbolic and political function to the Battle of Okinawa as much as it owes its heritage site status to its Ryukyu Kingdom origins. This nexus between premodern heritage restoration and modern war history in present-day Okinawa is both obvious and undisclosed. On the one hand, it is well advertised that the castle was completely destroyed by American bombardment in World War II; many tour guide books—including the official multilingual guide published by the park's authorities, *Shurijō monogatari: Shurijō ga tanoshiku manaberu* (*The Tale of Shurijo Castle: Enjoy Learning about Shurijo Castle*, in the official English translation)—mention that the reason for the bombardment was the placement of the Japanese Thirty-second Army Headquarters underneath the castle grounds in a complex of tunnels. A few popular books even mention or show the ruins of the bunkers that once protected the entrances to the cave headquarters (the antitourism tour guide *Kankō kōsu de nai Okinawa* discussed in chapter 2 prominently features them). On the other hand, in showcasing Okinawa's Ryukyu Kingdom past and presenting the castle as it might have looked in the early eighteenth century, the rebuilt castle works to bypass much of the site's troubled modern history and literally keep buried from visitors the details of the site's connection to the battle fought there. In the park area itself, there are no signposts or markers pointing out or identifying the concrete bunker ruins that visitors walk within fifty to one hundred feet of as they make the approach from Shureimon to the first gate (Kankaimon) on the castle compound's outer wall and then pass by again upon exiting the castle (see figure 4.2). As a major site in the history of the Battle of Okinawa—one that had received serious consideration to be turned into a significant tourist attraction in the manner of the Naval Headquarters Cave—the Army Headquarters Cave complex underneath the Shuri Castle Park and its visible ruins on the surface go unacknowledged and unseen by all but a handful of the thousands of visitors who pass by daily. The re-creation of Ryukyu Kingdom glory—"Shuri Castle resurrected" as local newspaper headlines proclaimed upon its public opening on November 3, 1992—trumps the historical remains of its conditions of possibility: the war that enveloped it and the army installations that made it a target.

The utter devastation of Shuri Castle, long-standing symbol of the premodern unified Ryukyu Kingdom, was assured by the Japanese Thirty-second Army's locating its headquarters in a system of tunnels under the castle grounds. The unlikelihood of rebuilding the castle also seemed assured after the University of the Ryukyus, under the direction of the United States Civil

**Figure 4.2.** Bunker ruins beside Shuri Castle Park. Trees are labeled; the ruins are not.
*Source*: Gerald Figal.

Administration of the Ryukyu Islands (USCAR), was founded on the site in 1950. Hopes for the resurrection of Shuri Castle, however, persisted against all odds—it now required the removal of the newly built university in addition to resources that Okinawa did not have under American occupation. In the meantime, however, the famed Shureimon (Gate of Courtesy), designated a Japanese National Treasure in 1933 and standing well outside the former castle walls and the new university campus, proved a more feasible project. In 1958, under the auspices of the Government of the Ryukyu Islands, it became the first major structure of the castle complex to be rebuilt. The gate's identification with Okinawa as "The Land of Courtesy" (*Shurei no kuni*, which is the inscription on the gate, originally given by the Chinese emperor to the Ryukyuan king in recognition of loyal tributary relations) stretches back to the sixteenth century when it welcomed foreign ambassadors, particularly official emissaries from China, on their approach to the castle's main compound (*una*) for audiences with the Ryukyuan king. In its postwar incarnation, it quickly resumed its status as symbol of Okinawa and the hospitality of its people toward foreign visitors, including an increasing number of Japanese tourists. In his 1962 assessment of tourism development in Okinawa, Senge Tetsuma comments regrettably about the "irrecoverable loss" of Shuri Castle and singles out the iconic nature of Shureimon:

> One would naturally expect that Shuri Castle, as a historical site, would be an important sightseeing spot, but the entire edifice and the surrounding forests were destroyed in the flames of the recent Great War and in vain the only thing you see are stone hedges and withered broken trees. This is truly sad. Moreover, at the center of the ruins the University of the Ryukyus was built in the modern concrete block architecture prevalent throughout the main island, and all traces of the castle have vanished. Shureimon, which today adorns postcards and posters as a symbol of Okinawa, used to be in the area between middle gate and front gate of the castle approach, but it too was burned down. The present one is a restoration. The stone gate of Sonohyan Utaki [a site of worship for Ryukyu royalty] was also restored. These two things are uniquely Okinawan structures, and because Shureimon is so completely different from the type of gate seen in the mainland, it somehow draws our interest as something expressing Okinawaness.[16]

Not only posters and postcards but also postal stamps issued by the GRI attest to Shureimon's place as icon of Okinawa/Ryukyu cultural heritage. Later the Japanese government used an image of Shureimon on special two-thousand-yen notes issued to commemorate the July 2000 G-8 summit held in Okinawa. The rebuilding of Shureimon gave both a material and a mental boost to the development of a fledgling tourist industry in postwar Okinawa; it was widely featured in tourism publications, and the successor of the Okinawa Tourism Association, the Okinawa Tourism Federation, adopted the image of Shureimon as its logo. A widely recognized piece of Ryukyuan heritage was restored, and despite the presence of the University of the Ryukyus on the old castle site, local boosters still lobbied for the eventual restoration of the entire castle complex, especially the Seiden.

As long as the United States occupied Okinawa and the University of the Ryukyus occupied the former castle grounds, rebuilding the Seiden was not a realistic proposition. The persistence of the desire among many Okinawans to do so, however, speaks to the cultural and political significance of Shuri Castle, a significance newly wrought only in the aftermath of war and under foreign occupation. As Tze May Loo has documented, the dilapidation and disrepair into which the castle had fallen by the 1920s prompted Shuri City to decide on dismantling it and reusing the space for a public park.[17] That plan would have been realized if not for Kamakura and Itō's intervention and successful effort to have Shuri Castle's principal structures designated National Treasures while converting the Seiden into Okinawa Shrine. In other words, during the prewar period, Shuri Castle was found valuable and worthy of attention within a national political and ideological context, as a part of Imperial Japan's—not Okinawa's—cultural heritage. The war and postwar occupation, however, brought about a very different context in which the meaning of the site was generated. What had been left to decay during Okinawa's modern times was, after the war, mourned as having represented the heart and soul of Okinawan culture and civilization. Shuri Castle had indeed stood at the very heart of the former Ryukyu Kingdom, the center of high court culture and intellectual life, but that context had vanished with the forced dissolution of the royal line in 1879. The wartime loss of Shuri Castle, the conditions under which that loss occurred, and Okinawa's detachment from Japan and subsequent uncertain political status from 1945 to 1972 all conspired to direct a renewed investment in the idea if not realization of restoring Shuri Castle to its prior premodern glory, regardless of the obstacles. Under these new circumstances, a project that was presented in cultural terms—restoration of lost cultural properties—took on charged political import that directly challenged the implications of the castle's prewar status of National Treasure even as that status was critical in arguments for rebuilding. It also served to hold Japan publicly responsible for the devastation that the war brought to Okinawa.

Public discussion for Shuri Castle's rebuilding escalated as reversion to Japan approached, propelled by the slogan "Okinawa's postwar will not end unless Shuri Castle is rebuilt."[18] This sentence can be read several ways. On the surface, it simply signals the importance that the castle held for at least some Okinawans. The absence of Shuri Castle will always be a gaping reminder of wartime loss; as long as it is missing, Okinawa will not be fully recovered and complete. In the context of Japan's impending reclamation of full sovereignty over Okinawa Prefecture, this rallying cry was freighted with political meaning as well. It signaled to Japanese government authorities that while the turnover of Okinawa from American to Japanese hands was popularly anticipated as the end of Okinawa's postwar, there remained the unfinished business of complete material recovery. More pointedly, when understood alongside the conviction among Okinawans that the Japanese—not the American—military was responsible for the destruction of Shuri Castle by placing the Thirty-second Army Headquarters beneath it, this slogan asserted that with full sovereignty comes full responsibility for the reckless devastation of Okinawa at the hands of Japan's military policy. This implication is driven home in the discussions among supporters of the rebuilding of Shuri Castle and in their appeals to the Japanese government to approve and finance such a project. While talk about someday restoring Shuri Castle began almost as soon as it was destroyed, serious discussions did not take place until 1970 in the context of Okinawa returning to Japanese sovereignty. In May and June of that year, the newly formed Okinawan Bunkazai Hogo Iinkai (Committee for the Protection of Cultural Properties) met with Yamanaka Sadanori, a Liberal Democratic Party (LDP) member of the lower house of the diet. Yamanaka was likely tapped by then prime minister Satō Eisaku to serve as his cabinet's

Okinawa Reversion liaison because of his experience in the southwest islands: he was born in Kagoshima, the mainland prefecture nearest Okinawa; graduated from a teacher's training college in colonial Taipei, Taiwan; and taught during the Pacific War at the Taiwan National People's School (Taiwan Kokumin Gakkō). In addition to becoming the director of the Okinawa Development Agency (ODA), he would also later become defense agency chief from 1973 to 1974 and international trade and industry minister from 1982 to 1983. He became best known as the head of the LDP tax commission for eight years from 1979 and the chief architect of a national consumption tax.

Records of Yamanaka's meetings in 1970 with members of the Okinawa Cultural Assets Protection Committee indicate relatively forceful efforts on the part of the committee, although public arguments asserting Japanese responsibility for Shuri Castle's destruction are muted at this point. The committee formally presented the following written request to Yamanaka:

> Points Concerning the Restoration of Cultural Properties and Protection of Traditional Arts and Crafts
>
> 1. As there is a great number of war-damaged cultural properties in Okinawa, we would respectfully like to work into the Okinawa Rehabilitation Legislation that Director General Yamanaka is planning restoration projects for war-damaged cultural properties.
> 2. We would respectfully like to take up the restoration of the Seiden of Shuri Castle as a governmental commemoration project.
>
> The Seiden of Shuri Castle is a building that remained as a monument to the era of great commerce that our ancestors actively engaged in five to six hundred years ago throughout Southeast Asia and was designated as a prewar National Treasure. If possible, we would like its restoration to receive consideration as a Reversion commemoration project. We respectfully request your consideration.
>
> 3. In addition: the protection of classical arts and dance; the large-scale reclamation of unique Okinawan folk crafts such as Tsuboya pottery and the weaving of *bingata* and *kasuri* textiles. We request aid from the Japanese government for the training, etc., of craftspeople in these arts.[19]

Of particular political significance in the Okinawan requests is tying the rebuilding of Shuri Castle with Okinawa's reversion to Japan. There was no natural connection between the two; framing the restoration as a commemoration of Reversion appears arbitrary and motivated more by political expediency than a true desire to have the castle serve as a remembrance of Reversion. In fact, insofar as Shuri Castle was the site and symbol of the glory days of the independent Ryukyu Kingdom (evoked in the request itself), it seems outright odd to have it mark the resumption of Japanese sovereignty over Okinawa Prefecture. This rhetorical gesture also has the unintended effect of tying any reconstructed castle even more tightly to the postwar U.S. occupation even as it is—in another rhetorical gesture—being rationalized as the structure without which Okinawa's postwar condition will not end. It marks the end of U.S. occupation but also, in the same stroke, reminds one of it. Finally, offering a rebuilt Shuri Castle as a memorial of Japan's resumption of rule over Okinawa seems doubly perverse given that Okinawans will cite the Japanese state's responsibility for bringing about the castle's destruction in the first place. In that context, Shuri Castle restored as commemorative device possesses a dark side—it serves as a reminder of the devastation that was brought to Okinawa the last time it was under Japanese rule.

In response to these requests for reconstruction of the Seiden of Shuri Castle—and likely oblivious to the complex economy of signifiers they implied—Yamanaka is quoted as having said, "Since I think that the Seiden of Shuri Castle is Okinawa's greatest cultural inheritance and is a fitting symbol for Okinawan culture, I would like to give these requests thorough consideration."[20] Yamanaka seems to have been genuinely sympathetic to the Okinawan plight and truly supportive of the requests. In a follow-up meeting with Yamanaka the next month in Okinawa, committee chair Minamoto Takeo "strongly pressed" the issue of Shuri Castle's restoration and then went back to Tokyo with Yamanaka to make his case directly to the newly formed Okinawa-Hoppō Taisaku Chō (Okinawa–Northern Territories Policy Agency), the Japanese government body founded on May 1, 1970, to prepare for Okinawa's reversion to Japan and to deal with the Northern Territories issue.[21] As a result, then prime minister Satō announced in November as part of the First Okinawa Reversion Policy Plan (Dai-ichi-ji Okinawa Fukki Taisaku Yōkō) preparations for the rebuilding of Shuri Castle, noting that "in light of the importance of Okinawa's cultural properties, [we] will promote the reconstruction, repair, and preservation of war-damaged cultural properties."[22] Satō's backing, at least in principle, seemed to have assured the rebuilding of Shuri Castle despite all the practical obstacles to realization: the existence of the University of the Ryukyus on the former castle site, the paucity of detailed architectural plans for the original structure, principled objections from various quarters, administrative legalities, and, of course, funding. A brief examination of these problems reveals the extent of the project's impact and brings to the surface political and cultural tensions among interested parties, tensions that typify the development of such large-scale heritage preservation and tourism.

The project to rebuild Shuri Castle was barely announced when a budget request through the Agency of Cultural Affairs (Bunkachō) for an initial excavation survey hit a legal snag in the Finance Ministry (Ōkurasho). Finance Ministry officials argued that because all tangible assets of Shuri Castle had been destroyed in the war, the project could not be properly called a restoration (*fukugen*) to be funded under the provisions for tangible cultural assets.[23] The Finance Ministry had a point. This was not going to be the restoration of damaged edifices as they had existed before the war. Rather, it would be an entirely new building, based on what Shuri Castle looked like just after its last complete rebuilding in 1715.[24] Caught between demands for restoration from the Cultural Assets Protection Committee and the Finance Ministry's rejection of the restoration as a project falling under the purview of the Agency of Cultural Affairs, Yamanaka was forced to find a way to circumvent this technicality. His solution was to submit all funding requests through the Okinawa–Northern Territories Policy Agency (which was under the Prime Minister's Office) to the Construction Ministry for a projected Shuri Castle Park. In January 1971, funds amounting to 1.02 million yen were finally appropriated within the Okinawa–Northern Territories Policy Agency budget for an excavation survey, marking the first concrete steps toward the restoration of Shuri Castle. With the aid of University of the Ryukyus students, a survey of the foundations of the Seiden was soon undertaken, followed by a survey of the remains of the Kankaimon, the first gate at the entrance to the castle proper, in order to prepare for its rebuilding. By the eve of Reversion, the groundwork had thus been laid for the long road to Shuri Castle's restoration. Upon Reversion in May 1972, the Cultural Assets Protection Committee was dissolved and replaced the following year by the Cultural Assets Protection Committee and the Shuri Castle Restoration Association (SCRA; Shurijō Fukugen Kisei Kai), which was closely attached to the Okinawa Prefectural Board of Education Cultural Section through association member Shuri-born Teruya Seishō, Culture Division chief and first SCRA chair.

The Finance Ministry's objection to the physical status of any planned reconstruction relates to other objections raised by an entirely different constituency within Okinawa—local historians and preservationists—after initial excavation surveys were completed. Okinawan historians objected vociferously to the plans on the grounds that the money necessary to build what would amount to an "imitation" or "replica" of the Seiden would be better spent on actually surviving historical edifices and cultural assets in dire need of repair and preservation.[25] They made their case in newspaper op-ed pieces and through flyers distributed on the streets to passersby in front of the main Ryubō department store complex across from the Prefectural Office. Such an objection throws into relief the cultural politics at play in the push to restore Shuri Castle—from a more sober point of view of historical assessment of surviving, historically significant items in need of restoration with limited funds, Shuri Castle would be low on the list. In other words, if interest and value lay in the repair and preservation of cultural properties possessing some tangible presence and historical value, there would be more effective ways to invest hard-fought-for funding. The SCRA's ardent pursuit of restoring Shuri Castle to its original state despite many obstacles implied an investment in a different set of values with a different kind of payoff, one that was political and, later, economic. This is not to say that these historians were without their own political and ideological positions. However, their critique exposed the extent to which the efforts to re-create Shuri Castle were driven as much by political symbolism as by a concern for historical preservation. They also forced debate on the issue among a public that at the time showed lukewarm interest in restoring Shuri Castle. Sensing that any internal opposition among Okinawans would jeopardize national funding for the project, Minamoto countered with his own editorials in support of the rebuilding. To galvanize and organize public support for the movement to restore the castle, he and Teruya then planned together the formation of the Shuri Castle War Damage Restoration Association (later simply Shuri Castle Restoration Association), which met for its first planning meeting on June 14, 1973. As reported by the *Okinawa Times*, Minamoto led the meeting—characterized by the slogan "Let's take pride in Okinawan culture"—with an account of the pre-Reversion efforts to gain Japanese government support for restoring the Seiden and the castle compound's first entry gate, Kankaimon.[26] The transfer of the University of the Ryukyus campus was also discussed, and it was emphasized that the entire area of foundation ruins around a restored Seiden would be zoned as a commemorative park and historical landmark. A full group of twenty-four members representing various sections of the prefectural government, education, business, and media met five days later and, to garner backing from the highest quarters in Okinawa, appointed Governor Yara Chōbyō committee chair.

After the Kankaimon's restoration was successfully completed in 1974, central government support for further restoration waned as attention and resources were being spent on preparations for the 1975 International Marine Exposition. In response, the work of the SCRA throughout the mid-1970s and 1980s consisted largely of quelling criticism, lobbying for further funding, and rallying public support for the rebuilding of the Seiden and, to a lesser extent, the Kyūkeimon (a side gate originally used mainly by females). Faced with persistent roadblocks set up by the Finance Ministry and some lingering local apprehension about the value and feasibility of this massive restoration project, the committee closed ranks with the Governor's Office, Naha City Hall, and the University of the Ryukyus to redouble its efforts in uniting public opinion. Pressure was kept up on the Okinawa Development Agency for funding while Ryudai president Kinjō Hidezō (1973–1978) shepherded the preparations for his university's transfer from Shuri to the Nishihara area, which began in 1975. University buildings were not fully cleared from the castle site until 1982, and the move was not entirely completed until 1985. Meanwhile, funding for the rebuilding of the Kyūkeimon was secured in the ODA's 1976 budget, and construction began in March of that year and was finished in 1983. With the former castle grounds cleared of the university, the two gates rebuilt, and the tenth anniversary of Reversion just passed, lobbying for the restoration of the Seiden reached a new intensity and saw a shift in rhetoric to match. The idea of framing the project as a national park to commemorate the 1972 Reversion remained consistent, but to that was added the open assertion that the Japanese government owed Okinawa a replacement for the destroyed castle because of the Japanese army's actions during the Battle of Okinawa. What might have previously been thought and privately expressed became, by the mid-1980s, a standard part of the public rhetoric in support of rebuilding the Seiden.

The details attached to this new trope—a trope that carried a political punch—were typified in SCRA member Matsukawa Kunio's 1984 essay "The Promotion of Shuri Castle's Restoration" ("Shurijō fukugen no suishin"). In it, Matsukawa cites, as did others before him in the early 1980s, unconfirmed American documentation indicating that, following the same reasoning by which Kyoto and Nara were spared aerial bombardment, General Douglas MacArthur proposed that the old parts of Shuri, with its abundant cultural antiquities, be off limits to bombardment and advised the Japanese army to evacuate its headquarters from the castle area. The Japanese Thirty-second Army Command decided, however, to maintain its operational headquarters underground in a series of tunnels beneath the front edge of the castle complex, running roughly north to south between the Shureimon and Kankaimon. The direct result of this placement, Matsukawa emphasizes, was the targeting and complete destruction of the castle. "For we Okinawans [*wareware ken-min*], this was truly regrettable. Shouldn't the state too feel the utmost responsibility for the fact that Shuri Castle was flattened as a result of this action by the army?"[27] Despite being unconfirmed, the story of the Japanese army's rejecting MacArthur's advice to vacate the castle grounds gained currency at a critical time in the campaign for restoration.[28] It opened a new political and moral dimension to the cultural and historical arguments in favor of Shuri Castle's restoration and was mentioned with regularity by the mid-1980s. That MacArthur's overture to the Japanese army was unconfirmed and yet spread throughout Okinawan appeals to the Japanese government attests to its rhetorical—rather than historical—value at the time. As ammunition for pressing the case for government support of restoration, it served to make a moral argument regardless of historical accuracy and was indicative of the lengths restoration supporters would go to promote their cause. It also likely played to the sentiments of many Okinawans at a time of increasing public scrutiny of Japanese actions in the Battle of Okinawa: Ishihara Masaie's volume of critical war testimonies *Shogen: Okinawasen—senba no kōkei* (Testimonies: The Battle of Okinawa—scenes from the battlefield) appeared in 1984; the first edition of *Kankō kōsu de nai Okinawa*—with a section on the army headquarters beneath Shuri Castle—was published in 1983; *Aruku, miru, kangearu Okinawa* came out in 1986; Chibana Shoichi had been researching the compulsory suicides at Chibichirigama since 1982 and burned the Hinomaru flag at the 1987 National Athletic Meet in protest of Japanese army actions. Tying the issue of Japan's responsibility for Okinawa's devastation to arguments for government-supported restoration of Shuri Castle made sense in this wider context of more open public discourse on Japanese conduct in the war. This strategy manifests yet another way in which the conditions of possibility for what would become a showcase for Okinawan heritage tourism were grounded in the experience of the Battle of Okinawa—both the total destruction of the castle and the ex post facto ascription of agency for that destruction were crucial in bringing Shuri Castle back better than it had been just prior to its loss.

After Matsukawa makes the moral appeal for Shuri Castle's restoration, he then quotes from a letter the SCRA sent to the ODA that contained the routine arguments for Shuri Castle's rebuilding: it recollected the "golden age" of the Ryukyu Kingdom; it was a symbol of Okinawa history; it was an important place to host dignitaries; it attracted scholarly attention in the 1920s and was designated a National Treasure then; and for Okinawans, culturally and psychologically, Okinawa's postwar will not end until Shuri Castle is restored.[29] As fervently as Matsukawa and the other members of the SCRA might have believed in these reasons to rebuild Shuri Castle, they faced a local population whose attitude toward the restoration project had from the beginning ranged from guarded enthusiasm to indifference to outright opposition. Similar to historians who derided such a use of scarce resources, Okinawans who struggled to make a living were not convinced of the tangible benefits a new "replica" of Shuri Castle would bring them. The rallying cry "Let's take pride in Okinawan culture!" did little to raise living standards in Japan's poorest prefecture and rang hollow coming from local boosters and government officials. Fresh approaches were needed to win over the skeptics.

One fortuitous event from unlikely quarters provided a new dimension to the standard appeal. The Sapporo Snow Festival, a famous annual event in Hokkaido featuring ice and snow sculptures, featured at the 1984 gathering an amazingly detailed two-thirds-scale replica of the Seiden of Shuri Castle sculpted from snow, a project sponsored by Hokkaido Television whose representatives had made three trips to Okinawa during the previous months to gather information on the real Shuri Castle. Shureimon had been similarly reproduced at the 1978 Sapporo Snow Festival.[30] Energized by the free publicity, the SCRA seized upon the Seiden in snow to advertise nationwide the campaign to restore the Seiden and to assert that "this has confirmed that the restoration of Shuri Castle is a Japan-wide—not only an Okinawan—issue." The desire to see Shuri Castle standing again, members claimed, was a national one.[31] Two association members, Vice Director Hamahiga Munemasa and Uezu Yasuhide, made the trip to Hokkaido for the unveiling and appeared on local television in front of the frozen replica. Uezu reported in the February 1984 special edition of the SCRA's publication *Shurijō fukugen kisei kai kaihō* (Bulletin of the Shuri Castle Restoration Association) that his Shuri-born-and-raised colleague, Hamahiga, became choked up to the point of tears when delivering his heartfelt appreciation to the builders of the sculpture and expressing his ceaseless efforts to bring about the castle's proper restoration in his hometown. For his part, Uezu related to their hosts that when he first told SCRA members that there were plans to re-create Shuri Castle at the Snow Festival, they too were overjoyed to tears and filled with renewed inspiration for their cause: "The Shuri Castle Main Hall will be rebuilt with snow in Hokkaido, but shouldn't we be ashamed that the real thing hasn't yet been rebuilt in its original place, Okinawa? Association members too must work harder!!" His address ended with a declaration of his intention to use the nationwide publicity of the Snow Festival Seiden as a springboard to garner more cooperation for the campaign to restore the real thing.[32] The excitement with which Uezu reports all of these details—from the dimensions of the structure to the volume of the snow used to build it—is palpable, but the highlight of the festival for him was when a dance troupe from Okinawa performed a traditional Ryukyu court dance in the plaza before the Seiden, braving the cold weather and falling snow. "Yes, you can say it was only a snow sculpture in Sapporo, but it was extremely moving that they danced in front of a Shuri Castle Main Hall that faithfully rendered the castle's ancient form. . . . I await the day when the real Shuri Castle Main Hall is restored and they dance before it."[33]

Immediately after painting this paradoxical and poignant scene of Ryukyuan dancers in the snow, Uezu abruptly turns to a thumbnail sketch of Shuri Castle's founding in the early fifteenth century and its unfortunate fate in the twentieth. In relating the circumstances of Shuri Castle's eventual wartime destruction—in the bombardment of Shuri on April 4, 1945—Uezu focuses on the question of why the castle was not leveled during the November 10, 1944, bombing raid of Naha or during the preinvasion shelling of the island in late March 1945. This is where he narrates his version of the story of the American command initially intending to spare the old capital of Shuri out of sensitivity to its important cultural assets. Like others, he draws the comparison with the other "old capitals" of Kyoto and Nara, effectively placing Ryukyuan cultural heritage on par with that of Japan. He notes that American forces had done detailed surveys of the geography and facilities of the island before the invasion, marking important cultural properties in the Shuri area, including the castle. "If the policy makers and military at the time, recognizing the importance of the cultural assets in the Shuri area, would not have built the underground army headquarters beneath Shuri Castle, then the American army would probably not have destroyed the old capital of Shuri. Noting that in this sense the Japanese state should be responsible for restoring Shuri Castle, the Restoration Association has from early on vigorously demanded of the state the restoration of Shuri Castle."[34] Suddenly shifting to this assignation of blame in a report on the Sapporo Snow Festival's re-creation of the castle and its accompanying Ryukyu dance performance, Uezu heightens the rhetorical effect of the appeal. The tone of his description of the snow castle and the court dance is filled with a sense of fragile beauty and nostalgic loss. It was not simply a castle that Japanese policy makers and the military were responsible for destroying; culture, beauty, and refinement—embodied by female dancers in traditional Ryukyuan costume—were the victims. These snowy re-creations of the Ryukyu Kingdom and court life were ghostlike figures close enough to the real thing to move the viewer emotionally, but ultimately they were ephemeral conjurations that served to remind one of the pain of their absence. They tantalizingly manifested the real possibility of reconstructing the Seiden and the cultural productions surrounding it and compelled restoration supporters to redouble their efforts. Uezu, currently (2010) the vice director of the Shuri Castle Restoration Association, recalls in retrospect the Sapporo Snow Festival as indeed a turning point in raising local interest, support, and confidence in restoring the castle for real in Okinawa.[35] Photos in newspapers of visitors in front of Hokkaido's "restoration" of the Seiden envisioned the tourist draw that a restored Shuri Castle could be, but that angle had not been pursued aggressively to this point in the public discussion of the rationale for rebuilding it. One begins to see the tourism angle introduced as a rationale among SCRA members in the early 1980s, but it is typically appended as an extra item, a bonus to the principal reasons for restoration. After the appearance of Sapporo's Seiden, the argument that Shuri Castle could offer significant economic impact for Okinawa became more readily attached to the list of reasons in favor of restoration and was one that gained traction among previously skeptical locals hoping for some economic trickle-down from a Shuri Castle Park.

One group of locals, however, fearful of the ill effects of a popular tourist destination in their neighborhood, remained opposed to the Shuri Castle Park plan after Okinawa Prefecture and Naha City announced it to the public in 1986. Calling themselves the Association of Residents Concerned over the Shuri Castle Park Project (Shurijō Kōen Jigyō ni Kakaru Jūmin no Kai), these were residents of the section of Shuri that would be directly impacted by the restoration project through forced removal and increased vehicular and pedestrian traffic. The criticism of the project that they self-published in the form of a twenty-page pamphlet in 1989 pulls no punches, beginning with the cover, which is composed of a frontal view of an architectural drawing of the Seiden set askew and above a frame from the manga *Barefoot Gen* depicting Gen's father and siblings crushed under their atomic-bombed house in Hiroshima. The cover thus hyperbolically turns the issue of war-damaged cultural assets inside out, suggesting that while Shuri Castle was destroyed in the war, its rebuilding now will destroy the daily life of people in the area. The inside cover contains as epigraph exclamations that also turn inside out the language often seen in promotion of the restoration project: "Do not allow city plans that ignore the local residents! Do not allow local destruction by tourism-centered plans! Do not allow development plans that destroy cultural assets!"[36] In other words, the cultural asset to be saved is not Shuri Castle but the daily life and culture of the local population. The pamphlet enumerates thirteen areas of criticism, centering on plans to move about fifty households in order to build a large-scale parking lot in anticipation of handling buses, taxis, and private vehicles transporting a forecast goal of 3 million visitors per year to Shuri Castle Park. While delivering point-by-point objections to this plan, the pamphlet begins by raising general questions concerning the rush to tourism development Okinawa was experiencing by the late 1980s within the context of the Comprehensive Recreation and Local Development Law (Sōgō Hoyō Chiiki Seibi Hō), otherwise known as the "Resort Law" that was passed in 1987 at the height of the bubble economy to stimulate the growth of vacation resorts and recreation facilities (see chapter 6). It notes that while there is considerable discussion in the 1986 Okinawa Prefecture Tourism Promotion Plan about designating recreational zones, addressing the issue of hospitality training, considering appropriate tourist products to sell, and projecting the number of visitors and revenue, there is little mention of the problems spawned by tourism development. It then proceeds to mock the slogan "Okinawa's postwar will not end unless Shuri Castle is rebuilt" by claiming that the campaign has nothing to do with rebuilding the castle in its role as a war-damaged cultural asset but rather simply in its role as "the crown jewel of Okinawa tourism." The group's criticism of Okinawa tourism policy exemplifies Erve Chambers's focus on source of agency as the yardstick for determining the authenticity of any given heritage tourism site. It is to this measure—not the accuracy of replication—that a restored Shuri Castle should be submitted, as the Shuri Castle Park protesters suggest:

> The residents' countermeasures don't come from the simple mind-set that monetary compensation solves everything. This is because the masses (the local residents) give birth to much of what we call historical and cultural heritage from their everyday lives; it's something that is fostered and protected within the local area. In other words, without the sympathy and support of the local residents, inheriting and developing historical and cultural heritage would be impossible. One cannot create an attractive tourist site that brings historical and cultural heritage alive at the cost of ignoring local residents. The development and maintenance of tourist sites is inseparable from town building [*machi-zukuri*], and tourist sites (town building) that bring historical and cultural heritage into play must be fine-tuned and carried out with long-term project planning and execution coherent to residents while obtaining the participation of local residents and planning for harmony with their everyday lives. There are many examples of such situations in mainland Japan.[37]

Turning around the trope of Japan having sacrificed Okinawa (*gisei ni suru*) during the war and postwar occupation, this general critique of Okinawa tourism policy ends by describing the Shuri Castle Park plan as tourist-site building (*kankōchi-zukuri*) that sacrifices local residents (*jūmin o gisei ni suru*). Rather than recovery from war damage, this kind of tourism development is equated with war damage when it comes to the harm it inflicts on the foundations of Okinawan heritage—the people and the land they inhabit. In short, their argument is that there can be no authentic cultural heritage on display without these Shuri residents participating in decision making about sites of heritage tourism in their neighborhood. This view aligned with those of historians who described any rebuilding of Shuri Castle as creating a mere replica of little true historical or cultural value despite its potential educative value; it would be artificially grafted onto—not rooted in—the former castle site.

Much of this local protest, while reacting to the particular issue of the forced expulsion of residents from their homes to build a parking lot to serve Shuri Castle Park, engaged larger political questions concerning local self-government. In addition to the concrete problems of harming the immediate environment and destroying the integrity of the neighborhood in order to cater to increasing numbers of tourists, the overarching theme throughout this document is the violation of people's rights to private property and self-determination in the face of state policy determined for the economic and political benefit of others. It is brutally critical of what it labels the "undemocratic" process by which the park plan was decided and insists that the voices of those most affected by these decisions must be heard. The pamphlet ends by again invoking and reversing the notion of preserving or destroying *bunkazai* (cultural assets). This is a loaded term, used throughout the campaign to have Shuri Castle rebuilt. To suggest that its rebuilding would achieve the opposite of preserving cultural assets is a stinging criticism and forces one to reconsider what constitutes a cultural asset. In fact, it reveals the constructed and arbitrary nature of the entire category of "cultural asset" at the same time that it demystifies the notion of the authenticity of such cultural assets.

In the same year that the Association of Residents Concerned over the Shuri Castle Park Project published its protest pamphlet, the ground-breaking ceremony for the construction of the new Seiden took place. On November 2, 1989, ceremonial lumber from the mountain forests of Hentona in Kunigami Village, the northernmost municipality of Okinawa Island, began a two-day trip passing through all parts of the island before arriving at the former castle site atop Shuri Hill for the ritual ground breaking on November 3. The ceremony itself involved a reenactment of a Ryukyu Kingdom–period tree-presentation procession that was viewed by throngs of people along the road up to Shuri, the first of many reenactments of Ryukyu court ceremonies that have since become a part of the annual festivities hosted at the park. The following fall, on September 11, 1990, another ceremony was held to mark the raising of the first central pillar of the Seiden. Completion of this main portion of the Shuri Castle restoration was projected for 1992, to coincide with the twenty-year anniversary of Reversion, the justification for its special designation as a national-prefectural commemorative park and thus its eligibility for funding under provisions for such parks. The architectural and engineering firm contracted for the project, the Naha-based Kuniken Ltd., has since been involved with the design and construction of many high-profile cultural, educational, and tourism-related facilities. These include the Okinawa Prefectural Archives, the Navy Headquarters Park Visitor Center, the Okinawa Churaumi Aquarium, the Yomitan Culture Center, the Onna Village Museum, the Bankoku Shinryōkan (site of the 2000 G-8 summit), the Busena Resort, the Busena Terrace Cottage, the Atta Terrace Club Towers, the remodel of the original Moon Beach Hotel, and the three regional airport passenger terminals on Miyako Island, Kumejima Island, and Minami Daitō Island. Advertising itself as specializing in architecture suited to Okinawan culture and climate, many of its buildings—including the beautiful Prefectural Archives overlooking Haebaru—could be described as neo-Ryukyuesque with a dash of the tropical. Iconic red-tiled roofs and Ryukyu limestone (real or concrete imitation) walls applied to modern designs mark the style, often complemented by large windows and quotations from traditionally styled rooflines, gates, hedges, and spirit walls (*himpun*). Shuri Castle's Seiden was completed more or less on time on October 31, 1992, and was opened to the public with

**Figure 4.3.** The rebuilt Seiden (Main Hall of Shuri Castle Park). *Source*: Gerald Figal.

much fanfare on November 3 and quickly rose to become the number one tourist site in Okinawa (see figure 4.3).[38] According to the slogan that had propelled its reconstruction, Okinawa's postwar period was now over.

## THE SEMIOTICS OF SHURI CASTLE PARK

By the late 1990s, after the Seiden had been rebuilt and opened to the public for several years, Shuri Castle's place within general tourism development became more prominent in accounts of its restoration. For example, in his introduction to the twenty-fifth anniversary retrospective of the Shuri Castle Restoration Association, Director Goya Shigenobu, while citing the work of the SCRA in pushing through this project, acknowledges the favorable tourism development environment of the late 1980s as key in allowing the actual construction to move forward. In fact, he triumphantly counters the naysayers who said that such a restoration would be a "mere replica" without true value as a cultural asset by citing Shuri Castle Park's central role and success in Okinawa tourism.[39] In a mutually beneficial relationship, the drive for concerted tourism development—especially resort development—during Japan's boom years in the late 1980s stimulated support for Shuri Castle's rebuilding as a national and prefectural park, and once established, Shuri Castle Park boosted the number of visitors to Okinawa. Its origins as a site to commemorate Okinawa's reversion to Japan and a marker for the end of Okinawa's postwar correspondingly faded into the background. During the time of Shuri Castle Park's construction and just after its public opening, discussions about what the revived castle would mean for Okinawa consolidated around "symbol of traditional Okinawan culture" as marketing it as a major tourist attraction was made more overt. But what was the meaning of "traditional Okinawan culture" for modern times? Or rather, what meaning should Shuri Castle be given now that it had assumed the center of attention as a symbol of Okinawan heritage, in effect expanding writ large the role Shureimon had held?

Shureimon, "The Gate of Propriety," had historically been treated as a welcoming gate, as a sign of courtesy and peaceful relations toward visitors. Shuri Castle Park would encompass that meaning but reinscribe it to accommodate Okinawa's peace discourse, which was expanding throughout its schools and universities, government offices, and, in hindsight, its historical and cultural institutions. Long before Shuri Castle Park was opened, tourism—particularly international tourism—had been promoted as a "peace industry." The logic behind this concept was simple: to be successful at tourism, one had to be an accommodating and friendly host, regardless of whence the guest hailed. When the United Nations designated 1967 "International Tourism Year," it was not only to recognize the surge in international tourism during the 1960s but also to encourage tourism in the interest of fostering peaceful relations among peoples (the previous international year was "International Cooperation Year" in 1965, while the following one was for human rights in 1968). Like many countries, the Government of the Ryukyu Islands issued a commemorative stamp in 1967 marking "International Tourism Year." At the same time, Okinawa tourism promoters seized upon the idea of tourism for peace and made the slogan for their Second Annual Okinawa Festival in August 1967 "Tourism is the passport to peace" (*Kankō wa heiwa he no pasupōto*).[40] There was thus an established foundation for placing Shuri Castle Park within a rhetoric of peace promotion as it existed in the tourism industry. In addition, idealized characterizations of Ryukyu Kingdom history increasingly highlighted the period as one of peace and prosperity (despite evidence to the contrary) to the extent that cultivating peaceful relations was identified as being at the heart of a pacifist Ryukyuan culture—that is, Okinawan cultural heritage. Private and public promotional literature on Okinawa is replete with expressions of this supposed native pacifism in the "Okinawan heart," backed by the myth of being a weaponless state during the reign of Shō Shin (r. 1477–1527). As Greg Smits has ably demonstrated, this romantic view of a peaceful and pacifist Ryukyu has no historical grounding and has been born and bred by contemporary Okinawan politics, especially under the administration of former governor Ōta Masahide (1990–1998), who, from a staunch antibase position and his own war experience, established a number of peace promotion initiatives, including a new branch in the prefectural government dedicated to peace promotion.[41] It is not surprising, then, that the campaign rhetoric surrounding the restoration of Shuri Castle acquired by 1990 an additional layer of peace discourse that seals the connections among Shuri Castle as the premier example of Okinawan cultural heritage, as the "crown jewel" of Okinawa tourism, and as a manifestation of war redemption.

Teruya Seisho's effusive characterization of Shuri Castle's symbolic role in the midst of its rebuilding in 1991 exemplified this positioning. In his essay "The Significance of Shuri Castle's Restoration: My View from Three Positions," he enumerates what he believes the value of the restored castle will be. First, he cites its cultural value and role in communicating an appeal for peace. "Culture" and "peace" are explicitly brought together in this instance through his wholesale acceptance of the myth of a weaponless Ryukyu and his characterization of Shuri Castle as unique among castles in Japan and the world. The old castles on the mainland and abroad were, he points out, marked by tall, fortified castle towers that evidence their function as manifestations of power and military might while "our Ryukyu promptly forbade the carrying of swords and issued peace proclamations before others in the world. In other words, banning weapons, we established benevolence and virtue as national policy." He continues by describing the hallmarks of the former Shuri Castle's relatively low-profile design itself—a blend of Japanese, Chinese, and local styles—as having been particularly Ryukyuan and having constituted "a hall that was not a figure of power but, rather, of unparalleled peace in the world. Okinawa's superb traditional culture displayed in the form of Shuri Castle can indeed be thought of as something that has been formed with poetic sentiment and a deep desire for peace." For him, the restored Shuri Castle will reembody the best of Okinawan culture, a culture that was putatively formed from a fundamental peace principle fostered under the Ryukyu Kingdom. He makes no mention of the civil wars through which that kingdom was forged or the resentment of the outer Ryukyu Islands forced to submit to Shuri. Neither is there mention of the armed conflicts within the Ryukyus that Smits documents. This supposed history of peaceful culture and the values stemming from it form the core of Teruya's second point: the educative and spirit-enhancing function of the restored castle. Teruya paints a picture of a spiritually bankrupt, materialistic postwar society in need of a restoration to a more "spiritual climate." Shuri Castle, he claims, as an embodiment of traditional culture and "an unparalleled symbolic cultural asset of peace," could serve as a platform to bring younger generations in touch with native spiritual roots and foster an "education of the heart." It would bring great psychological benefit to Okinawans in general. Teruya's third point turns to the economic benefit for Okinawans. Reflecting the enthusiasm for and confidence about tourism development that was growing throughout the bubble economy years, he makes the argument that the restored castle will contribute richly to the tourism industry. He notes that for many years, photos and logos of Shureimon have been used on pamphlets and posters as the symbol of Okinawa tourism and hospitality, but "I have often heard that many tourists who actually visit Shureimon say that their expectations are betrayed [because that is all that is there]." The complaint "Is that all?" among visitors to Shureimon was cited frequently among SCRA members. Teruya, like many, argues that rebuilding Shuri Castle's Seiden within a Shuri Castle Park will silence those criticisms, provide a grander symbol for Okinawa tourism, and become a "mecca" (his word) for visitors. At the same time, the supposed pacifist nature of Okinawan history and culture will be spread beyond the prefecture. Teruya ends on that note, foreseeing the castle as a monument to the peaceful foundations of "Okinawan heart": "Now, the Kannon Peace Statue stands atop Mabuni as a symbol of world peace, and then Shuri Castle will be up atop Shuri Hill, royal castle ground, as an unparalleled symbol of traditional culture. In a plea for peace and as icons of traditional culture, both of these will then jointly become grand structures that will surely set forth forever a brilliance and splendor as great historical undertakings in Okinawa."[42] If not for Shuri Castle's pulverization in the Battle of Okinawa, such an opportunity for this "great historical undertaking"—offering up a paramount example of Okinawa's putatively peaceful heritage while sidestepping the castle's compromised prewar condition—would not have been possible. But nor would it have been possible to rebuild Shuri Castle without a concerted drive during the 1980s to turn Okinawa into Japan's "Tourism Prefecture" and to wed that effort to an overdetermined peace discourse born not from a pacifist cultural essence but from war experience, postwar occupation, and an abiding militarized status under the U.S-Japan security arrangement.

By the time of Shuri Castle Park's opening on November 3, 1992, twenty years after Okinawa's reversion to Japanese rule, a simultaneous "reversion to Ryukyu" had taken place, offering a sense of local cultural and historical autonomy, an identification with premodern native origins that looked past the war and Okinawa's entire history as a modern Japanese prefecture. The restoration of Shuri Castle constituted a symbolic "Ryukyu Restoration." The accuracy of the popular portrayal of the Ryukyu past from which the restored castle derived its form and meaning mattered little; what propelled Shuri

Castle Park to the head of a widespread (re)discovery of the Ryukyu Kingdom was the resonance of that portrayal with the cultural, political, and economic winds of the present. As the *Ryūkyū Shimpō* reported in its wrap-up of the big news events of 1992, Shuri Castle Park "quickly blew wind into the Ryukyu Kingdom boom." Mainland—and even some local—attitudes toward Okinawan culture and customs could not have been more distant from what had been expressed during prewar and early postwar times when "Ryukyuan" was a pejorative, and Okinawan ways were considered backward. Okinawa as Ryukyu became cool.

Ironically, the United States previously had an indirect hand in making Ryukyu fashionable. USCAR's purposeful promotion of Okinawa as Ryukyu—with a history and culture distinct from Japan's—served as a political strategy to assert the "natural" separation of Okinawa from Japan until 1972 and involved the encouragement of traditional "Ryukyuan" cultural arts, from music and dance to pottery and textile dyeing—the kinds of things that would subsequently fuel the Ryukyu Kingdom boom that was in full swing by the early 1990s. That decade began with Okinawa Prefecture's sponsoring the first Worldwide Uchinanchu Festival (Sekai no Uchinānchū Taikai) in August 1990, a gathering of Japanese Okinawans and about twenty-four hundred Okinawan immigrants from across seventeen countries, billed as a forum to foster linkages among Okinawans worldwide and to contribute to Okinawa's (and by association, Japan's) internationalization. This event featured displays and celebrations of *Uchinā* (Okinawan/Ryukyuan) culture and, like the restoration of Shuri Castle, was officially—and somewhat awkwardly—cast as being held in commemoration of the twentieth anniversary of Okinawa's reversion to Japan. The pointed use of the Okinawan term *Uchinānchū* as an ethnic identifier in the name of the festival signals an identity apart from mainland Japan and in this context particularly signifies Okinawan immigrants abroad who identify themselves as of Okinawan rather than (simply) of Japanese descent. As Wesley Ueunten, writing on the Third Worldwide Uchinanchu Festival (2001), points out, the themes and representations of Okinawan identity at the festivals have been managed by the Okinawan prefectural government and stress the idea of outward internationalism through the metaphors of "bridges," "crossroads," and "bases of exchange," limiting the flexible and changing reality of Okinawan identity.[43] In addition to this global use to bring together diasporic Okinawans, *Uchinānchū* is also used in general to identify with non-Japanese Ryukyuan roots. In this instance, *Uchinānchū* are "Ryukyuan people." And Ryukyuan people—those imagined at the court of Shuri Castle in the past and those artists, craftspeople, writers, and musicians performing this nativist ethnic identity in the present—were at the center of the Okinawa-as-Ryukyu Restoration that increasingly spread over Okinawa's touristscape and popular culture. Okinawa was being styled a Ryukyu theme park.

While the Worldwide Uchinanchu Festival may have helped popularize on a limited scale an ethnic identity drawn from an imagined Ryukyuan heritage that brought together disparate Okinawan immigrant communities, the widespread theming of Okinawa as Ryukyu Kingdom through nationwide media came only in the wake of Shuri Castle Park's opening. As seen in the previous chapter, contemporary media images of Okinawa until this point largely depicted Okinawa as tropical beach resort. Outside of base-related issues and high-profile political events, mainstream national media coverage of Okinawa was dominated by tourism—its development and its advertisement—ever since Marine Expo '75. To see featured images of an Okinawa that was not defined by bases or beaches and not a part of a historical documentary on the Pacific War was a novelty. The bright vermillion, Chinese-influenced Seiden and Ryukyu Kingdom court styles were exotic sights for mainland Japanese and were conducive to framing the ensuing Ryukyu Kingdom boom as a newfound discovery among Japanese. Okinawa was both outside Japan's history as a previously independent state and inside it—at least since the 1879 dissolution of the Ryukyu Kingdom and establishment of Okinawa Prefecture, if not since the Satsuma domain's invasion of Ryukyu in 1609. It possessed the status of an internal exotic, familiarized enough to be navigable yet strange enough to draw interest. In this sense, the "Discover Japan" and "Exotic Japan" travel campaigns that behemoth advertising agency Dentsū launched on behalf of Japan National Railways in 1970 and 1984, respectively, converged in 1990s Okinawa (Okinawa had not been a part of the JNR campaigns for the simple reason that Okinawa did not have railways). Shuri Castle Park materialized this status of Okinawa as an exotic Japan to discover, and NHK's Taiga Drama Series *Ryūkyū no kaze*, which followed soon after the park's public opening, spread it to households throughout Japan for forty-five minutes every Sunday evening starting at 8 p.m., spanning twenty-six episodes from January 10 to June 13, 1993.

## RYUKYU STAGED

*Ryūkyū no kaze* (Winds of the Ryukyus), set in the late sixteenth and early seventeenth centuries and straddling the time of the Satsuma domain's invasion of Ryukyu, was NHK's thirty-first Taiga Drama Series and the first to feature the Ryukyu Kingdom. As such, its subject matter—the existence of a separate state and kingship within Japan that a Japanese domain invades—was considered daring and even progressive for normally conservative NHK.

However, according to the series director, Yoshimura Yoshiyuki, there were three main reasons it made it to television as part of NHK's venerable Taiga Drama Series. First, the 1993 Taiga Drama Series was planned and produced by NHK affiliate NHK Enterprises, which had a freer hand in deciding material for a series whose guiding principle was to find fresh historical subject matter that had meaning for the present. Second, the 1991 Taiga drama *Taiheiki* broached the previously taboo topic of the fourteenth-century division of the southern and northern courts, so a recent precedent existed for taking on controversial subject matter. Third—the biggest reason—was the 1992 opening of Shuri Castle Park. The timing of *Ryūkyū no kaze* with the opening of Shuri Castle Park was not coincidental; both the TV series and the park served as mutual promotions for each other as the castle complex was used for sets throughout the series. As cultural anthropologist Hara Tomoaki has commented, it was almost as if the rebuilding of Shuri Castle was for the sake of staging the series.[44] Great expectations for making Okinawan history, culture, and identity more widely known to Japanese as a whole were openly expressed throughout the media by public officials, businesses, tourism promoters, and ordinary citizens in the run-up to the inaugural episode. Tourist agencies ran special "Shuri Castle Tours" and "Ryūkyū no Kaze Tours" while commemorative and souvenir goods were produced.[45] The Okinawa Convention & Visitors Bureau held a major Ryukyu history symposium while the Prefectural Museum displayed a special exhibit titled "Ryukyu Kingdom: The Age of Great Trade and Castles," and local municipalities hosted public talks and discussions. An open set depicting Naha Port and the Chinese traders' quarters of Kume Village was also built on the coast of Yomitan Village. Given that this secondary set was located on prime real estate nearby a resort hotel, it was planned that the set would be a "theme-park-like facility," which, after the end of the series, would be converted into the Nankai Ōkoku Ryūkyū no Kaze (South Seas Kingdom Winds of the Ryukyus) "living history" theme park.[46] The close affinity of *jidaigeki* (historical drama) stage set and theme park is evidenced in this decision; both are fundamentally themed environments, one for televisual spectatorship and the other for direct sightseeing. It is noteworthy that while Yomitan's South Seas Kingdom Winds of the Ryukyus and Onna's Ryukyu Mura are classified as theme parks in the 1998 survey cited at the outset of this chapter, Shuri Castle Park, despite physically sharing much in common with the former, is not. This different treatment at Shuri Castle Park might be explained by the lack of daily dance or musical performances and hands-on experience exhibits, typically involving the visitor taking part in producing a traditional craft or participating in a performance. The lack of those elements is in keeping with the regal grandeur of the castle and its promotion project. Designating Shuri Castle Park a "theme park" would somehow diminish its dignity and draw unnecessary attention to the fact that the Seiden and its adjacent buildings are, strictly speaking, wholly new constructions, not restorations of original structures.

As new constructions, Shuri Castle Park and the Ryūkyū no Kaze Studio Park (as the site was known before its conversion to theme park) were literally set to stage a depiction of the Ryukyu Kingdom during a time of great change in China (fall of the Ming dynasty), Japan (rise of the Tokugawa *bakufu*), the Ryukyus (invasion by the Satsuma domain), and East Asia at large. This was the time when Ryukyu was forcedly brought more directly into Japanese history, an action dramatically portrayed for hundreds of thousands of television viewers on the heels of the twentieth anniversary of Okinawa's reversion to Japan and featuring the castle built to commemorate that political event. The symmetry between Satsuma bringing Shuri Castle under its control in scenes shot at the castle that was ostensibly rebuilt to commemorate Japan's reclamation of sovereignty over Okinawa is almost too perfect to call symbolic. Indeed, opening with the death of Oda Nobunaga and subsequent ascent of Toyotomi Hideyoshi and then passing through the Battle of Sekigahara (1600), the founding of the new order under the Tokugawa regime, and the Satsuma invasion, the series could be read as an ideological retelling of the origins of modern (Imperial) Japan, this time taking Okinawa—now rejoined with modern Japan—into account. As Carol Gluck suggests, the *jidaigeki* that NHK produced for its long-running Taiga Drama Series probably constitute the single most-important force shaping popular understanding of Japanese history.[47] Immediately following Shuri Castle's rebuilding and amid a mainland boom in Okinawan music, film, and traditional arts that had been going on for a few years, *Ryūkyū no kaze* certainly functioned for many viewers as an introduction to the parts of Okinawan history deemed most relevant to mainland Japanese who knew little about Okinawa, let alone premodern Ryukyu. As part of the wider Okinawa/Ryukyu boom, it is credited with stimulating tourism to Okinawa from the mid-1990s despite a slumping domestic economy. The presumed unfamiliarity of Okinawa/Ryukyu to most Japanese viewers accounts for the extra time and care taken by production staff in researching and accurately reproducing aspects of Ryukyu culture—dress, hair, food, customs, and so forth—depicted in the series. Nothing could be taken for granted as had been possible with previous Taiga dramas. Ryukyu was new, and its culture was treated as "foreign" in producing it for a mainland television audience. The meticulous display of Ryukyu cultural items in *Ryūkyū no kaze* also did double duty as guide to Okinawan heritage tourism.

The Ryukyu Kingdom during its golden era of maritime trade from the mid-fifteenth to the mid-sixteenth centuries is the research focus of Takara Kurayoshi, the historian who served as historical consultant for both the restoration of Shuri Castle and the production of *Ryūkyū no kaze*. As such, he represented another direct connection between the castle and the TV series. The trajectory of Takara's work—some would say agenda—has been to relate fully Ryukyu's history as an independent state in a wider East and Southeast Asian regional history apart from Japanese history. His 1990 book *Ryūkyū no jidai* gained audience beyond academia, sparking within Okinawa popular interest in Ryukyu-period history through television and radio programs. Such popularization was among Takara's goals, subscribing to the ideal of teaching younger generations a history of Okinawa for the formation of a historically grounded regional identity. He insists, however, that all sides of that history be told, that one not simplify Ryukyu's so-called golden age, for example, as being without its dark side or Ryukyu's so-called weaponless state as being without its violence. That Takara would be an enthusiastic consultant for both the rebuilding of Shuri Castle and for *Ryūkyū no kaze* therefore comes as no surprise. Referring to his work on *Ryūkyū no kaze*, he considers it "one part of the grand endeavor of how to tell the story of Okinawa" and "the first step to tell the story of Okinawa in contrast to 'Old Japan.'"[48]

Given the audience's general unfamiliarity with Ryukyu history, *Ryūkyū no kaze* was required, in Takara's opinion, to describe the era and events with more deliberate detail. Takara's role in the production was therefore significant and, for the first time in the thirty years of the NHK Taiga Drama Series, the screenwriter (Yamada Nobuo), the director (Yoshimura Yoshiyuki), and the actors themselves engaged in serious historical study, reading both secondary and primary historical materials.[49] Takara considered a primary task of *Ryūkyū no kaze*—besides entertainment—to be to provide fundamental knowledge about Okinawa's independent past and the circumstances surrounding the loss of that independence in the early seventeenth century. He and director Yoshimura were also keen on displaying Okinawa's cultural differences amid current discussions on multiculturalism that were reaching Japan at the time; *Ryūkyū no kaze* provided an effective vehicle to counter the ideology of Japan as a single culturally homogenous nation state. Yoshimura recognized, however, that the Taiga Drama Series was first and foremost enjoyable entertainment that should not be dragged down by history lessons. To meet this requirement he innovated with a "Churaumi Kikō" (Beautiful Ocean Travels) information corner at the end of each episode, which provided accessible explanations about the history and culture of the Ryukyus that aimed, according to Yoshimura, to relativize mainstream Japanese history and culture by displaying Ryukyuan/Okinawan difference. Following a familiar travelogue-edutainment format, the "Churaumi Kikō" inserts effectively doubled as tourism promotion. In addition, more than the usual number of popular histories and guides to the program accompanied the release of *Ryūkyū no kaze*, reinforcing in bookstores the "Ryukyu boom" that paralleled the Okinawa beach resort boom (see chapter 6).

While staging a generation of dramatic historical change in Ryukyuan-Japanese-Chinese history, *Ryūkyū no kaze* went to great lengths to showcase for mainland Japanese viewers Ryukyuan/Okinawan cultural differences. Echoing tourist guides past and present, what are considered defining elements of this cultural difference are overtly displayed throughout the series. Items of clothing, hair styles, language, sacred sites (*utaki*) and priestesses (*noro*), turtleback tombs, shamisen (*sanshin*), song, karate, and so on are prominently featured during the story and in the postepisode "Churaumi Kikō" inserts. The single most-prominent item is the newly rebuilt Seiden of Shuri Castle. Picture-postcard shots of the Seiden routinely mark a subsequent scene within, which is typically an official audience with King Shonei or a meeting among officials. Ceremonies in the *una*, the courtyard before the Seiden, are also featured. Dance and musical performances held within and outside Shuri Castle hold special significance; in the first episode, dance is described as "the homeland of the heart of Ryukyuans" (*Odori wa, Ryūkyūjin no kokoro no furusato*) and "a treasure in the heart of Ryukyuans" and is placed in opposition to politics and warfare. After the Satsuma invasion, one of the Ryukyuan male leads, Keizan, in contrast to his older half-brother and star of the series, Keitai, gives up the political life and pursues dance as a gesture of peace. Ryukyuan dance in particular comes to exemplify the peaceful inner heart of the Ryukyuans while "nonmilitary" Shuri Castle, behind its welcoming Shureimon, is its outward material manifestation.

The requirement by NHK Enterprises that content for the Taiga Drama Series have relevance for the present foregrounds pedagogical content and invites allegorical readings. For example, Hara's analysis of the eleventh episode of the series—during which King Shonei is faced with the decision of whether to cede the northern island of Oshima to Satsuma or go to war—reveals the contradictions among the messages director Yoshimura publicly stated that he intended to convey through the program: (1) peace without military power, (2) a sense of borderlessness, and (3) the independent existence of the Ryukyu Kingdom.[50] All of these points had their analogs in Japan and Okinawa at the time *Ryūkyū no kaze* aired: the antibase peace movement in Okinawa; the question of immigration and multiculturalism in Japan, which was a hot-button issue at the end of the bubble economy, when previously needed illegal immigrant laborers were in the center of a new *sakoku* (closed country) versus *kaikoku* (open country) debate (Japan passed the Immigration Control Act in 1990); and the question of local autonomy and regional devolution, which was being debated in the Japanese Diet during 1993 (the Regional Devolution Act was eventually passed in 1995). Throughout the series an essential pacifist nature among Ryukyuans and their sense of openness to foreigners are represented by serene scenes of performing arts (song, dance), appeals for peaceful negotiations by certain characters, and the peaceful trade Ryukyu conducted with various East and Southeast Asian countries. These attributes—presented as residing in the "Ryukyu heart"—come into conflict in relation to Yoshimura's third point, which is captured by a phrase repeated often by characters in the series: "Waga Ryūkyū Ōkoku wa dokuritsu no kuni de aru" (Our Ryukyu Kingdom is an independent country). As Hara points out, in episode eleven the peace-loving Shonei is pressed to go to war to have any chance to preserve the integrity of Ryukyu as an independent state. Hara draws the comparison with the Shōwa emperor during the Asia-Pacific War, noting that both he and Shonei are popularly portrayed as desiring peace and possessing the power, as sovereigns, to stop war, but both ultimately cite the need to protect the home of their ancestors and reluctantly set their countries on a path to war. He sees this parallel as commentary on the Shōwa emperor's war responsibility, a topic that was very much alive in the wake of Hirohito's death in 1989. The prospect of having to defend Ryukyu also prompts discussions among court officials concerning the necessity of a country in the first place. The issue here involves risking a war for the sake of preserving the independent Ryukyu Kingdom, a war that will inevitably kill Ryukyuan people. While some—expressing the pacifist position—believe that people can live without a country, that it is not worth risking lives to preserve Ryukyu's independence, others—most notably emissary and senior adviser Jana Uekata—insist that people who lose their country are pitiable and without a real life. Pacifist, borderless Ryukyu is at direct odds with the proposition that Ryukyu exists as an independent state with defended borders. That Satsuma—with Tokugawa blessings—upsets the status quo and forces the issue of war, peace, and borders opens up a critique of modern Japan's forceful dissolution of the Ryukyu Kingdom and full annexation of its former territory as Okinawa Prefecture. In other words, the Satsuma invasion is treated as the first step in Japan's eventual overall conquest of the Ryukyus. It also invites reflection on Okinawa's postwar experience of American occupation, the terms of reversion to Japan, and the continued concentration of U.S. military bases in Okinawa. Mapping the positions presented in *Ryūkyū no kaze* onto modern Japanese-Okinawan cultural politics is not difficult; the creators of the series provided ample opportunities to do so, but the extent to which the average viewer did is unclear. One could happily watch the series straight, without twisting it with the present. Nonetheless, while falling short of being overtly allegorical, *Ryūkyū no kaze* does suggest a range of positions relevant for modern Okinawa, from secessionist at one extreme to assimilationist at the other. The tension, contestation, negotiation, and compromise among the majority in the middle provide the drama in both the television series and in contemporary real life.

Despite its occasional bluntness, the effort throughout *Ryūkyū no kaze* to relativize mainstream Japanese history and culture is laudable. Also to its credit is the attempt to relativize the centrality of Chūzan (Shuri) within Ryukyu. In episode eighteen, the far southwestern island of Yonaguni—from which Taiwan is visible on a clear day—makes an appearance that moves Shuri's position from periphery in relation to Japan and China to center in relation to Ryukyu's own peripheral islands such as Yonaguni. Concerned about the defense of the southwest boundaries against European encroachment, Tokugawa Ieyasu dispatches an entourage to Yonaguni led by Keitai. In the same way that Ryukyu culture is presented to the mainland viewer as foreign and fundamentally more peace loving than Japan's, Yonaguni culture is presented to Keitai as different from and fundamentally more peace loving than Shuri-centered culture. The ideal of peace without weapons in a borderless state is repeated to Keitai by a wise old Yonaguni woman who relates to him an ancestral saying: "Taking up weapons will lead a country to ruin. There is no country that prospers in weaponry. Take a look at the ocean. There are no borders among countries [*kunizakai*] anywhere. No matter how far you go, the ocean is one." She implores Keitai to remember, upon returning to Shuri, that despite their differences the islanders of Yonaguni are also Ryukyuans like him and should be treated accordingly. This utopian ideal is held onto at the poor and powerless periphery of Ryukyu where the impact of the political reality of power being contested at the center is minimal. This convolution of what the Ryukyu Kingdom stands for in relation to Japan works to put into perspective the ideals attributed to "the Ryukyuan heart" and opens up critical reflection upon the representation of the Ryukyuan inheritance as it is articulated throughout the series.

While this national exposure of Ryukyuan culture and the program's edutainment effort were perhaps flattering for Okinawans whose history and culture were often overlooked and misunderstood, the representation of Okinawa/Ryukyu in the series did not go uncriticized, as Hara's overview of the *Okinawa Times* and *Ryūkyū Shimpō* reportage on the reception of *Ryūkyū no kaze* reveals. There were two main divisions among the criticism: that which emanated from residents of Okinawa Island and that which came from other islands within Okinawa Prefecture, principally Miyako and the Yaeyama group. There was also a critical reaction among professional writers and intellectuals, which overlapped with both. The prospect of having Shuri Castle and the Ryukyu Kingdom on the NHK Taiga Drama Series generated much excitement and positive anticipation on Okinawa Island. Surveys during the first month of episodes showed 80 percent and above viewership, and reaction was generally positive, although some wondered why the series was focused on the time around the Satsuma invasion rather than on Ryukyu's earlier "Golden Age of Maritime Trade." Others began to question why actors portraying Ryukyuans were not Okinawa-born and why only a smattering of local language (*Uchināguchi*) was sprinkled—unnaturally—here and there in the dialogue. By the end of the second month of episodes these latter two complaints had grown, more open criticism of the historical accuracy appeared, and ratings among Okinawans slipped. That local actors and language were not being used struck a chord and was treated more and more as an affront to Okinawans despite intentions to better educate Japanese about Okinawan heritage. Some suggested that NHK should have treated *Ryūkyū no kaze* as it would have a foreign-based historical drama, complete with subtitles and "foreign" actors.[51] In response to such reactions, eight months after the original series ended, NHK-Okinawa Broadcasting released *Ryūkyū no kaze: Uchināguchi Version* in February 1994, which more broadly used local language and actors. This version was generally well received—at least on Okinawa Island.

The reception of *Ryūkyū no kaze* on other islands within Okinawa Prefecture brought to the surface a history of center-periphery relations among the Ryukyu Islands, which are often eclipsed within larger center-periphery relations between the prefecture and mainland Japan. In other words, while *Ryūkyū no kaze* set out to relativize Japanese history and culture, Shuri-centered Ryukyuan culture itself, according to critics on outlying islands, needed to be relativized as well. Observers from the Yaeyama island group treated *Ryūkyū no kaze*, the rebuilding of Shuri Castle, and the entire "Ryukyu boom" itself with indifference at best and harsh criticism at worst. The media blitz surrounding the series on Okinawa Island was absent in Yaeyama. In fact, soon after the broadcast of *Ryūkyū no kaze* began, the *Yaeyama Mainichi Shinbun* serialized a set of articles on the history of the severe taxation to which Shuri subjected Yaeyama residents and on Oyake Akahachi, who defied Shuri's demands for taxes and tribute and led a rebellion against the government in the late fifteenth century (King Shō Shin sent an army from Shuri in 1500 and crushed the rebellion, capturing and beheading Akahachi; so much for the "peaceful native heart"). In the annals of the Ryukyu Kingdom Oyake Akahachi is a traitor, but on his adopted home of Ishigaki Island and in the surrounding area, he is memorialized as a heroic freedom fighter. In Yaeyama, there has historically been little to celebrate about the Ryukyu Kingdom. It was viewed as an oppressor, not an Okinawan cultural heritage in which to share. To those in Yaeyama, focus on and praise of the Ryukyu Kingdom in the early 1990s was merely an extension of a long history of marginalization of the outer islands that consistently placed Okinawa Island

and Chūzan (the government at Shuri Castle) at center. The release of *Ryūkyū no kaze: Uchināguchi Version* only exacerbated the situation by employing *Uchināguchi* central to Shuri and unintelligible to most in Yaeyama, despite the fact that Yonaguni figured into one episode. Locals in Yaeyama acknowledged that national exposure of Yonaguni in *Ryūkyū no kaze* increased the number of tourists there by 9 percent (from 24,373 to 26,750) from 1992 to 1993, but even that was a mixed blessing; the spike in tourism to Yonaguni ever since the expansion of airline service from Ishigaki to Yonaguni in 1987 has raised concerns about the safety and the social and environmental impact of increasingly larger numbers of visitors.[52]

By the end of *Ryūkyū no kaze*'s run of twenty-three episodes, it was evident to many that, as some critics characterized it, the series and the entire contemporaneous "Ryukyu Kingdom boom" represented a mediated "Yamatoization" (*Yamatoka*; i.e., Japanization) of Okinawa-as-Ryukyu designed for mainland Japanese consumption.[53] Local interest in learning *uchināguchi*, practicing traditional arts and performance, and rediscovering an Okinawan identity in the Ryukyu past had been going on previous to the high-profile boom of the early 1990s. It became a boom through external interest propelled by national media and in conjunction with the concerted effort to market Okinawa further as tourist destination for mainland Japanese. In *Ryūkyū no kaze,* the Ryukyu Kingdom had been shaped to fit the NHK historical drama mold, despite the best intentions of its director, writer, and historical advisers to offer a fresh break from that mold. The content of Japanese history and culture could be relativized by introducing Ryukyu difference, but the power of the genre and form of *jidaigeki* in the Taiga Drama Series and the concern about capturing and keeping a national audience ultimately put limits on how far that relativization could go. In this respect the production of *Ryūkyū no kaze* bears much in common with general tourism development and the manufacture of Tourist Okinawa under the gaze from the north. With respect to heritage tourism, historical and cultural authenticity (however defined) often must be compromised by concerns over marketability—including efficient and effective means of packaging and delivering services. Most of the "practical" reasons for not using Okinawan language (aversion to subtitles) and actors (not enough known to mainland viewers) and deviating from the strict history of the period (to enhance the human drama) involved accommodating the mainland Japanese consumer based on the previous experience of broadcasting historical dramas. The lack of awareness of (or simply not much concern over) internal historical, cultural, and linguistic differences within the Ryukyus also speaks to the homogenizing and simplifying tendencies of the tourist gaze. The destination—whether in person or through media—has to sustain enough of the exotic, of the nonquotidian and unfamiliar, to capture interest, but in the end it needs to be conveniently consumable by the widest profile of average consumers if the goal is to maximize the number of visitors (which, judging by annual announcements the Tourism Division of Okinawa Prefecture makes, is indeed the perpetual goal). Amid the mix of aggressive beach resort development, the Japanese "discovery" of *Uchinā* pop music, and the rediscovery of Ryukyu that accompanied the opening of Shuri Castle Park and the broadcast of *Ryūkyū no kaze*, a convergence of overdetermined Okinawan identities flourished from the early 1990s, identities that, although produced for mainland Japanese consumers through national media, cannot be so easily cordoned off from a presumably more authentic identity rooted in the local soil. Performing "Tropical Okinawa" and "Ryukyu Kingdom Okinawa" within a staged Tourist Okinawa eventually seeps into the landscape and insinuates its way into everyday life, at the very least compelling one to negotiate more consciously among affiliations and personas.

All Nippon Airways' (ANA) Okinawa tourism campaign at the time *Ryūkyū no kaze* was broadcast seized upon this convergence in one compact image and two words: "Ryukyu blossoming" (*Ryūkyū kaika*, see figure 4.4). Appearing on the inside front cover of an NHK-published guide to the sets, actors, and Ryukyuan history and culture behind the series, ANA's advertisement was tied directly with the newly opened Shuri Castle Park and NHK's historical drama without directly showing either. Instead, sand, sea, and sky—the *real* reasons to take an ANA jet to one of the ANA-owned beach resorts in Okinawa—form the backdrop for Rinken Band, the colorful icons of *Uchinā* pop music whose members, posing earnestly in flamboyant Ryukyuesque/*eisā* costumes, are clearly not suited up to swim and sunbathe. Shuri Castle and *Ryūkyū no kaze* are implicit in the dragon logos used in NHK's promotions ("Dragon Spirit" being the series' subtitle) and in the ad copy that appears below the image, which offers this invitation to (re)discover the Ryukyu Kingdom within Tropical Okinawa:

> A Ryukyu Dynasty that boasted prosperity from the 14th to 16th century.
> A unique culture nurtured by relations with various Asian countries.
> The most Okinawan heart of Okinawa—Ryukyu.
> This winter's theme is about rediscovering the splendor of the Ryukyu Spirit that has continuously flowed and is deeply rooted throughout Okinawa even today.
> It's the Ryukyu Spirit itself that allows you to sense a new Okinawa because it reveals to you the Okinawa you didn't know until now.[54]

Recasting Okinawa—the most Okinawan heart of Okinawa—as Ryukyu conveniently bypasses the troubles of Okinawa's modern history as a Japanese prefecture, the tragedies of war, and the controversies of Okinawa's

**Figure 4.4.** Ryukyu blossoming. *Source*: Advertisement on inside front cover of *Ryūkyū no kaze: Dragon Spirit*.

postwar status as host to the majority of U.S. bases in Japan. It displaces false preconceptions one might have of Okinawa with the assertion of a splendid, idealized Ryukyu "spirit" that forms the true basis of Okinawan cultural heritage. As a catchphrase, "Ryukyu blossoming" was brilliant for marketing Okinawa tourism at this time. It not only suggested Okinawa's now famous faux-tropical flowers; it simultaneously tapped into the Ryukyu Kingdom craze that peaked with the opening of Shuri Castle Park and manifests itself today in neo-Ryukyuan architecture and the branding of "Ryukyu style."

Predictably, the ANA ad on the inside back cover of the same *Ryūkyū no kaze* guide highlights seven ANA resort hotels in Okinawa pictured under a huge hibiscus blossom: nature and culture—and package tours—blossom. *Kaika* (blossoming) is also homonymic with the *kaika* in the Meiji-period slogan *bunmei kaika* (civilization and enlightenment), suggesting a coming of age for this newly discovered Okinawa as well as a commingling of past and present that epitomized the 1870s *bunmei kaika* era in Japan. And, ironically, it was at the end of that decade, in 1879, that Imperial Japan dissolved the Ryukyu Kingdom and incorporated the islands as Okinawa Prefecture.

By the 1990s, the creations and re-creations of landscape and culturescape—cultivating a progressively tropical *nangoku* look and rediscovering the Ryukyu Kingdom as Okinawan heritage—had generated layers of images of (Tourist) Okinawa, which to this day sometimes strain to coexist harmoniously in a configuration we might call "Tropical Kingdom Okinawa." Okinawan cultural and historical identification with an independent premodern Ryukyu Kingdom—often with political overtones—was set alongside an Okinawa wishfully cast as "Japan's Hawaii." Accommodating the gaze from the north by invoking an exotic, tropicalized South located conveniently within Japanese political and linguistic boundaries, Okinawa also offered to the Japanese sightseer a suitably "foreign" but translatable history and culture. That distinct inheritance, however, faced its own compromises in translation, as seen in the accommodations made for mainland Japanese viewers in the broadcast of *Ryūkyū no kaze*. Visions of the tropics and revisions of Ryukyu, which have dominated Okinawa image making during much of the postwar period, have been taking place in the long historical shadow of the bloodiest conflict of the Pacific War and in the face of bereaved family members, historians, politicians, and peace activists who each in their own, often conflicting ways insist on the maintenance of war history and memories. This encounter among war, tropics, and Ryukyu has involved negotiations between emotional and economic exigencies, between local self-representation and outsider expectations, between historical faithfulness and marketing savvy. The results of these negotiations vary from thoughtful transitions to crass juxtapositions of war history, tropical paradise, and cultural heritage. Some war legacies, however, have found a different path into the sightseeing itineraries of tourists drawn to both Okinawan beaches and American bases.

## NOTES

1. Okinawa Sōgō Jimukyoku, *Tēma pāku no dōnyū ni yoru kankō sangyō shinkō chōsa* (Naha: Kuniken, 1998), 61–65. It should be noted that the publisher of this report, Naha-based Kuniken LTD., is a major Okinawa construction company

responsible for high-profile projects that cut across the tourism spectrum, such as the remodeling of the original Moon Beach Resort (1975), the upscale Busena Resort (1997), the Bankoku Shinryōkan (which hosted the 2000 G8 Summit), the Navy Headquarters Cave Visitor Center (1999), the Churaumi Aquarium (2002), the Okinawa Prefectural Archives (1995), and the Seiden (Main Hall) of the rebuilt Shuri Castle (1992). It is not surprising that this report would advocate the building of more tourist attractions.

2. If there were train stations with *eki-ben* in Okinawa, odds are they would have *gōyā* (bitter melon) and Spam, items decidedly outside the Japanese culture-nature matrix. Regional dialect is one item where (linguistic) exoticism of peripheral areas may be comparable to that of Okinawa, although Okinawan (and its own dialects) are popularly perceived as more radically different from mainland regional dialects. The status of Okinawan—dialect of Japanese or separate language—was the focus of much scholarly debate during the prewar period when native ethnologists such as Yanagita Kunio were preoccupied with defining the core and outlines of Japanese culture. See Hugh Clarke, "The Great Dialect Debate: The State and Language Policy in Okinawa," in Elise K. Tipton, ed., *State and Society in Interwar Japan* (London: Routledge, 1997), 193–217.

3. Jennifer Robertson, *Native and Newcomer: Making and Remaking a Japanese City* (Berkeley and Los Angeles: University of California Press, 1991), 1.

4. Marilyn Ivy, *Discourses of the Vanishing: Modernity, Phantasm, Japan* (Chicago: University of Chicago Press, 1995), 40–48.

5. Details of the *furusato nōzei seido* can be found at http://f-tax.jp (accessed September 8, 2011).

6. Guidelines and applications are available online at http://www3.pref.okinawa.jp/site/view/contview.jsp?cateid=6&id=16689&page=1. Links to various municipal *furusato* tax payment home pages are available at http://www3.pref.okinawa.jp/site/view/contview.jsp?cateid=38&id=18360&page=1 (accessed September 8, 2011).

7. See the Okinawa-ken Nakijin-son website at http://www.nakijin.jp/nakijin.nsf/doc/furusatonozei (accessed September 8, 2011).

8. See the Okinawa-ken Yomitan-son website at http://www.yomitan.jp/5/4025.html (accessed September 8, 2011).

9. See "Naha-shi furusato-zukuri kifukin no go-annai," Naha City, http://www.city.naha.okinawa.jp/kikaku/furusato/index.html (accessed September 8, 2011).

10. "Kifukin o katsuyō suru jigyō," Naha City, http://www.city.naha.okinawa.jp/kikaku/furusato/katuyou.html (accessed September 8, 2011).

11. Nagasaki—with its historical connections with "exotic" Dutch and Chinese traders and a relatively warmer climate for the cultivation of tropicalesque flora—is perhaps the closest comparison with Okinawa. The Ainu areas of Hokkaido in the northern extremes of the archipelago offer a different kind of comparison with Okinawa's exoticism from a mainland perspective.

12. See Tze May Loo, "Treasures of a Nation: Cultural Heritage Preservation and the Making of Shuri Castle in Prewar Japan" (PhD diss., Cornell University, 2007),

especially chs. 1, 4, and 5 for the modern prewar history of Shuri Castle and how it became designated a National Treasure.

13. When referring to Shuri Castle, most people have in mind the *Seiden*, or Main Hall, where the throne of the Ryukyu kings was located, even though the castle complex is comprised of several dozen separate structures.

14. Although the official English translation for the park is the redundant "Shurijo Castle Park" (Shuri Castle Castle Park), I will henceforth simply refer to it as "Shuri Castle Park."

15. It must be noted here that Okinawa tourism dropped precipitously in the wake of the September 11 terrorist attacks in the United States. The concentrated presence of U.S. military bases on the main island of Okinawa—amounting to about 20 percent of the land and upward of forty thousand military personnel and their dependents—brought fears from would-be mainland Japanese tourists that these bases would be targets of terrorism as well as sources of nuisance, given the heightened security alerts and exercises in and around the bases. School field trips from the mainland to Okinawa—a growing mainstay counted on by many midsized hotels and bus companies—also experienced a severe drop post-9/11. This economic downturn prompted the prefectural government, tourist industry officials, and local businesses to unite in a high-profile campaign aimed to assure travelers that Okinawa was a safe tourist destination. By 2003 the number of visitors to Okinawa had recovered to pre-9/11 levels.

16. Senge Tetsuma, *Okinawa kankō shindansho* [A Diagnosis of Okinawa Tourism] (Naha: Okinawa Kankō Kyōkai, 1962), 16.

17. Tze, "Treasures of a Nation," ch. 6.

18. The annual bulletin of the Shurijō Fukugen Kisei Kai (Shuri Castle Restoration Association), *Shurijō fukugen kisei kai kaihō* (Proceedings of the Shuri Castle Restoration Association, first published in 1982), contains frequent references to the phrase and its use in lobbying efforts for the castle's rebuilding.

19. Goya Shigenobu, "Shurijō Fukugen Kisei Kai ni-jū-go no ayumi" [The Past Twenty-Five Years of the Shuri Castle Restoration Association], *Shurijō fukugen kisei kai kaihō*, no. 17 (July 1998): 42.

20. Goya, "Shurijō Fukugen Kisei Kai ni-jū-go no ayumi," 43.

21. The Okinawa-Hoppō Taisakuchō was discontinued on May 14, 1972, and replaced by the Okinawa Kaihatsuchō (Okinawa Development Agency) and the Northern Territories Policy Office.

22. Goya, "Shurijō Fukugen Kisei Kai ni-jū-go no ayumi," 44.

23. Goya, "Shurijō Fukugen Kisei Kai ni-jū-go no ayumi," 44.

24. Shuri Castle is thought to have been first built circa 1427 and to have been burned down three times prior to the Battle of Okinawa: in 1453 during civil war; in 1660 by accident; and again in 1709 as the result of an accident.

25. Goya, "Shurijō Fukugen Kisei Kai ni-jū-go no ayumi," 44–45.

26. "Okinawa bunka no hokori ni," *Okinawa Taimusu*, June 14, 1973.

27. Matsukawa Kunio, "Shurijō fukugen no suishin," *Shurijō fukugen kisei kai kaihō*, no. 3 (July 1984): 12.

28. See, for example, Zaha and Kuba, "Okinawa sensai bunkazai nado fukugen ni kansuru koiinkai sanka no kiroku," *Shurijō fukugen kisei kai kaihō*, no. 2 (June 1983): 4; Uezu Yasuhide, "Shurijō ni yuki ga furu: Sapporo yuki-matsuri o mite," *Shurijō fukugen kisei kai kaihō* (February 1984): 8.

29. Matsukawa, "Shurijō fukugen no suishin," 12–13.

30. Hokkaido has long maintained a special relationship with Okinawa as parallel peripheral prefecture, as having sent the largest contingent and suffered the largest losses in the Battle of Okinawa, and as having erected the first prefectural war memorial in April 1954.

31. "Shurijō fukugen wa kokumin no ganbō," *Okinawa Taimusu*, February 8, 1984.

32. Uezu, "Shurijō ni yuki ga furu," 6.

33. Uezu, "Shurijō ni yuki ga furu," 7.

34. Uezu, "Shurijō ni yuki ga furu," 8.

35. "Shurijō o meguru hitibito," Wonder Okinawa, http://www.wonder-okinawa.jp/001/005/004_01.html (accessed March 11, 2010).

36. Shurijō Kōen Jigyō ni Kakaru Jūmin no Kai, *Shurijō kōen keikaku hihan* (Shuri Kinjō-chō: Shurijō Kōen Jigyō ni Kakaru Jūmin no Kai, 1989).

37. Shurijō Kōen Jigyō ni Kakaru Jūmin no Kai, *Shurijō kōen keikaku hihan,* 1.

38. A 1995 *Ryūkyū Shimpō* publication of the top 100 tourist sites in Okinawa ranked Shuri Castle Park first. The older Ryukyu Mura and the onetime set for the NHK Taiga Drama Series *Ryukyu no kaze* (see below) also received citations. *Ryūkyū Shimpō*, ed., *Shin Okinawa kankō meisho 100 sen* (Naha: *Ryūkyū Shimpō*, 1995).

39. Goya Shigenobu, "Sōritsu 25 shūnen o mukaete," *Shurijō fukugen kisei kai kaihō*, no. 17 (July 1998): 33.

40. *Okinawa Taimusu*, August 1, 1967, inset.

41. Greg Smits, "Romantic Ryukyu in Okinawan Politics: The Myth of Ryukyuan Pacificism" (paper presented at the Association for Asian Studies Annual Meeting, San Francisco, April 7, 2006).

42. Teruya Seisho, "Shurijō fukugen no igi—mitsu shiten kara no shigen," *Shurijō fukugen kisei kai kaihō*, no. 10 (1991): 35–36.

43. Wesley Ueunten, "Okinawan Diasporic Identities: Between Being a Buffer and a Bridge," in David Willis Blake and Stephen Murphy-Shigematsu, eds., *Transcultural Japan: At the Borderlands of Race, Gender, and Identity* (New York: Routledge, 2008), 174–75.

44. Hara Tomoaki, *Minzoku bunka no genzai: Okinawa • Yonagunishima no "minzoku" he no manazashi* (Tokyo: Dōseisha, 2000), 157.

45. Hara, *Minzoku bunka no genzai*, 182–86.

46. Hara, *Minzoku bunka no genzai*, 162.

47. Carol Gluck, "The Past in the Present," in Andrew Gordon, ed., *Postwar Japan as History* (Berkeley and Los Angeles: University of California Press, 1993), 74–75.

48. Hara, *Minzoku bunka no genzai,* 166–67.

49. Hara, *Minzoku bunka no genzai,* 168–69.

50. Hara, *Minzoku bunka no genzai,* 158–59.

51. *Ryūkyū Shimpō*, op-ed, May 15, 1993.
52. Hara, *Minzoku bunka no genzai,* 192–93.
53. Hara, *Minzoku bunka no genzai,* 198.
54. NHK Shuppan Kyokai, ed., *Ryūkyū no kaze, Dragon Spirit: NHK taiga dorama sutōrī* (Tokyo: NHK Shuppan, 1993).

# Part III

# BASES AND BEACHES

# 5

# Military Bases as Tourist Attraction

The American military base construction boom in Okinawa began about forty years before the beach-resort-building boom of the early 1990s. After its victory in the Battle of Okinawa in the spring of 1945, the United States, knowing Okinawa's strategic location for a forthcoming Cold War context, immediately set about establishing a more permanent base on the island, but it was not until the Korean War broke out in 1950 that "permbase" was realized. The following decade was one of tension-filled confiscations of land from local residents and contention over what constituted fair compensation for the loss of prime real estate to the U.S. military.[1] One physical result of this surge in base building was a perforation of the island, especially the central area, by large zones of territory off-limits to Okinawans, except for those who worked on base. The central location of the bases guaranteed direct contact between American military personnel and the local population, most notably in adjacent "base towns" such as Koza (present-day Okinawa City) that provided pawnshops, bars, clubs, and brothels for the foreign occupiers. Today many of the bases abut densely populated residential areas. It was in this physical context of a heavily militarized island that the first glimmerings of postwar tourism promotion, discussed in chapter 1, began in the mid-1950s. In the wake of the catastrophic physical destruction and human loss the Battle of Okinawa left, tours of this subtropical island focused on battle sites and war memorials, not the sea, sky, and beaches promoted today. This is not to say the natural attributes of the landscape were not featured. Rather, mainland tourists had as their destination—outside of shopping areas—the concentration of war-related sites on the far southern end of Okinawa Island. The other concentration of war-related sites—American military bases—piqued tourist interest in the central area of the island despite never being fully and openly promoted as tourist attractions. Throughout the postwar period, American bases could not be actively advertised as sightseeing spots without encountering logistical obstacles or political controversy. There was perhaps a more open attitude pre-Reversion among Okinawa tourism promoters toward the possibility of including U.S. bases within guided tours, but the ideas floated for that never took off. Post-Reversion, however, even mild attempts to include the U.S. military within mainstream tourism promotion have met with loud objections from peace activists. And yet, the desire to see the spectacle of installations, weaponry, aircraft, and real-live American military personnel has held a deep fascination among visitors, young and old alike. Officially promoted or not, American military bases and their personnel did, in practice if not in principle, become and still are tourist attractions in Okinawa. An excavation of this scarcely recognized form of tourist activity, which coexists with cultural heritage and beach resort tourism, opens up a broader understanding of the scope of the war's abiding impact and of the kind of compromises and negotiations that followed from building Japan's "Tourism Prefecture" in Japan's "Military Base Prefecture."

## BASES AND BASE PERSONNEL WITHIN PRE-REVERSION TOURISM

Perhaps the single most-persistent problem hampering any full-fledged tourism development in Okinawa before reversion to Japan in 1972 was lack of money among Okinawan investors, compounded by American restrictions against Japanese capital investment in the Ryukyu Islands. The other nagging problem was the high profile of the U.S. military there. This concern appears in the record of planning meetings of the Okinawa Tourism Association (OTA) at its first attempts in 1954 to consider how to portray Tourist Okinawa in photos and postcards. One note reads, "It's best to leave out military installations. It's better to do photos and postcards of Okinawaesque [*Okinawarashii*] sites."[2] This attitude to downplay the base presence throughout the mid-1950s is understandable given the friction over lease land, the freshness of war memories, and the corresponding focus on war memorial pilgrimages that dominated early Okinawa tourism. By the 1960s and the boom in tourism to Okinawa that followed Reversion, U.S. bases had become just as much a part of the landscape on Okinawa Island as transplanted palm trees—the two were often side by side—and arguably just as "Okinawaesque," but simply not in a positive way. While travel posters, guidebook covers, and industry literature featured sea, sky, sand, flora, and the latest hotels and improvements to infrastructure on the one hand, newspapers, magazines, and television documentaries pictured permbase and PR shots of American and Government of the Ryukyu Islands (GRI) officials in displays of joint cooperation on the other. Browsing through issues of *Kankō Okinawa* one would scarcely realize that the American military was on the island. And yet, the fascination among Japanese visitors for the U.S. military presence, on the sheer level of the exoticism of the foreign and the modernity of the hardware, had to be squared somehow within the framework of general tourism promotion. It was too obvious to ignore, but at the same time it was not the *Okinawarashii Okinawa* that Okinawans desired to put on display.

The formula for fitting the base presence within general tourism was worked out in the early 1960s when U.S. authorities began to encourage more actively tourism development. Simply put, it involved seizing upon the exoticism and modernity that the bases and their personnel represented while ignoring the negative impacts. We see this strategy best in the scenario drawn up for the first Okinawa tourism-promotion film produced in 1962. The actual film that was eventually produced differed in details from this scenario, but the general structure and spirit of the scenario remains intact, and the marginal notes are revealing. Halfway through the scenario, after a series of natural and historical assets, a section describing the American presence begins with a shot of Route 1 (present-day Route 58), the bloodline of the U.S. military on Okinawa. The notes indicate that "jazzy Okinawan theme music" is playing in the background. The next shot pans over the bases of central Okinawa, keying in on "American modern-style residences and families" and "golf courses" while eliding the raison d'être of the bases. Notes for the narration here read, "In complete contrast [to previous images of local agriculture and manufacturing], here is machine civilization and contemporary living. Associating with America." The planned film then elaborates on what "associating with America" means with the next scene depicting "the details of everyday life around the bases where Americans and Okinawans are on the same plain [*sic*]." Of course, Okinawans were hardly on the same plain (*dōitsu jigen*) as Americans, but so saying coincides with the fiction of Americans bringing mutual friendship and democracy to Okinawans.[3] After framing the bases in this fashion, the scenario moves on to the positive attraction they should hold for the Japanese tourist—namely, the experience of shopping in a dollar economy for foreign goods (golf clubs, perfume, jewelry, alcohol, etc.) that are considerably less expensive than on the mainland because of the absence of mainland duties and tariffs.[4] The imagined shots here are of Okinawan shopkeepers speaking English to Americans and Japanese to Japanese customers at various well-known "American" shopping areas. The tentative catchphrase for this segment is "Savor the taste of foreign travel in Japanese!" (*Nihongo de gaikoku ryokō no ajiwai o!*). The closest the scenario comes to suggesting nightlife activities in base towns like Koza is a scene depicting a group of Japanese tourists window shopping at night. The scenario then uses a shot of foreign goods mixed in with Okinawan craft items (fabrics, pottery) to segue to a section depicting a variety of local cultural items. It then shifts to a tour bus ride south to the final battle site zone, beginning at the famed Himeyuri-no-tō. It ends, as did the battle, on the cliffs of Mabuni, at the site of the suicides of commanding officers Ushijima Mitsuru and Cho Isamu. A scene of traditional Okinawan turtleback graves follows. The Okinawa Island section of the scenario ends with an American jet, a line of cars, a busy intersection of military vehicles on Route 1, and the description "the contrast of new and old among the pedestrians on the street." The notes emphasize this theme of "old Okinawa" existing side by side with a "new, modern Okinawa," thus naturalizing the U.S. military presence as part of a progressive evolution of the island. In this way, a potential source of problems for tourism development is neutralized, even capitalized on.

Among all of the mainstream tourism materials I have seen—pre- and post-Reversion—this scenario for a promotional film that was distributed to tourism information offices in mainland Japan comes closest to actively embracing U.S. military bases as part of an Okinawan identity, as part of the Okinawaness of the place as tourist destination. One half of the strategy employed to do so—the American presence is part and parcel of Okinawa's own modernization—could only be plausible before Reversion. Missing out on the rapid economic growth and postwar modernization happening in Japan while under American control, Okinawa could cast the modern (military) technology and new construction that the United States brought to Okinawa as a sign of progress, however dubious that claim might be. After Japan resumed full sovereignty over Okinawa in 1972, boasting about modern ferro-concrete buildings, newly paved roads, and neon lights in the Koza nightlife would appear quaint at best. Mainland Japan, having undergone its own American-inspired postwar modernization, would henceforth be the measure of Okinawa's progress, and in that it would appear sorely lacking. Reading this scenario and watching the film now, one cannot help but feel the pathos of Okinawa's earnest efforts to put forth its best face. The other half of this image-making strategy—packaging the American presence as part of Okinawa's exotic appeal—has proven more enduring and effective both pre- and post-Reversion. The slogan "Savor the taste of foreign travel in Japanese!" could be taken as representative of the ideal of much tourism as it was being defined and packaged in the 1960s—experiencing something outside the everyday but within one's comfort zone. Beyond shopping with U.S. dollars in American-style stores staffed by Japanese-speaking clerks, the film scenario highlights Japanese visitors mingling among Americans as one would on a trip to the United States. The difference, however, is the presence of the female Okinawan clerk in relation to the two types of guests (American and Japanese). Her position—and Okinawa's position—as host places both the Japanese and the Americans together as guests. In other words, in the instance of interaction with the Okinawan, the Japanese and the Americans are on the same side of the host-guest relationship and share in an uneven power relationship with the Okinawans, although the Japanese and the Americans cannot be fully identified with each other. Hospitality—a form of subservience in this instance—masks the implicit colonial relationship of this scene of exchange between host and guests. In itself, this situation is not surprising or particular to Okinawa; much of the international tourism developing in the post–World War II period involved the travel of first worlders to decolonized areas of the globe. Even the successful case of Hawaii, the tourism business of which skyrocketed after American statehood in 1959 brought the first commercial jet service to Honolulu, must be considered in a context of a history of semicolonial relations with the United States and as a U.S. military outpost. As in Okinawa after Reversion, in Hawaii after statehood increased tourists brought an escalating concern among locals and visitors that overdevelopment was ruining the image of a beautiful tropical island featured prominently in promotional materials. While differing in their relationship to World War II, both also had a military presence to contend with and war-related sites prominent among tourist attractions: the Pearl Harbor Memorial and the National Memorial Cemetery—the Punchbowl—in Hawaii's case.

Another early glimpse of the allure of U.S. bases as tourist attractions in Okinawa appeared just prior to the planning of the first tourism-promotion film. Although not verifiable, it is possible that the material in the scenario and final film concerning bases and base towns as sightseeing spots was in fact partly a response to suggestions that Senge Tetsuma made in his 1962 tourism assessment report discussed in chapters 1 and 2. In it, Senge first describes Koza, which abuts Gate 2 of Kadena Air Base, as a "rare city" with a "marvelous" main drag full of English-language signs identifying rows of pawnshops, bars, "cabarets," Hong Kong–style department stores, and East Indian tailors frequented by locals and foreigners alike. The street scene he describes uncannily resonates with the lyrics of the 1996 song "America Dōri" (America Street) by the *Uchinā* pop music group the Nenes ("Sisters" in Okinawan), which continues this idealized view of Koza (present-day Okinawa City), now tinged with nostalgia:

"America Dōri" (Remix) by Nenes, from the CD *Koza*

(Koza, Koza . . . Gate, Koza . . . Gate)
Words from many countries
Flooding the town
In the space between day and night
The bustle of pawnshops
The neon of audio shops
The East Indian clothing stores
Like a town in a foreign country
Horizontal letters dancing
America Street twilight
rock, *shima-uta* [island songs], rap, reggae
our island, this Koza town
mixed up, mixed together
mixed up, mixed together
America Street
Thread-like vapor trails
Painting pictures in the sky
In the space between day and night
White-skinned women
Black-skinned men
Brown-skinned island people
in the storefront windows
lovers reflecting
America Street twilight
rock, *shima-uta*, rap, reggae
our island, this Koza town
mixed up, mixed together
mixed up, mixed together
America Street
Stores like a movie set
brighten up the town
in the space between day and night
smiles of GIs
blond hair flowing with the wind
the odd English of merchants
the town's like a box of toys
with dreams and romance spilling out
America Street twilight
rock, *shima-uta*, rap, reggae
our island, this Koza town
mixed up, mixed together
mixed up, mixed together
America Street

Multicultural, multilingual harmony reigns as jet trails are aestheticized and bars and pawnshops become movie set facades. As James Roberson comments about this song,

> "America Dōri" valorizes a vision of a dreamlike *champuru* [mixed up] Okinawa that does not really exist but, perhaps, could. Here, there are no confusions, no conflicts. The music, which prominently features *sanshin* in a light pop frame, is also used to construct an upbeat hybridity, while background English interjections provide an added "hip" feel. Koza, the reference town, is a fantasy town of beautiful people and colorful sights and sounds, where U.S. military jets don't make noise or crash into elementary schools, where children of mixed parentage don't encounter discrimination, and where GIs don't fight or rape twelve-year-old girls. The musical construction of imaginary sites inside Okinawa such as "America Dōri," with its blond American GIs and East Indian merchants, simultaneously indexes the evolving set of real and imagined external relationships between Okinawa and other outside forces, places, and peoples.[5]

Roberson rightly points out that the song "creatively constructs Okinawa as distinct and different from homogeneous mainland Japan."

This creative construction of exotic and hybrid difference is not unlike the Tourist Okinawa that Senge was urging and that lies at the heart of most attempts to fashion an attractive tourist destination. In Senge's vision of the place, "America Street twilight" would give way to nighttime tourism, "to the extent that it could be made safe," a gesture to Koza's bar and brothel scene.[6] Sightseeing buses during the 1960s did have Koza on their list of stops, but that was for daytime shopping there. He also suggested tours inside Kadena Air Base itself if permission could be had to do so, a plan that thirty-nine years later was briefly realized before the 9/11 terror attacks. As a mainland Japanese observer, Senge was far more candid about the potential appeal of the bases and their environs to tourists who did not have to tolerate their nuisance on a daily basis. He played up the advantage of being able to experience firsthand this level of the foreign within a relatively familiar social and cultural context. All the while, as discussed in chapter 3, he urged the overt tropicalization of the landscape to turn Okinawa into "Japan's Hawaii," a place that held out the example of beach resort tourism on small islands that hosted military bases. Okinawa did not come anywhere near being transformed into the same kind of international tropical tourist destination as Hawaii; a byzantine process to secure passports to travel to the U.S.-controlled Ryukyu Islands, lack of sufficient local capital, restrictions against Japanese investment, and meager non-Japanese foreign investment (despite many queries from abroad from potential developers) mitigated against that happening. The relatively steep rise in the number of visitors to Okinawa that did occur during the 1960s was attributed mainly to war memorial and shopping tours; experiencing a quasi-foreign vacation in the comfort of one's own language was a bonus. Tour bus and taxi routes through central Okinawa Island that skirted U.S. bases did provide spectatorship and commentary by guides, effectively turning military installations into unofficial tourist sites. However, by the late 1960s the idea to integrate U.S. bases as an officially recognized part of the tourist experience waned in appeal as U.S. involvement in the Vietnam War heated up. As a staging site and R&R area for U.S. troops involved in that war, the bases and base towns changed in character, complicating attempts to package them in a way that dissimulated their true nature and function. Regular flights of troop transports and B-52s on bombing runs to and from Vietnam meant serious noise and traffic nuisances as well as accidents. Base town clubs, bars, and brothels boomed with increased numbers of troops, rendering places like Koza a more dangerous proposition for the casual Japanese tourist. Senge's vision of safe nighttime recreation for regular tourists was put on hold.

## BASES AND BASE PERSONNEL WITHIN POST-REVERSION TOURISM

The U.S. pullout from Vietnam coincided closely with Okinawa's return to Japan, and yet the majority of the bases remained, leaving the same problem of negotiating tourism promotion around a conspicuous military presence and constant reminder of Okinawa's wartime past. On the other hand, the perpetual problem of a dearth of funding to realize visions of "Japan's Hawaii" was less severe given government and private investment in the newly recovered prefecture. To help ameliorate the base presence and mute protests against the terms of Reversion, which allowed a continued high-profile U.S. military presence, Tokyo established the Okinawa Development Agency and promised large infusions of capital for infrastructure projects and for Marine Expo '75 that rapidly accelerated the number of visitors to Okinawa. Like the Tokyo Olympics a decade earlier but on a smaller scale, Marine Expo '75 brought improvements, cash, and tourists to Okinawa, although the majority of profits from that event ended up with mainland investors, while overbuilding left many vacant hotel rooms. Despite the mixed economic results of Marine Expo '75 for the local economy, Okinawa was now clearly on the maps and minds of mainland Japanese tourists as a less expensive alternative to—albeit a pale reflection of—a trip to Hawaii or the South Pacific. After a predictable drop of about 40 percent in the number of tourists to Okinawa in 1976 in the wake of Expo '75, numbers climbed steadily—from about 1 million to about 4.5 million—until the end of the century before temporary setbacks following the G-8 summit in 2000 and the 9/11 terror attacks. The latter served as a distinct reminder of the reality and impact of hosting a significant contingent of American military in the midst of Japan's self-proclaimed "Tourism Prefecture," which has gone to great lengths to project a tropical resort image. In *Okinawa imēji no tanjō* (The Birth of the Okinawa Image), Tada Osamu provides a detailed analysis of Expo '75 as the formative watershed event that set in place the image (now cliché) of "blue sea Okinawa" with abundant greenery and subtropical foliage. He characterizes "parallel worlds of bases and tourism," which, through the apparatus of Okinawan image making, are kept apart, especially since Reversion and Expo '75.[7] On the level of visual imagery and narrative description in mainstream official and most private Okinawa tourism promotion, Tada is certainly correct. However, he is dealing mainly with the image, not the practice, of Okinawa tourism. If we examine the practice of tourism in Okinawa, we find another set of "parallel worlds": the world of mainstream corporate and government promotion on the one hand, and the world of nonmainstream private promotion and actual tourism practices on the other. Extending Tada's analysis to the latter world, we find that these parallel worlds are not so far apart.

One specialized form of Okinawa tourism that takes U.S. bases as one principal focus is the *shūgaku ryokō* (school field trip), for which Okinawa is famous. Such field trips are big business, catering to tens of thousands of mainland schoolchildren per year. Since the opening of the Cornerstone of Peace and the institution of "peace guides" in 1995, the renovation of the Peace Memorial Museum in 2000, and an expansion of tours into refugee caves over the recent years, school field trips to Okinawa have developed into rather sophisticated programs often identified as peace study tours. The trips typically cover cultural, historical, natural, and militarized aspects of Okinawa and involve pretrip study of its role as host to U.S. military bases. Outside of time spent at the beach, it is questionable how much middle and high school students take away from the experience.[8] Nonetheless, it is significant that the tours they participate in directly treat U.S. bases as sightseeing opportunities. This sense comes across most strongly at the locally famous and ironically dubbed Anpo ga Mieru Oka (The Hill from Which the Security Treaty Can Be Seen) or simply Anpo no Oka (Security Treaty Hill), a small hill along Route 74 just outside the north perimeter of Kadena Air Base that allows a clear view of landing strips and hangars on base. The idea behind its name is that the U.S. base, lying before one's eyes, is the concrete manifestation of the security arrangement between the U.S and Japan. It is a typical stop for school field trips and its status as a well-known alternative tourist sight is evidenced by its sign, originally posted at a makeshift parking lot that used to be across the road, and its mention in editions of *Kankō kōsu de nai*

*Okinawa*. Until Michi-no-Eki Kadena (Roadside Station Kadena) opened at the site of the parking lot in August 2003, aircraft fanatics virtually camped on Anpo no Oka with professional-grade cameras on tripods, walkie-talkies, and radio receivers tapped into Kadena's air traffic control in order to be prepared to take photos of incoming and outgoing planes. Copies of photos they have taken are for sale as souvenirs to the tourists. Postcards of Anpo no Oka have also been available in souvenir shops, a testament to its status as a homegrown sightseeing spot. I had visited the place on numerous occasions before Michi-no-Eki Kadena opened and siphoned visitor traffic away from the hill itself across the road. Spending hours observing, filming, and listening in on the stream of school kids and other tour bus groups passing through, I was generally impressed by the level of detail tour guides provided about the base (its size, number of inhabitants, range of facilities, types of aircraft, as well as basic information about the Japan-U.S. Security Treaty and Status of Forces Agreement) (see figure 5.1). Information given to adult groups was especially detailed, with guides fielding a range of questions from visitors. Aside from casual sightseers and regular school field trip groups, specific peace studies groups composed of high school and college students as well as older adults also visited the site. One of the school group bus guides whom I interviewed indicated that the school kids do not usually come away having learned much about the Anpo of Anpo no Oka. They are, however, predictably fascinated by

**Figure 5.1.** The view of Kadena Air Base from Anpo no Oka. *Source*: Gerald Figal.

the jets landing and taking off. To witness an F-15 roaring down the runway and banking off over the East China Sea in the distance is what draws most people to Anpo no Oka and, more recently, to the adjoining Michi-no-Eki Kadena. Indeed, the experience, which I have had, is exhilarating.

Completed in 2002 and opened for use on August 8, 2003, Michi-no-Eki Kadena was constructed partly in response to threats by U.S. authorities after the 9/11 attacks to raise the perimeter wall in front of Anpo no Oka to obstruct the view onto the base. Ironically, just prior to the attacks, plans were in place to conduct civilian bus tours through parts of Kadena Air Base, but they were abruptly halted. Also suspended post-9/11 was the annual "AmericaFest," a weekend-long event in late June or early July (often coinciding with American Independence Day) when American and non-American civilians were allowed on base to observe aircraft and other military hardware up close, eat hot dogs, drink Coke and Bud, listen to American music, play carnival games, and pose in battle gear for photos with marines and airmen. Sponsored by the U.S. Air Force and "designed to promote friendship and foster mutual appreciation and understanding between the local community and Americans assigned to Kadena," AmericaFest was toned down following the 9/11 attacks and suspended entirely from 2004 to 2008.[9] Base security—already high pre-9/11—became even stricter post-9/11, making it difficult even for friends and relatives of base personnel to go on base. Indications from Kadena authorities that a higher wall would be put up next to Anpo no Oka fell within this context. Ultimately, the wall was left as is, but as if to defy authorities, the Kadena Town government, with the support of local businesses and residents, built Michi-no-Eki Kadena. As one of over eight hundred *michi-no-eki*—essentially rest areas for highway travelers—across Japan, Michi-no-Eki Kadena is distinctive in the scope of its facilities. In addition to offering the usual functions of refreshments, toilets, parking areas, phones, souvenirs, and information about local history and culture, the four-story, seventy-one-hundred-square-meter building houses a "learning exhibition room" that presents a history of the Kadena Town area from prehistoric times to the present. Despite the chronological span, half of this room is given over to an implicitly critical history of Kadena Air Base, which seems fitting since the base takes up 83 percent of Kadena Town. At the end of the exhibit is a corner explicating types of aircraft that operate out of Kadena, accompanied by four video monitors placed against a wall-sized photo of the base and connected to live feeds from cameras mounted atop the building and trained at four specific spots on base. Fitted with user-controllable remote zooms, the cameras allow visitors to obtain a real sense of secretly snooping in on military activities that authorities would rather not broadcast publicly (see figure 5.2). In the face of the threats to raise the perimeter wall of Kadena, there is little

**Figure 5.2.** Surveillance of Kadena Air Base from Michi-no-Eki Kadena.
*Source*: Gerald Figal.

doubt that the addition of these cameras was a gesture of defiance. Beyond the political statement being made, what is particularly interesting about this gesture is its effect on bringing real-time images out of the base and into the critical frame that the exhibition provides. The present-day base is scrutinized on local terms. The past history of the town and base—told together in text, documents, maps, models, and photos along a timeline—relates construction, local impact, accidents, protests, and statistics, and then suddenly is made "live" in the juxtaposition of black-and-white historical photos and live color video cams that the visitor controls. The effect is ambiguous and disconcerting. On the one hand there is a sense of stealthily having control over access to activities on base, of domesticating and manipulating it, but on the other hand, there is the reminder that it is only through a zoom lens and at a distance that any access is possible. What appears close-up on screen is at the same time distant; what seems in one's control is ultimately not.

While the video surveillance monitors of base locations within the Kadena Town history exhibit are fascinating in their effects and implications, the real draw of Michi-no-Eki Kadena is the open-air observation deck on the top floor. With a covered shelter area, picnic tables, vending machines, and restrooms, it has all the trappings of a regular tourist sightseeing spot and offers panoramic views of the airbase's runway from a better vantage point and more comfortable surroundings than on the hill itself (see figure 5.2). It invites one to spend a leisurely time waiting for aircraft to take off and land, or simply to enjoy an unobstructed view from Kadena to the East China Sea in the western horizon, with or without the aid of the telescopes mounted along the railing. The aircraft fans with their long-lens cameras and radios tuned to the frequency of Kadena Air Base's air traffic control are still there among the casual visitors, but something of the homegrown, guerrilla nature of such crews on the original Anpo no Oka is lost with this new building with modern conveniences. What is gained, however, is a higher-profile site serving tourists and passersby alike who would have been unlikely to stop at—or even know about—Anpo no Oka. In this sense, Anpo no Oka has been mainstreamed into the larger institution of *michi-no-eki,* representing one of the few instances of direct promotion of U.S. military bases as tourist sights. Other buildings along other base perimeters afford similar opportunities to peep—for example, the upper floors of certain buildings of Okinawa International University, situated next to the U.S. Marine Corps Air Station (MCAS) Futenma and the site of the August 2004 crash of a marine transport helicopter; the upper floors of the Sakima Art Museum, also in Ginowan and often host to war-related exhibits; and, at a greater distance away, the globe-shaped observation tower on Kakazu Heights (see figure E.1), dedicated in Ginowan in January 1964 as a "new Okinawa famous place" (*shin Okinawa meisho*) according to the marker at the site.[10] Despite the initial post-9/11 fears about the presence of U.S. bases and the corresponding drop in the number of tourists to Okinawa in the immediate aftermath, the bases have returned to the tourist gaze with perhaps more fascination than before.

The issue of the visibility of the bases and their formal and informal display to the public has existed since their initial construction and the first days of organized tourism in the postwar period. From the Okinawa Tourism Association's concern in the 1950s about not depicting them within tourism promotion, to Senge's suggestion in the early 1960s about being able to tour them, to Kadena Town's present-day active encouragement to view and think critically about them, the bases have been variously mapped—even by their absence—in tourism promotions and practices. In addition to specialized school field trips, general guided bus tours of sightseeing spots have been one principal platform for spectatorship of U.S. bases, despite their not being overtly advertised as such. Much as Okinawan tour bus guides accrued fame for their dramatic renditions of Battle of Okinawa sites in the pre-Reversion period, bus tours after Reversion have increasingly gained a reputation for the observations and anecdotes they relate about the bases and base personnel. Tour bus routes conducted by two of the three major Okinawa tour bus companies—Okinawa Bus and Ryukyu Bus—are typically divided into three geographic regions that roughly correspond to the areas of the three kingdoms (Hokuzan, Chūzan, and Nanzan—Northern, Middle, and Southern Mountains) that reigned over Okinawa Island during the so-called Sanzan (Three Mountain or Kingdom) period from 1322 until the Chūzan king Shō Hashi conquered Hokuzan (1419) and Nanzan (1429) to establish a unified Ryukyu Kingdom.[11] With the highest concentration of U.S. bases being in central Okinawa, it is those on the *chūbu kōsu* (central course) or *hokuchūbu kōsu* (north-central course) that receive the majority of attention. The Okinawa Bus central course plans, scripts, and reference materials to which I obtained access at the company's headquarters in 2001 reveal a typical tour around several bases just prior to the September 11, 2001, attacks. They make very visible the military installations that are indeed physically very visible but nonetheless are virtually invisible in usual tourism promotional materials.

Traveling from south to north from Naha through Ginowan City on the Okinawa Bus central route, MCAS Futenma is the first base that Okinawa Bus's 2001 model script mentions, followed by Marine Corps Camp Foster and Kadena Air Base.[12] Among the basic statistics narrated in the script about Futenma is the fact that it comprises one-quarter of the area of Ginowan City and is sited so that it gives the remaining civilian area a "doughnut shape." These observations segue into the issue of the base's close proximity to residents and their corresponding complaints about noise and fear of accidents (such as the helicopter crash onto the Okinawa International University campus in 2004). These issues, in turn, naturally lead to a comment explaining that in the wake of the September 1995 gang rape of a twelve-year-old Okinawan schoolgirl by three U.S. servicemen, the Special Action Committee on Okinawa (SACO) was established in November 1995 to investigate ways to reduce the burden of the base on local civilians.[13] SACO's final report concluded, the script relates, that Futenma Marine Air Station will be moved and the land it occupies returned.[14] This point is the basis for the prolonged (and, as of August 2011, stalemated) negotiations to move the functions of Futenma elsewhere, either to other locations within Okinawa Prefecture or beyond. The degree of information and the implicit political commentary inserted here during an otherwise incidental portion between stops on the central course is rather remarkable when compared to a typical tour guide narration. A similar critical edge can be detected in the section that offers background on the foliage that borders Camp Foster. After a rundown of the vital statistics of the facility, which happens to house the Okinawa office of the United States Forces Japan, an explanation is offered for the hedge of *kyōchikutō* (Indian oleander) that forms a natural fence along the actual perimeter fence:

> The *kyōchikutō* growing along the fence is something the Japan Self-defense Forces [JSDF] planted in 1976 for the purpose of improving the living environment of the area around the base. At times they bloom lovely little flowers and delight the eyes of passersby. They're tolerant of pollution and exhaust fumes, but some people say they're to hide the insides of the base. There's also a sense of irony because the "Warning, Danger" signs apply to the plants. Now, entirely as base plants, a strange aroma seems to come wafting over from the other side of the fence.[15]

The irony of the plants, like the base, posing a risk to people in the area lies in the fact that oleander is among the most toxic plants in the world. Because of its hardiness and easy maintenance, it is also among the most commonly used plants in parks and roadsides, especially in subtropical regions, where it flourishes. As veteran Okinawa Bus tour guide trainer Shiroma Sachiko confirmed in an interview, local residents do refer to the hedges as "base flowers" and view with cynicism the attempts to beautify (camouflage) base perimeters with them and other foliage.[16] That it was the JSDF—rather that the U.S. military or local government—who planted the hedges adds another layer of irony. One can only speculate on the timing for the planting (1976), but this landscaping initiative might very well have been a response to the unprecedented number of visitors to Okinawa—over 1.5 million—the previous year during Marine Expo '75. In addition to these oleanders, hundreds of nonnative palm trees flank Route 58 where it winds past several bases, representing the largest concentrations of palms in Okinawa outside the now closed Southeast Botanical Gardens. As discussed in chapter 3, these palms began being transplanted there in the mid-1960s. By the end of the century, they had spread north and south along the central stretch of Route 58 and also along many of the east-west arteries between base areas. One of the more dramatic juxtapositions of base and palm is on the take-off and landing axis that stretches from the main runway on Kadena Air Base, across Route 58, and out over the East China Sea.

Kadena is the next base that the script takes up, but not before commenting on Chatan Beach, which lies between Camp Foster and Kadena. Being so close to both Camp Foster and Kadena Air Base, the beach, restaurants, and shopping areas of Chatan, as the script explains, are heavily frequented by U.S. military personnel and their families. As if offering accounts of exotic zoo animals and their behaviors, the script enumerates typical weekend beach activities of these American families—windsurfing, diving, swimming, picnics. History then intrudes upon this peaceful present-day beach scene in the next paragraph: Chatan Beach is where, on April 1, 1945, thousands of American marines landed as part of the invasion of the island, which stretched north past the Hija River—the northern boundary of Kadena Town—onto the beaches of Yomitan. The effect of this sharp juxtaposition from playful American beach scene to violent American beach landing is not without its critical irony; it jars the audience into a conscious recognition of what lies behind the site. While the tour guide does not narrate details of the landing and invasion on this particular route in the same dramatic fashion as her predecessors of forty years earlier, the seed for imagining the beachhead the Americans secured on that first day is planted in the minds of the audience.

Tying this wartime history back to the present, the narration recounts the base building that began soon after the war's end, noting that Chatan Town contains 57 percent of the total area of the bases in Okinawa. There is a palpable sense that what lies before the tourist is the direct legacy of the invasion of spring 1945. It is as if the marines who landed then never really left; they merely transformed as the island itself did as it was rebuilt, bases and all. Now, however, they are offered as a live spectacle for Japanese tourists. Some sightseeing buses make a stop at the Chatan shopping area—"American Village"—that borders the beach. Ironically, the buses park in the same lot where Kadena Air Base Staff Sergeant Timothy Woodland raped a twenty-four-year-old Japanese woman on the hood of a parked car in the early hours of June 29, 2001.[17] The signified of the signifier "American" in the area's name is ambiguous—does it designate the putatively American-esque shops and restaurants or the foreigners one can view there? There is indeed a concentration of originally American eateries—Tony Roma's, A&W, Kentucky Fried Chicken, McDonald's, Baskin-Robbins, Starbucks—and Americana souvenirs can be had here, but these can be found elsewhere in Japan as well. Besides their concentration in one spot, they do not stand out as particularly special in Chatan. What sets such a collection off from the usual Japanized American establishments on mainland Japan is the number of Americans—single marines and airmen as well as whole families—who can be seen among them, making "American Village" yet another undesignated tourist destination.

Just north of Chatan Beach lies the main event of this part of the central-north sightseeing bus tour, Kadena Air Base. The explanation of the air base commences at Gate 1 off of Route 58 and describes a veritable town. As the script puts it,

> On everyone's right is Kadena Air Base Gate 1. It may be a bit of an exaggeration, but they say it has everything besides a prison: on top of schools, hospital, restaurants, PX, commissary, churches, movie theater, it even has a foreigner-only golf course. This is why it's known as "Little America."

The details of Kadena-as-Little America segue into another historical juxtaposition concerning Okinawa in general: "The Okinawa that was called the 'Paradise of the Pacific' in prewar is now also known as the unsinkable aircraft carrier and has become the cornerstone of the American military's Far East strategy." The image of pristine island beauty set against that of an American-occupied aircraft carrier succinctly captures the modern historical condition of Okinawa. As in the narration of Chatan Beach as American playground and invasion landing point, this one-line commentary on Okinawa's dual attractiveness—as place of natural beauty and as place of natural strategic interest—forces the sightseer to register, if only momentarily, the historical and political realities beyond the present-day façade. Implicit too is the charge that invasion and occupation have compromised Okinawa's full promise as tropical paradise. What is missing here, however, is any overt mention of Japan's role in bringing on the conditions for that invasion and occupation. That is reserved—in small doses—for the Southern Battle Sites Tour route, the scripts for which have changed noticeably in tone from the past generation, moving from tear-jerking melodrama to more sober accounts of certain engagements and of the experience of civilians during and immediately after the war.[18]

The Okinawa Bus tour around Kadena Air Base that ran before Michi-no-Eki Kadena was built had as one highlight a pass-by at Anpo no Oka. While there is much extemporizing from the guides beyond the standard script, the summer 2001 draft version makes an explicit self-reference to the transformation of this little hillock into a tourist spot by virtue of the view it affords onto the base: "Because you can see various aircraft and the planes here sometimes put on the spectacle of a veritable air show, airplane freaks also come out to take photos at 'Anpo no Oka,' which has turned it into a sightseeing spot [*kankōchi*]." Never planned as a sightseeing spot, the little hill that peeks over the wall at Kadena became one because some local aircraft buffs wanted to watch U.S. planes operate there. Peace study groups also popularized the spot to dramatize the Japan-U.S. Security Treaty and the base issue in Okinawa, and now it figures regularly on school field trips and general bus tours, with Michi-no-Eki Kadena serving as its more convenient substitute since August 2003. The gradual public mainstreaming of Anpo no Oka as a regular sightseeing spot—and not simply as an alternative site for aircraft maniacs and antibase activists—is evidenced by its institutionalization and commodification in the form of Michi-no-Eki Kadena, which now appears on Okinawa Bus tour route advertisements in a way that Anpo no Oka never was, but it is still not overtly identified as a spot to observe U.S. base activities. The long-latent desire among many regular tourists to see the bases was finally accommodated, but only in the familiar, user-friendly form of a *michi-no-eki*. Nevertheless, the transformation of the site from grassroots word of mouth to a spot in a glossy bus route brochure speaks to the deep fascination that tourists to Okinawa have harbored for the bases, their hardware, and their inhabitants, as they would have for any other sightseeing spot. It also demonstrates the willingness of tour operators to exploit this fascination as long as it can be done in a convenient, profitable, and inoffensive way.

After completing this circuit of base-related sights, the 2001 Okinawa Bus central area sightseeing route continues from Kadena Air Base directly to the Southeast Botanical Gardens, again seesawing the tourist back onto the other side of the unavoidable juxtaposition between transplanted foreign military and transplanted tropical flora in this part of Tourist Okinawa. Only as analytical categories do *churashima* (beautiful island) Okinawa and *fuchinkūbo* (unsinkable aircraft carrier) Okinawa run parallel as Tada suggests. As the physical practice of touring the place demonstrates, the war related and the nature related intersect and coexist. They are entangled in such a way as to contribute to the cultural ideal of *champuru* (mixed-up, as the Nenes sing in "America Dōri") that Okinawan enterprises and individuals actively promote: Okinawa is the place where U.S. military bases are mixed in with palm trees, hibiscus, and beaches; it is also the place where the sound of jet engines intermingles with the soothing background music of the enclave of lush tropical flora that is (now was) the Southeast Botanical Gardens. This kind of *champuru* hybridity as a strategy to suture discursively the disjuncture between military presence and tropical mood is an advance upon earlier attempts simply to try to ignore the bases and promote a localized version of a stereotypical tropical resort image imported from Hawaii and the South Pacific. It has an advantage of actually having some local historical roots and cultural manifestations and thus an aura of credibility. And yet, because of the long shadow of war experience and the political thorniness that the postwar bases carry, there is a hesitation in mainstream tourism promotion to embrace fully and openly the U.S. (or JSDF) military presence as a vital part of modern Okinawan culture worthy of inclusion within historical and cultural tourism. One retired Okinawa Convention & Visitors Bureau worker, Takushi Katsuo, is somewhat exceptional in this regard. In my interview with him, he recalled, for example, continuing efforts on his part after Reversion to include U.S. military marching bands in the annual Naha Matsuri parade simply because, in his words, "they were a good band," but once peace activists caught wind of such plans, their public protests always shut the initiative down. Takushi was also among those who for years lobbied to arrange guided bus tours through Kadena Air Base but met with similar opposition from protesters, doubts from colleagues, and concerns over logistics and security from U.S. authorities.[19] Despite such political resistance from peace activists and hesitation from tourism officials because of the politics involved, the actual practices among tourists and tour guides in the field demonstrate little hesitation to treat the U.S. military as another extraordinary object that makes Okinawa a destination worthy of a visit.

## MILITARY *MEIBUTSU*

Like any of the photo-ops in Okinawa, from Manzamō to Shuri Castle, military bases, hardware, and personnel are counted among the things to view, photograph, and, if possible, obtain a little part of to bring back home for friends and relatives. The touristic commodification of the American military in Okinawa is not limited to souvenir photographs of Kadena aircraft taken and sold by hobbyists at Anpo no Oka and posing among men in uniform at annual on-base festivals. Varied military-related *omiyage* (souvenirs) are now an Okinawan specialty as much as *awamori*, *bingata*, and *gōyā champuru*. An integral part of the practice of Japanese tourism in general, gift giving in the form of *omiyage* has forced tourism officials and shop owners throughout the postwar period to consider what from Okinawa is suitably characteristic of the region and, preferably, small in size and/or consumable. This question obsessed Okinawa Tourism Association members from the late 1950s after they received complaints that there were few suitable *omiyage* available in Okinawa. Selection, quality, price, and distinctiveness were all concerns. As in the cases of enhancing hospitality and cuisine, the OTA conducted surveys of shops and their offerings, researched what other tourist destinations in Japan offered, and sponsored numerous workshops and exhibitions to improve souvenir quality and quantity, although it was not immediately clear what should be sold as exclusively Okinawan souvenirs. OTA members recognized this problem during their 1958 meetings when they first discussed the new trend of "shopping tourism" in Okinawa, which complicated the question of *omiyage*. Unlike other areas of Japan where local *meibutsu* (specialties) identified a place, Okinawa became well known for foreign goods that were less expensive than in mainland Japan because of much lower import tariffs. Its *meibutsu* were "watches, jewelry, lighters, Western clothes, whiskey, golf clubs, and the like," which, the OTA notes, was in stark contrast to the flourishing prewar production of "dried bonito, lump brown sugar, lacquerware, pottery, *bingata* textiles, Panama hats, and Ryukyu *kasuri* cloth," which suffered first because of the war and now was in competition with foreign goods.[20] This situation was, of course, the direct result of the outcome of the Battle of Okinawa and the postwar settlement that placed the Ryukyu Islands under U.S. control. The dollar limits that the United States Civil Administration of the Ryukyu Islands imposed on the amount of cash visitors could bring with them to pre-Reversion Okinawa exacerbated this condition despite growing per capita income among Japanese throughout the 1960s. In a zero-sum game that pitted prestige Western items at a discount against local products, only a compelling "Made in Okinawa" *omiyage* could survive. These low-tariff foreign goods were indeed distinctive of postwar Okinawa and arguably fit the function of *omiyage*, but foreign goods could not stand in for native specialties. Annual OTA-sponsored exhibitions therefore aimed to reestablish languishing craft production and encourage innovation, particularly in lacquerware, pottery, textile weaving, and such things as the use of coral for jewelry. *Awamori*, a rice-distilled spirit, was also targeted as a high-profile souvenir item on the order of foreign whiskey (and is today one of the most conspicuous and successful souvenir items). In addition to the issue of production, marketing and distribution strategies preoccupied the OTA and the Tourism Division of the GRI as they continually lobbied American authorities to raise the limits on the amount of cash Japanese could bring into Okinawa. Reversion would eventually eliminate this problem and open up large capital investments to develop tourism in general, but the issue of what kind of items qualified as Okinawa *omiyage* lingered as competition shifted from discounted foreign watches, jewelry, and golf clubs—because special tariff status for those items was discontinued upon Reversion—to army and navy surplus items and their derivatives.

In a way similar to the upgrading and commodifying of Anpo no Oka as the Michi-no-Eki Kadena roadside stop, the once truly army-navy surplus that shoppers rummaged through is now thoroughly commodified as the cool Okinawa *omiyage*. The storefront of the Americaya on Kokusai Dōri—with its oversized World War II–style aircraft nose art pinup girl sign emblazoned with "Surprise Attack!"—is probably the most conspicuous souvenir shop dealing in new and used military surplus on this main tourist drag (see figure 5.3). The allusion to the Japanese surprise attack on Pearl Harbor in the context of the army-navy surplus that American military conquest and occupation of Okinawa has brought reads as a not-so-subtle and, as Ruth Ann Keyso suggests, insensitive jab, but against whom is not clear. Keyso's account of her first reaction to Okinawa begins with a description of the store and its contents:

> My initial reaction to Okinawa was shock. The shops surrounding the U.S. military bases and lining Kokusai Dōri [International Street] in Naha, the island's capital, were disturbing reminders of Okinawa's past. "Surprise Attack!" one colorful sign read, luring shoppers inside with displays of military surplus items, from shiny silver dog tags to key rings and cup holders made from glinting brass bullet casings. Crowding the sidewalks in front of other stores were racks of camouflage jackets and pants and stacks of olive-green helmets, exhibits that appeared to taunt the islanders, forcing them to remember their island's wartime past. The insensitivity of those displays on an island that had suffered such heavy human losses struck me.[21]

Putting Keyso's shock at and assessment of the effect of such displays aside—she does not take into account that most of these displays are willingly done by "the islanders" themselves, many of whom also willingly and actively

**Figure 5.3.** Americaya army-navy surplus store, Kokusai Dōri, Naha. *Source*: Gerald Figal.

cultivate memories of Okinawa's wartime past—her description is accurate and could be applied to many other shops. What certainly stands out with a display like "Surprise Attack!"—and to some degree at all of these types of military surplus stores that target tourists—is the irony, and yet the appropriateness, involved when mainland Japanese tourists purchase U.S. military items as *omiyage* from Okinawa. The branch of Americaya (America House) in Chatan's "American Village" is an even better example of the slick marketing of military junk transformed into Okinawa *omiyage* as well as items for everyday use—the company's motto (in English, as seen in figure 5.3) is self-conscious about this transformation: "It may be junk to you but it's bread and butter to us." There is a profit to be made from recycled military cast-offs as long as there is a market for them, especially if they are proven "authentic." The frequently asked questions page on the Americaya website reveals a concern for the authenticity of the items it stocks—to the question "Are the products you handle real?" the answer is that all of the used items are authentic military surplus, but new items—such as replicas—are not.[22] Of course "real" (*honmono*) in this context means "authentic" in the sense of items produced for and used by the U.S. military. If, however, we define "real" (authentic) in the way Erve Chambers encourages—as a function of present agency over the production of an item rather than an item's past provenance or accuracy in representing the "original"—then even replicas and items newly fashioned from military gear could be thought of as "real" insofar as they represent the determination of locals to put forth certain items for tourists as emblematic of Okinawa. Travel *omiyage* practices generally require that the gift given be a specialty product of the place visited, so in this respect, tourists who buy army-navy surplus items in Okinawa for friends and relatives back home confer the status of Okinawa *meibutsu* on such goods through this specific form of consumption of them.

Many of the used surplus items that Americaya offers—in store and online—come with their own provenance, typically post–Vietnam War All-purpose, Lightweight, Individual, Carrying Equipment (ALICE) items. For example, one can purchase online for 750 yen (as of May 2010) a Vietnam-era ALICE LC-1 M-16 30-round mag (ammo magazine) pouch with hand grenade pockets. Spent ammo shells and casings are also available, as are land mine canisters, smoke grenades, and pistol belts. Among the new military-related items for purchase are jewelry fashioned from bullet shells, dog tags, unit insignia patches, replica World War II–era Zippo lighters, aviator shades, bomber jackets, body armor, suspenders, and a range of camouflage apparel from standard-issue fatigues to bikinis and mini-tees. Camo-wear, along with Okinawa's version of aloha wear, is in fact a distinct sartorial subculture associated with Okinawa. It can be seen and purchased in shops around bases and on Kokusai Dōri and even in general gift shops at non-military-related sightseeing spots. Although they are not exclusively marketed to tourists as souvenirs—local residents and Americans based on Okinawa also purchase them—mainland Japanese visitors, particularly the younger ones, treat them as one of the *meibutsu*, alongside coral jewelry, sugar cane candy, and mythological *shiisā* (lion-dog) figures, that qualify as *omiyage* for themselves and friends and relatives. One will never see a U.S. LC-1 M-16 mag pouch or camo mini-tee among the souvenirs typically advertised in Okinawa tourist literature, but in day-to-day tourist practices on the street, that is what they effectively are. Again, the "parallel worlds of bases and tourism" find themselves fully enmeshed in a way one never sees in the words and images of official tourism promotion. As with the tropical adornments to Ryukyu heritage sites, it is not uncommon to see camo-wear side by side with aloha wear, or palm trees and hibiscus motifs mixed among dog tags and combat boots in addition to live palm trees lining base perimeters.

What is one to make of this arguably crass commodification of things military? Keyso's reaction—shock and opprobrium—is understandable, but it is formed from a predetermined notion of what should and should not be appropriate given Okinawa's history of wartime tragedy, and it rests on surface appearances. It is a reaction that offers no real analysis. I would rather encourage consideration of this phenomenon within historical, cultural, and socioeconomic contexts—not to forgive it but to understand it as a strategy of making do with what is on hand and, in this case, placing some control over it to one's own advantage. I do not think one can automatically assume that military surplus qua souvenir represents, for example, a glorification of war or even an insensitive gesture toward war survivors and their descendants. The first context to consider is Okinawa's long history of accommodating and even profiting from relations with stronger foreign powers as a survival strategy. Transforming surplus military items into souvenirs for tourists to buy and take home rather than adding them to landfill or paying to dispose of them some other way is arguably an economic benefit, even if perceived by some as culturally insensitive. Until that artillery range near one's neighborhood is removed, the spent shells it produces might as well to be put to some kind of productive use, economic, artistic, or otherwise. One is reminded here of the plight of the desperate and pushy flower sellers at the Himeyuri and other war memorial sites whose means for scraping together a living came under attack by sightseers as rude and disrespectful. Dire straits do not forgive rude or insensitive marketing as such, but outright condemnation without regard for contexts is equally problematic. Likewise, if a bricolage-like *champuru* such as that idealized by the Nenes in the song "America Dōri" is a live cultural practice, then that local context needs to be acknowledged and understood before appropriateness is judged. Outside of some local residents, little complaint is heard about the inauthenticity of transplanted nonnative tropical foliage, a testament to the power of expectations of the tourist gaze that preempts any questioning of the landscape—from the position of the mainland Japanese traveler, Okinawa is *nangoku* and thus *should* have palm trees and other exotic South Seas flora. The transposition of a South Pacific or Hawaiian image—itself idealized—onto Okinawa is thus naturalized. One could argue the same case with respect to the effective integration of the American military presence into aspects of Okinawa tourism, whether it is advertised in mainstream tourism promotional literature or not. This phenomenon is the result of Okinawa's reputation as host to the majority of U.S. bases in Japan, a reputation that also feeds the expectations of mainland tourists, many of whom regard this military presence positively among the exotic sights Okinawa has to offer rather than as a security risk and impediment to travel. Only in the months immediately following 9/11 was there an overtly negative reaction to the U.S. presence, which manifested itself as a drop in visitors to Okinawa. By the following year, numbers had recovered to their pre-9/11 levels and continued their steady ascent toward 5 million visitors per year, a goal that the prefectural government had set years earlier and finally crossed in 2003. The next milestone targeted, 6 million, is projected for 2012.[23] The vast majority of that number will visit Shuri Castle Park, go to a beach if not stay at a beach resort, see at least one World War II–related tourist site, and run into the U.S. military in some form. There is a good chance that among their photos and souvenirs one will find a melange of Tropical Okinawa, Ryukyu Okinawa, and Anpo Okinawa. And each one will be considered by tourists as a token of an authentic Okinawa experience.

Thus, in spite of the official public treatment of American military bases in Okinawa, which does not include them in the tourist landscape, they and their personnel remain de facto tourist attractions. As such, they are another instance of the abiding impact of the Battle of Okinawa and its legacies on the production and consumption of (Tourist) Okinawa. While the fascination with the U.S. military presence is often parlayed into advancing education about Okinawa's situation as principal host to U.S. forces in Japan—as in school field trips and peace tours orchestrated by teachers and activists—it also carries consequences for Okinawa's reputation and its inhabitants. Lessons taught to school groups are eclipsed by the flash of military hardware; visual spectacle can trump thoughtful reflection and engagement; fetishization of military surplus items can lead to questionable taste in souvenirs to the point of offending onlookers. However, recognizing bases as among the sites that distinguish contemporary Okinawa in their now rooted material presence is not only intellectually honest; it also opens up new and more nuanced channels for understanding and critiquing their position and role in Okinawan everyday life. There is no denying that the bases have shaped postwar Okinawan culture and landscape in general and the development and practice of tourism in particular, despite efforts to keep them out of mainstream tour guidebooks. Some of the ways that U.S. military culture has manifested itself within Okinawa tourism certainly deserve criticism for trivializing warfare, exploiting stereotypes, and glamorizing weapons and their use. But dogmatically dismissing all attempts by local businesses, private organizations, and individuals to find accommodations—however unpleasant to some—to make the best of a difficult situation over which they have little control shows an insensitivity to contexts and forgoes attempts at understanding. The extended U.S. military presence in Okinawa joins a long history of Okinawans dealing flexibly with foreign powers in the Ryukyus and concomitantly cultivating a practice of mixing cultural elements and making the product their own. To some observers inside and outside Okinawa, such contact and accommodation constitute complicity with occupiers and blunts political opposition to the bases or at least signals a passive acceptance of an unfortunate status quo. One can cringe at crass souvenirs (as I have), and one should condemn brothels that have spun from the base-related prostitution business and attract male Japanese tourists. Rapes and other violence perpetrated by military personnel against the local population and tourists alike should be prosecuted vigilantly and protested vigorously. I do not think, however, such things out-of-hand preclude exploiting the bases as tourist sights while they are there. Or, at the very least, if and how they are exploited should perhaps be included in general discussions on the best use of resources, and that "best use" might not be limited to the economic but might also make calculations of social, political, and cultural value as well. I can understand why such Japanese consumption of U.S. bases as tourist sights in Okinawa happens. For better or for worse, and against protestations claiming otherwise, they do contribute significantly to the transformation of Okinawa from mere place to destination, a fundamental prerequisite for any kind of tourism development anywhere.

Finally, seeing Anpo Okinawa as intersecting, not paralleling, Tourist Okinawa invites a view of high-end beach resorts as types of bases themselves—established beachheads, if you will—that launch their own kind of invasion upon Okinawan space (physical, cultural, social). Although their guests, like those at military bases, rotate in and out, the physical and institutional presence of beach resorts is, since the resort-building boom of the late 1980s and early 1990s, virtually permanent and ironically complements U.S. military installations. In this sense too, I see greater integration, or least complementarity, between beaches and bases than other commentators have seen. The next chapter examines the extent and effects of this complementarity.

## NOTES

1. For an overview of the land issue, see Kensei Yoshida, *Democracy Betrayed: Okinawa under U.S. Occupation* (Bellingham: Center for East Asian Studies, Western Washington State University, 2002), 41–75; Ōta Masahide, *Essays on Okinawa Problems* (Gushikawa City, Okinawa: Yui Shuppan, 2000), 139–55.

2. Okinawa Kankō Kyōkai, *Okinawa kankō jū shūnen shi* (Naha: Okinawa Kankō Kyōkai, 1964), 19.

3. "Kankō eiga shinario," 1962, OPA R00070386B.

4. After twelve years of using the "B yen" note under U.S. occupation, Okinawa was switched to the U.S. dollar in 1958 until the end of the occupation. For details and photographs of Okinawa's changing currencies, see Yamauchi Masanao, *Sengo Okinawa tsūka hensen shi: Beikoku tōji jidai o chūshin ni* (Naha: Ryūkyū Shinpō, 2004).

5. James E. Roberson, "Uchinā Pop: Place and Identity in Contemporary Okinawan Popular Music," in Laura Hein and Mark Selden, eds., *Islands of Discontent: Okinawan Responses to Japanese and American Power* (Lanham, MD: Rowman & Littlefield, 2003), 202–3.

6. Senge Tetsuma, *Okinawa kankō shindan hōkoku sho*, OPA T00009152B, 49.

7. Tada, *Okinawa imēji no tanjō*, 3–5.

8. I have tagged along on parts of many school field trips in Okinawa, observing behavior and listening to conversation among students.

9. The official U.S. Air Force fact sheet and poster for the 2008 event is available at http://www.kadena.af.mil/library/factsheets/factsheet_print.asp?fsID=12644&page=1. The final AmericaFest before 2001 took place in the shadow of an investigation of a U.S. airman accused of raping a local woman two days before. At the 2009 festival a sixty-two-year-old local man choked to death on a hot dog after it took sixteen minutes for emergency vehicles to cross the base from Okinawa City (Koza). David Allen, "Local Man Dies at AmericaFest; Okinawa Ambulance Delay Decried," *Stars and Stripes*, http://www.stripes.com/article.asp?section=104&article=63619 (accessed April 20, 2010).

10. This particular tourist site on Kakazu Heights is where Japanese government officials who visit Okinawa to inspect the Futenma base are inevitably taken by Ginowan's mayor. At the time of this writing, the last such visit was in April 2010 by members of the Lower House of the Diet.

11. The third bus company that runs sightseeing routes, Naha Bus, has a standard southern tour and two northern routes (one is longer than the other and passes through more base areas).

12. A pamphlet advertising the current Naha-Shuri and Chūbu courses is at http://www.okinawabus.com/top/kikaku-tour.html (accessed April 22, 2010).

13. For the details of the rape and an examination of its impact on Okinawa society, politics, and gender relations, see Linda Isako Angst, "The Rape of a Schoolgirl: Discourse of Power and Gendered National Identity in Okinawa," in Hein and Selden, *Islands of Discontent*, 135–57.

14. A copy of SACO's Final Report is available online at http://www.mofa.go.jp/region/n-america/us/security/96saco1.html (accessed April 22, 2010).

15. Okinawa Bus Company Chū-hokubu tour guide script, transcribed and translated from original document read in company study room, Naha, June 14, 2001.

16. Interview with Shiroma Sachiko, Okinawa Bus Company, Naha, June 14, 2001.

17. Woodland was convicted in a Naha district court on March 28, 2002, and received a sentence of thirty-two months in jail.

18. Ishihara Masaie, sociologist and historian at Okinawa International University, related to me in June 2001 his stealth recording of tour bus guide narrations on the Southern Battlefield Tour in the early 1970s and subsequent criticisms of them for their uncritical stance toward Japan's aggressive war. His campaign to improve the historical quality of the scripts has paid off—tour guide trainer Shiroma Sachiko of Okinawa Bus acknowledges having benefited from Ishihara's research and input in crafting more historically informed scripts.

19. Interview with Takushi Katsuo of the Okinawa Convention & Visitors Bureau, Naha Office, May 25, 2001.

20. Okinawa Kankō Kyōkai, *Okinawa kankō jū shūnen shi*, 46.

21. Ruth Ann Keyso, *Women of Okinawa: Nine Voices from a Garrison Island* (Ithaca, NY: Cornell University Press, 2000), viii.

22. Americaya Frequently Asked Questions: http://www.americaya-int.co.jp/contents/faq/index.html (accessed April 20, 2010).

23. Kakazu Hiroshi, *Island Sustainability: Challenges and Opportunities for Okinawa and Other Pacific Islands in a Globalized World* (Bloomington, IN: Trafford Publishing, 2009), 220.

# 6

# Beach Resort Invasion

Beach" and "resort" are practically synonymous with "Okinawa" to the younger generation of Japanese in the same way that "Battle of Okinawa" and "base issue" are to their elders. Whether expressed among the mainland high schoolers on field trips who come decked out in shorts, sandals, and sunglasses or asserted on travel posters and in mass media, the image of sunbathers on white-sand beaches, water sports in a blue-green sea, and poolside tropical drinks at a resort hotel forms the foreground for present-day Okinawa even when its background of war history and military bases is occasionally in the spotlight. As natural as "the beach" might seem, however, it has a history as a concept, a tourist destination, and built environment, especially when groomed into a "resort." As Lena Lenček and Gideon Boskar remind us, the beach as a place to go to for leisure in the form of sunbathing, swimming, surfing, and so on is a modern phenomenon: "In fact, it took hundreds of years for the seashore to be colonized as the pre-eminent site for human recreation. Although the coast was the birthplace of history, before it could be transformed into a theater of pleasure, it had to be discovered, claimed, and invented as a place apart from the messy business of survival."[1] "Colonized" is a particularly appropriate choice of words when describing the history and present state of the beach resort invasion that has taken place in post-Reversion Okinawa.

Internationally, premodern attitudes about the sea and seashore among Europeans and Americans—that the shore was a place of business, harvest, and danger with perhaps occasional medicinal immersions and moments of religious and artistic inspiration—shifted by the early twentieth century to the increasingly willing embrace of the beach as a site for healthful recreation. Overcoming old myths about liminal coastlines and fears about salt water, sea creatures, and sun exposure and creating new ones with the eighteenth-century European "discovery" and subsequent romanticization of South Pacific islands, upper-class trendsetters led the way to the grooming of the shore as beach resort, a place of recreation and relaxation. The idea of a "resort" was hinged on shifting attitudes about the health benefits of a sojourn by the shore, away from influences of industrialized cities, and expanded to include a range of leisure amenities and entertainments. Some nineteenth- and early-twentieth-century entrepreneurs—often connected to rail companies—invested in high-end resort building in complexes of hotels, restaurants, clubs, casinos, and manicured parcels of sand from the French and Italian rivieras to Palm Beach, Florida, while others developed more popularly oriented facilities and entertainments aimed at middle-class markets of day-trippers at places within easy rail travel from large cities, as in the case of Britain's Brighton Beach, New Jersey's Atlantic City, and New York's Coney Island. Once legitimated by medical doctors, scientists, and celebrities, the beach resort joined the ranks of leisure destinations for mainly upper-class Westerners before "the beach" was popularized as a simpler and less expensive destination for middle-class vacationers. In most every instance, the earlier romantic image of a palm-lined white-sand stretch of shoreline along azure South Pacific seas shaped both the expectations and the landscaping of beach resorts outside the South Pacific. Hawaii, to which Okinawa tourism developers frequently turned, probably has best manifested this vision, although rows of palms—that convenient signifier and artifice of the tropical—grace beaches across all latitudes that will sustain them.[2]

The case of beaches in postwar Okinawa is doubly complicated and the cultivation of its beaches as resort sites doubly difficult: cultural and social relations with the seashore from the premodern to modern eras remained largely defined by spiritual beliefs and "the messy business of survival"; and, more immediately, the images of beaches burnished in the minds of the postwar generation were hellish rather than paradisiacal—these were beaches of invasion and death. Lenček and Boskar note that whereas the darkness of the Great War helped stimulate a popular social, cultural, and physical interest in the sun as a source of vitality during the 1920s, World War II turned some of the world's most beautiful beaches "into death traps, where thousands of men were mowed down, ripped apart, and incinerated by the most modern tools of destruction."[3] Beaches throughout the Atlantic and Mediterranean were no longer resort havens; Pacific islands—Iwo Jima, Guadalcanal, New Guinea, the Marianas, Okinawa—had their beaches strewn with corpses. Beach landings and beachheads—not beach resorts—made headlines. From the massive landing on the west-facing beaches of Okinawa—specifically on a several-mile-long stretch from Yomitan to Chatan—on April 1, 1945, to the messy mop-up operations among seaside caves along the coast of Mabuni in late June and July, whatever favorable associations Okinawan beaches may have previously had were dashed. In the aftermath, amusements on "sacred ground" in the southern part of Okinawa Island were considered in bad taste if not outright sacrilegious; establishing swimming beaches along the coast where the enemy had come ashore seemed out of place (although, as we will see, beach resorts would come to Yomitan). While the shoreline to the north did not suffer the same wartime fate, the idea of "the beach"—let alone a "beach resort"—required an active refashioning and reorientation of what a shoreline meant and how it should be used in the wake of wartime devastation. The beaches and resorts in Okinawa that today are taken for granted required for their emergence the grooming of both material and conceptual foundations.

## TEACHING THE BEACH UNDER U.S. OCCUPATION

One of the main points of advice appearing in Senge Tetsuma's 1962 assessment of tourism prospects in Okinawa is the development of swimming beaches. In surveying the coastal areas, Senge expresses astonishment that there is such a dearth of public swimming beaches. Much of Okinawa's coast, he points out, possesses gentle surf, coral reefs, and white sand—ideal for attracting vacationers. The few public beaches he names—Imbu Beach, Moon Beach, Nashiro Beach—represent a small fraction of the potential even when taking into account the recreational beaches (Ishikawa and Okuma) that the U.S. military reserved for its personnel. He explicitly compares Okinawa's long swimming season (April to November) to that of Hawaii and describes it as having "great appeal" to mainland Japanese, who have about two months during which ocean waters on mainland beaches are comfortably swimmable. Although he does not use the word "resort"—a word not in great currency at the time—he clearly envisions and encourages the development of the kind of longer-term beach resort present at Waikiki by that time. "As in the case of Honolulu that has developed centrally around swimming and surfing, how about Okinawa too taking the plunge and planning for the construction of new seashore tourist destinations designed ideally around selected sites suitable for swimming to establish newly conceived, comprehensive facilities having inns, restaurants, shopping and various entertainments? In order to extend the current 4-night, 5-day sightseeing tourism, I think it best to consider such methods; to make Okinawa Japan's Hawaii and draw large numbers of tourists, it seems that this kind of big thinking is needed."[4] Senge then continues to criticize the concentration of hotels in Naha and concomitant neglect of the coastal areas. With the rare exception of the Moon Beach Hotel (discussed below), the very idea of the beach as a place to stay and center one's leisure activities appeared alien to Okinawa tourism planners in the early 1960s, whereas to the mainland observer, it was an obvious way to develop, given the natural conditions. The physical prerequisites were there; it was the concept—and capital outlay—that were lacking.

A survey of Okinawa Tourism Association (OTA) documents, issues of the trade journal *Kankō Okinawa*, and early tourism guidebooks confirm this neglect of beach development in pre-Reversion Okinawa. Imbu Beach in north-central Okinawa, for example, ranked among locals as probably one of the most popular—if only one of the few—public beaches. It is mentioned only a few times in OTA records of the late 1950s and early 1960s, and in those cases it is in the context of upgrading the public restrooms there and making certain they include Western-style toilets to accommodate the large number of foreign visitors.[5] Over ten years' worth of *Kankō Okinawa* contains only a few passing mentions of Imbu Beach, the most telling of which is a short July 1965 article titled "Let's Talk about Swimming in Okinawa." The piece begins by noting the recent steep rise in the number of mainland visitors to Okinawa and, among them, an increasing number of students and youngsters. In response to this trend, the article reports, the Showa Tourism Company began offering an alternative to the usual pattern of staying in a Naha hotel and making day trips along established bus tour courses. Rather than going first to a city hotel, visitors would take a Showa Tourism bus directly to Imbu Beach, where the company had previously established a campground. Though not exactly providing a stay at a beach resort, this option was offered as only a one-night, two-day package and targeted the more outgoing younger set, which could not afford a more expensive hotel and desired direct access to a swimming beach. A small photo accompanying the article displays not the campground but instead lounging U.S. military personnel with an ice chest of beer in the foreground and indistinct figures—probably Okinawans—manning a boat in the background. The captions reads, "Gaijin mo nakayoku" (The foreigners too are amicable). The photo of sunbathing off-duty U.S. marines and the article's encouragement of camping and swimming at Imbu and other beaches have the effect of suggesting that these foreigners know how to enjoy the beach as beach, and Japanese should learn from—not fear—them.[6] A similar presentation of a beach in *Kankō Okinawa*—one of only a few photos of any kind of a beach scene in a journal full of photos—appeared on the cover of a special issue on Ishikawa City in May 1959. Showing the curve of Ishikawa Beach over a barbed-wire fence, the explanation of the cover photo states that as a beach procured for use by American military personnel, it is outfitted with swimming areas, tennis courts, a baseball diamond, showers, and so on, for exclusive weekend use by Americans: "When Ryukyuans see these facilities they realize enviously that Americans are indeed a people who enjoy daily life. It's regrettable that Ryukyuans are forbidden entrance."[7] In contrast to Americans, the caption implies, Okinawans do not really know how to take full advantage of the beach as a modern leisure venue, although they certainly have a deep historical and cultural engagement with the sea and shore. In turn, they are not fully attuned to grooming Okinawa's beaches for modern leisure seekers such as the younger generation of Japanese tourists. The attempts made were, as at Imbu Beach, limited in scope. For example, Nashiro Beach in Itoman to the south underwent improvements to establish it as a "new tourist site" much like what the Americans had at Ishikawa Beach. The first phase, completed in August 1961, comprised a swimming area, showers, toilets, rest shelters, and a convenience store. Later it was planned to add tennis courts and a baseball field. Notably, the author reporting this development concludes by opining, "If tropical [*nangokuteki*] flora such as cactus, *adan*, palms, *deigo* were planted and facilities expanded, it would probably become Okinawa's top bathing beach."[8] A vision of a tropical beach resort without the high-end hotel exists in these comments, but at this time more typical images of the seaside in tour books were not of swimmers in the surf but rather of Itoman City's famed fishermen plying their trade. "The messy business of survival" still dominated the definition of the shore and was reflected in how it was presented to visitors.

The one exception to the state of beach development in pre-Reversion Okinawa is Moon Beach, a crescent that opens out onto the East China Sea along the coast of Onna Village. Originally land reserved for American military use, businessman and then president of Okisan Corporation, Heshiki Yoshihisa, formed the Tsuki no Hama Suiyokujō (Moon Beach) Corporation and obtained permission to purchase approximately three acres in 1956 to realize his plans for a "modern tourist site" on the beach. The gated for-pay, private bathing beach that opened to much fanfare in July 1957 boasted a well-groomed white-sand beach, coconut palms and tropicalesque flora, showers, restrooms, lockers, changing rooms, a "luxury" Western restaurant, a Japanese-style restaurant, and a game room.[9] It is featured in one of the Okinawa Tourism Association's earliest guides to Okinawa, where it is described alongside a small photo as "Okinawa's one and only bathing beach" with "sand so white it hurts the eyes."[10] The same guide does indicate Ishikawa and Okuma beaches as bathing spots, but both were for exclusive use by Americans. A self-consciously created "manmade beach" (as its detractors pointed out), Moon Beach fit more squarely within the modern concept of "the beach" as leisure site. Both Showa Bus and Okinawa Bus began to run daily direct express service from Naha to Moon Beach after it opened. Entrance fee to the beach was ten yen, a relatively large sum for Okinawans at the time who could swim for free at no-frills public beaches, so Moon Beach struggled to attract the locals who were among the target customers. Initially without on-site overnight accommodations, it was also difficult to draw mainland tourists who were not inclined to spend half a day of their limited sojourn in Okinawa on the bus to and from Moon Beach. After its opening as a private bathing beach, other such ventures—none with any lasting impact—were attempted along Okinawa's seashore. All faced the problem of being caught between Okinawans unwilling to pay for access to the sea, which had always been free, and mainland tourists based in Naha hotels unwilling to trek to a beach up the coast that was outside established sightseeing routes. Nevertheless, Moon Beach was then and is now looked upon as a pioneering beach resort, finally adding to its grounds the Hotel Moon Beach in 1975 in time for the International Marine Exposition (Expo '75). With a hotel on the beach and a critical mass of mainland visitors after Reversion, Moon Beach proved the viability of a Waikiki-like beach resort in Okinawa and maintained a lead in such accommodations until the great wave of resort building in the late 1980s and early 1990s. Having to compete in recent years with the more well-appointed and up-to-date resorts up and down Okinawa Island's west coast, Moon Beach has somehow survived through ownership changes, renovations, and smart marketing that now includes the site's nostalgic history as "Okinawa's first resort" as a selling point.[11]

The exception of Moon Beach aside, the visual presentation of Okinawa's seashore before Expo '75, while central to the place's image as a destination, notably lacked the element of leisurely engagement with sand and water. When guide books and promotional material from this period depict the coastline, it is as scenic natural beauty viewed from afar—it is something to look at, not luxuriate in—or as workplace for local fishermen or occasionally as sacred space for native religious practices. In fact, the earliest postwar sightseeing guides make little distinction in general between showcasing sites of natural, historical, or cultural interest on the one hand and exhibiting industrial and manufacturing progress on the other. The 1955 and 1956 editions of *Ryūkyū no bussan to kankō* (Products and Sightseeing in Ryukyu) published by the Government of the Ryukyu Islands (GRI) look and read like reports on Okinawa's postwar recovery, first highlighting agricultural and manufactured products before moving to a section on sightseeing that is dominated by war memorials, castle ruins, shrines, and temples. The few scenic spots at the end of the 1955 guide include the famed Manzamō cliff overlooking the East China Sea, Unten Port, and Shioya Bay, all depicted from a distant perspective. The 1956 edition adds to this modest sample several photos of the fishing industry in action: fishermen landing tuna on boats, pulling up nets of oysters, and mooring boats at docks and on the beach. It also adds for the first time a photo and brief explanation of the famous annual *hārī* (dragon boat races), which originated from a ritual for fishermen to pray for safety and a plentiful catch. In other words, the seaside is portrayed as a static tableau to admire from a distance or as a workplace for fishermen. This pattern of portrayal of the Okinawan seashore in guidebooks continues throughout the pre-Reversion period, although there is a notable shift in placing primary emphasis on scenic, historical, and cultural sights over industry, manufacturing, and general infrastructural improvements, all of which still make appearances in ways not usual in tourist guidebooks. It is clear that alongside selling sightseeing spots, there is an expressed need to assure the potential visitor of Okinawa's modernity and civilization.

There is also in later publications the beginnings of framing the seashore as a place of leisure activity, thanks in part to Moon Beach's initiative and GRI chief executive Ōta Seisaku's enthusiasm for promoting Okinawa tourism during his administration (November 1959 to October 1964). The June 1960 inaugural issue of a new "colorful pictorial magazine" called *Kankō Okinawa* (subtitled/translated in English as "Sightseeing of Okinawa" and not to be confused with the trade journal *Kankō Okinawa*), which Ōta was personally involved in publishing through the Okinawa Tourism Association, displays a greater consciousness of the beach as playground than the GRI's first effort in 1955. The progression of *Kankō Okinawa*—carried by photos captioned in Japanese and English—is broken into five major sections: introduction and transportation, sightseeing spots arranged by region, tourism-related facilities, examples of major industries and shopping venues, and examples of local crafts and festivals. While there is still a notable amount of space devoted to showing off local industry qua modernity, it follows rather than precedes the focus on tourist sights and accommodations and segues into shopping venues and souvenirs. It also includes a rare example of acknowledging the U.S. military presence, albeit indirectly in the form of a large, dependent on-base housing tract looking very much like a 1950s suburban subdivision of ranch-styled homes in California. Moon Beach and Imbu Beach are highlighted in the north region section with shots not found in earlier guidebooks: lifeguard towers on the beach in the case of the former and people wading at the shoreline in the latter. Paired with the Imbu Beach photo is another depicting a smiling family unloading their car in front of one of the Imbu Beach campground cabins. A half dozen other scenic shots of the seashore—Manzamō predictably among them—complement these beach scenes, creating together a noticeably stronger impression of the beach as tourist destination than in previous publications, despite the lack of a true beach resort complex. As is frequently the case in Okinawa promotional material, however, the cover of this inaugural issue features a beautiful smiling woman dressed in formal Ryukyuan kimono and headdress accented by a hibiscus.[12]

Larger, commercially produced pre-Reversion guidebooks, as opposed to governmental or OTA-sponsored publications, display a similar stance toward beaches. While the idea of "the beach" is sensed more strongly throughout examples in the 1960s, the reality of beaches as tourist destinations was not fully pursued outside Moon Beach. The 1964 Blue Guide Book Series volume on Okinawa, for example, eschews any discussion of beaches outside those developed for use by U.S. military personnel. In fact, this guidebook represents somewhat of an anomaly among its counterparts in that it addresses the presence of U.S. bases much more frankly and at greater length than dozens of other guides from this period; as a kind of prototype of the critical *Kankō kōsu de nai* series, it offers a base-related touring course that hits Camps Zukeran, Kadena, Hansen, and Henoko, as well as Ishikawa Beach, the U.S. Army Headquarters, the Plaza House America shopping area, the base town of Koza, and, for contrast, Moon Beach.[13] Visual treatment of the seashore is limited to the usual shots of nature, ports, and scenes of fishermen working the waters. *Karā tabi* [Color Journey] *14: Okinawa*, published in 1968, contains many more truly beautiful scenic photographs of Okinawa's coastline and several of fishermen, *hārī* preparations, and the related *unjami* ritual that is conducted on Iheya Island to invoke the sea gods for prosperity and fertile fishing. Again, the emphasis is on nature, workplace, and sacred space, not on leisurely engagement with the beach. This volume, however, does distinguish itself in offering a section on Okinawa's coral reefs that includes several underwater photographs and mention of scuba diving. Marine sports such as scuba diving later become central to widening the appeal of the seashore for tourists, especially younger ones, but except among U.S. military personnel, it was a rare activity for visitors to pre-Reversion Okinawa. After Japan regained sovereignty of Okinawa Prefecture in 1972, however, radical changes occurred in the depiction and use of Okinawa's coastline—the beach was born.

## THE COLONIZATION OF OKINAWA'S BEACHES

Okinawa's reversion to Japan eliminated the bureaucratic and economic barriers to travel to the island that the United States Civil Administration of the Ryukyu Islands had imposed under U.S. occupation. Travelers from the mainland were no longer required to go through a lengthy visa process and no longer restricted to carrying a maximum of $400 cash to Okinawa.

Coupled with the general interest in the place that Reversion brought, easier access to the reclaimed prefecture rapidly accelerated the flow of mainland visitors. This context generated a fresh demand for information about Okinawa, especially for those who now seriously planned to take a trip there. It also generated a fresh demand for the tropical beach resort Okinawa that existed in the mainland Japanese imagination. Under this new mainland gaze, and with the 1975 International Marine Exposition on the horizon, the pressure was on to refashion and re-present Okinawa's seashore as "the beach" in the modern conception of seaside leisure site. Even before Expo '75 cemented the "blue sea" image to Okinawa's public identity, sightseeing guides were already at work redefining Okinawa with an orientation toward seashore in a way unseen just a few years earlier. Gone was the self-conscious concern for the portrayal of Okinawa's modern infrastructure and industry; in fact, simpler and quainter arts and crafts production was preferred, as long as visitor accommodations were clean, the service efficient, and the food palatable. This new tourist-driven search to discover Okinawa went beyond its historical culture, war memorials, souvenirs, and scenic beauty; it now included finding the beach in Japan's Hawaii.

To aid the new surge of mainland tourists to Okinawa—total numbers jumped from 203,768 in 1971 to 443,692 in 1972 and jumped again to 742,644 in 1973[14]—many new guidebooks were produced. Basic content among them varies little; differences lie in emphasis and packaging more than in fundamental content. All feature at least a few color scenic photographs before turning to black-and-white images, tables of accommodations, and maps ranging from tour routes throughout Okinawa Island to block-by-block details of shops on Kokusai Dōri. All also actively depict the seashore—the beach and its immediate water—as play and leisure space in addition to site of scenic beauty. One such guide from the early post-Reversion period, *Mensōre Uchinā* (1974), is particularly noteworthy in its attempt to be accessible and comprehensive within a compact format and in its overt inclusion of base-related content alongside beaches. Clearly targeting travelers planning to attend Expo '75, it manages to cover superficially but effectively for the average would-be tourist a wide range of material to provide a variegated cross section of Okinawa. The hand-illustrated cartoon front cover colorfully captures the breadth of content and the tone of presentation within a small 4.5-by-7-inch space (see figure 6.1). On it is a *champuru* of iconic Okinawan figures—Ryukyuan dancers, *eisā* performers, *hārī* races, bullfighting, *shīsā*, hibiscus, and palm trees—but also crowds on Kokusai Dōri, war memorial cenotaphs in Mabuni, campgrounds in Motobu, golf courses, botanical and zoological gardens, amusement parks, pineapple fields, underground caverns, the Expo '75 site, the underwater viewing platform in Nago, sailing, fishing, swimming

**Figure 6.1.** A *champuru* of Tourist Okinawa icons. *Source*: Cover of *Mensōre Uchinā*, reproduced courtesy of Gekkan Okinawasha.

beaches, and U.S. military bases. This initial hodgepodge cover, a metonym for the entire guide itself, enhances the sense of difference if not outright exoticism of Okinawa, a theme that begins in the name of the book itself, which employs the Okinawan words *mensōre* (welcome) and "Okinawa" written with standard characters but glossed with the furigana *Uchinā* (the Okinawan word for the place). After several pages of brief historical highlights of the Ryukyu Kingdom period done in manga follow face-to-face one-page graphics of the Battle of Okinawa and current U.S. bases. The text then jumps to a section on local festivals, myths, legends, ghost stories, folk music and dance, and cuisine before providing detailed lists of hotels and local transportation. Examples of local dialect and folk songs appear as appendices. These opening and ending sections serve to frame Okinawan history and culture as exotic and unfamiliar.

Within this framing appears a juxtaposition of beaches, battlefields, and bases that also impart—unwittingly, I think—a sense of the unusual even though the portrayal of beaches is normalized to modern tourist expectations regardless of the actual realities on the ground. Three shots of swimmers and sunbathers at Moon Beach, Imbu Beach, and Tiger Beach are among the set of color photographs that open the book. Unlike all previous tour guidebooks, *Mensōre Uchinā* also contains a playfully drawn "Beach Guide" manga graphic map, as if beaches have also been a central part of Okinawa tourism. The map echoes the "Distribution of Principal Military Bases" map appearing earlier in the book. Nineteen beaches are pointed out, sprinkled with illustrations of swimming, sunbathing, fishing, boating, and scuba diving. A foreground image depicts a somewhat strained black-haired and small-eyed (= Japanese?) man positioning a beach umbrella behind a taller standing blond and big-eyed (= American?) bikini-clad woman who is holding a towel innocently but suggestively over the crotch of the man's swim trunks. Three cities are indicated on the map: Naha, Nago, and the base town of Koza, the last of which includes a racial caricature of an African American nestled amid small buildings presumably representing bars and clubs frequented by U.S. military personnel. The juxtaposition of beachgoers and base personnel—although subtle on this map—is more obvious as one progresses through the rest of the guide. The section on central Okinawa contains details on the bases and base towns mentioned in passing in pre-Reversion guides and scarcely at all in later guides, which is perhaps indicative of a kind of frontier mentality in depicting Okinawa for the new wave of mainland visitors right after Reversion. A description of Gate Street leading from Kadena Air Base through Koza City—from Koza Gate (i.e., Kadena Gate No. 2) past the rows of shops and clubs that the Nenes sing nostalgically about—opens the section, painting a scene of recent pre-Reversion days full of "horizontal script signs," pawn shops, and round-the-clock activity among drunken soldiers waiting for the next paycheck.[15] Statistics about the base itself are offered before an explanation of the basic layout of the adjoining base town with its "white," "black," and "Okinawan" entertainment areas. An accompanying comic depicts the outside of a bar with an apparent streetwalker/hostess, another caricature of an African American off-duty soldier with his arm around a woman, and two other puzzled-looking males—a Caucasian soldier and a man of unspecific ethnicity in civilian clothes—looking on the scene. A two-page block-by-block street map, reminiscent of the earlier map of Kokusai Dōri, marks the location of the segregated entertainment districts and a few particular clubs and music venues. These five pages probably represent the bluntest inclusion of base-related material in a mainstream tour guide that otherwise focuses on the seaside, beaches, and marine sports more than previous guides, while still covering classic battlefield tours and local cultural attractions. The matter-of-fact appearance of this variety of seemingly incompatible items within a quick succession of pages is initially disconcerting, but the text description does not self-consciously make an issue of it. The result is a representation of Okinawa that appears intriguing, lively, foreign, and inviting in a mixed-up variety of offerings wrapped around a central image of blue sea and white-sand beaches. Notably lacking, however, are beach resorts or any kind of seaside accommodations. The small color photos of sunbathers and swimmers at Moon Beach and Ocean Park, which appear within the teaser material at the front of the book, are the closest thing to a depiction of a beach resort in the entire guide. The hotel section within the guide consists only of a utilitarian list of names, addresses, and phone numbers, without a single photo of an actual hotel—most likely because of the relative lack of seaside accommodations and high-end hotels in general at the time. While beaches were certainly being discovered, it was also being discovered that they did not fully live up to tourist expectations of "Japan's Hawaii." This situation changed radically over the following twenty years.

As Tada Osamu has argued, Expo '75—with its concerted focus on the sea in its official theme—was the single most-important event in the formation of the image of "blue sea" Okinawa. Soon after Reversion, the planning committee's basic concept for the marine expo made clear the goal to "put as much focus of the place as possible on the sea, to have the visitor subjectively experience the sea."[16] A half year before Reversion, the GRI had already decided on some kind of marine expo, and representatives from across the Ryukyus discussed ideas about it. The guiding principles and goals for such an exposition were that it would (1) be an event to commemorate Reversion, (2) make Okinawa's subtropical marine environment come alive as emblematic of the place, (3) advance the touristification of Okinawa, and (4) upgrade infrastructure. The first and fourth items were closely tied together in the sense that the return to Japanese sovereignty would bring the promise of public and private investment in the improvement of basic infrastructure (roads, waterworks, electrical, sanitation) along the lines that areas of mainland Japan experienced during the high-growth period of the 1960s. Such improvement would in turn benefit the third item, tourism development, while item two addressed the issue of branding Tourist Okinawa. Although the realization—at least in part—of these goals has been associated with Reversion and hosting of Expo '75, it is important to stress the longer historical view wherein the advancement and branding of Tourist Okinawa, as well as modest infrastructural improvement, had already been going on for over a decade and included many of the elements that the influx of mainland post-Reversion Japanese capital could better realize. In other words, despite a dearth of funding, the conception of Okinawa as a would-be "tropical paradise" and "Japan's Hawaii" was already to a large degree in place and had even been attempted on a small scale at places such as Moon Beach and the Southeast Botanical Gardens. What was lacking was mainland capital and the critical mass of a more intense and widespread tourist gaze upon Okinawa's landscape, particularly its beaches. With the advent of hundreds of thousands of mainland visitors to Okinawa, the pressure to meet their expectations increased even if those expectations existed more in fantasy than in fact. In this context, the staging of "blue sea Okinawa" and the primping and promotion of Okinawa's beaches in conjunction with the marine exposition can be seen as exercises in the creation of a themed environment and imaginary space.

Across the divide of both Reversion and Expo '75, after the initial enthusiasm from the mainland to reintegrate Okinawa as Japan's forty-seventh prefecture and improve conditions there, the Okinawa prefectural government and the reformed Okinawa Prefecture Tourism Federation took up in earnest the task of redefining Okinawa's seaside as potential tropical beach resort. In 1976 Okinawa Prefecture issued the first of a series of tourism development plans, marking out goals and guidelines for sustaining the jump start it received from hosting the marine expo. By this time "beaches" (*bīchi*) became a regular category of terrain in such official publications and received more attention than previously as a natural resource to exploit. "Resorts" (*rizōto*) too became a part of the industry lexicon with Hotel Moon Beach serving as an early (1975) precursor on Okinawa Island, joined by All Nippon Airways' (ANA) Eef Beach Resort on Kumejima to the west in the East China Sea, opened in 1977. "Beach resort" then, as now, implied blue sea and white sand wrapped in a tropical atmosphere, items Okinawa could provide even if it meant lending nature a helping hand. The *Okinawa Prefectural Plan for Tourism Landscaping and Afforestation* discussed in chapter 3 in the context of the tropicalization of "tourist-exposed" thoroughfares and public places included specifications for the floral infrastructure of beach areas as well. As one arm of the prefecture's first tourism development plan, the survey conducted in February 1979 for this report offers recommendations for landscaping along prominent shorelines throughout the prefecture, but distinguishes ports, seaside parks, and seashore (*kaigan*) from particular beaches (*bīchi*). From northern beaches such as Okuma Beach to Nashiro Beach in the south, nonnative "tropical-type" flora—notably coconut and other palms—and native tropicalesque "*adan*-type" flora dominate. Plans for the beaches of the outlying islands of Kumejima—Eef Beach in particular—and of the Kerama Islands to the west of Okinawa Island, as well as for the beaches of Miyako and the Yaeyama Islands to the south, follow a similar pattern of "tropical-type" and "*adan*-type" plants. The specification of (necessarily transplanted) coconut palms on Eef Beach is particularly conspicuous and is in line with the ANA beach resort development opened there.[17]

In contrast to the pre-Reversion period, it becomes more evident that the natural beauty praised in tourist literature dating from Expo '75 is as much built environment as it is natural resource. It is not simply a beach but rather the beach—the one existing in the mainland tourist's tropical imaginary. As Matthew Allen notes for the beaches on Kumejima, the native residents of Kumejima do not have a history of using Eef Beach or the beautiful white-sand strand of Hatenohama for leisure recreation outside early morning fishing before the arrival of tourists.[18] The local residents' daily experience of the island is worlds away from the "island experience" manufactured for tourist consumption. Likewise, the actual condition of natural beaches often does not match the image of them presented in promotional literature, especially during this early period of post-Reversion development. As resort development accelerated and matured following the 1988 Resort Law (discussed below), the cosmetic improvement of resort beaches intensified in an attempt to fulfill mainland expectations of what a southern beach resort paradise should be. In this context, the dilemma for Okinawa tourism promoters was—and still is—how to reconcile the physical reality of Okinawa with its media image, how to sell an "authentic" Okinawan experience of environment, culture, and history while meeting familiar standards of comfort, convenience, and recreation. By the 1980s, in the midst of Japan's bubble economy boom, Okinawa Prefecture had fully embraced the beach resort concept, backed by the major airline carriers All Nippon Airways and Japan Air Lines (JAL), both of which established *keiretsu* business affiliations with local Okinawan tourism companies leading to beachheads in major resort development throughout Okinawa Prefecture.[19] The economies of scale that ensued brought forth the standardization of package tours (flight and accommodations), hurting independent inns and hotels that have since then struggled to compete with the newly built beach resorts dotting the coastline.[20]

One mid-1980s guidebook published by the Okinawa Prefecture Tourism Federation (Okinawa Kankō Renmei, successor to the pre-Reversion Okinawa Tourism Association) is representative of this accelerated trend in branding and marketing Okinawa. *Okinawa: Minami wa, rizōto paradaisu* (Okinawa: The South, Resort Paradise, 1984) buries the war-related and historical sightseeing that used to be foregrounded in Okinawa tourism promotion. In its place is an unabashed display of beach resorts, marine sports, and tropical flora sprinkled with Okinawan icons (Shureimon, *shīsā*, red-tiled roofs, *bingata*, Ryukyu dance) and bikinied young women posing with snorkeling gear and fishing harpoons or else simply sunbathing or smiling invitingly at the reader. The brief four-page section on the southern part of Okinawa Island—what used to headline as the Southern Battle Sites Tour—is incongruously introduced by a photo of an aggressively posed, harpoon-wielding woman smiling at the reader against a backdrop of crystal-clear azure sea that is likely not found anywhere in the area. The list of sightseeing spots above her includes only a skeletal version of the traditional Southern Battle Sites Tour—the Naval Headquarters Cave, the Okinawa Peace Memorial Hall, the Himeyuri Memorial, and the Reimei-no-tō and the original Peace Memorial Museum in Mabuni. Small photos of these sites, spread across the upper half of two facing pages, are eclipsed by the block of blue sea across the lower half against which the Okinawa Battlefield National Park is advertised in five short lines of copy. Two of those lines make prominent mention of the hibiscus and bougainvillea that bloom there, as if to reassure the potential visitor that bright tropicality can be found even within the somber setting of battlefields and war memorials.

The use of young women—as hosts and guests, typically in swimsuits or light summer wear—from cover to cover in this guidebook is overwhelming. Sixty of eighty photo-filled pages and all but three pairs of facing pages include at least one young woman, usually more. In other words, the reader encounters an image of a young woman in all but three page turns before reaching the utilitarian, monochromatic "Okinawa Information Guide" of timetables, transportation maps, and lists of accommodations and fares. The one prominent model—the one posed in a bikini with diving gear and harpoons—serves as a kind of virtual companion for the reader in her eight major appearances in different sections throughout the guidebook. At times she is functionally replaced by a cartoon drawing of a young woman done in typical manga style with light brown hair, round eyes, and blushed cheeks, thus appearing more Caucasian than Japanese. The majority of the other young women depicted in the guide—appearing to be in their late teens and twenties—are pairs of visitors enjoying together everything from tennis and kayaking to dining and sunbathing. A few solo women are also depicted sunbathing on beaches, walking the shoreline, and lounging on seaside decks with "tropical" drinks. Even when marine sports like parasailing and catamaran sailing are depicted, women hold the foreground. The few men in this guidebook serve as background material. Local men are shown in bullfighting matches, in an *eisā* performance, and in a *hārī* boat race—all strongly gendered male events—while unidentifiable men (locals and/or mainland Japanese) appear alongside women at a roller-skating rink, a disco, and a golf course. Male-female couples as such are virtually nonexistent: there is one small photo of a young couple on a golf green and, interestingly, two more-mature couples shown intently examining exhibits within the Naval Headquarters Cave. In the case of the latter, the man, camera slung around his neck and one arm around the woman's shoulder, has the active role of pointing at and explaining something to the woman, presumably his wife, judging by their age and conservative dress. The message conveyed in this photo is that serious historical tourism is gendered male and done by older, more staid people. The beach and the leisure activities associated with it are the domain of active young women—and the young men who might gaze upon them.

The gaze implicit in *Okinawa: Minami wa, rizōto paradaisu* raises the issue of its target audience and marketing strategy. The target is clearly the younger, active set—and those wishing to identify with youth—seeking seaside activities in a modestly exotic but comfortable, tropical atmosphere. Cute and sexualized images of young women work to grab the attention of the heterosexual male viewer while also providing models on which potential female visitors can project their desires, especially when the women depicted are in the position of tourists freely enjoying a wide variety of leisure activities. The front cover alone captures the mix of venues, activities, tropicalia, and exotica detailed within and waiting for the would-be traveler: snorkeling, windsurfing, white-sand beaches, poolside lounging, *shīsā* on an old red-tiled roof, a jungle of palm trees, and an oversized red hibiscus burst from the page and over the Okinawa Tourism Federation logo that is composed of a silhouette of Shureimon floating on stylized waves, suggesting that Shuri Castle as seat of the Ryukyu Kingdom had the sea as its foundation and signaling that the sea has joined Shureimon as symbol of Okinawan hospitality. The 1984 ANA Okinawa campaign girl—identified only as "Miniyon, residing in Hawaii, age fifteen"—meets the reader on the inside cover with that year's tagline—"kai, kai, karada ga waratteru"—running parallel to her body stepping through the sand with ocean blurred in the background (see figure 6.2). The copy's bold white font echoes her white bikini, graphically asserting the connection between the word *karada* (body) and the girl's body. The tagline itself might

**Figure 6.2.** Sea, sand, and hot smiling bodies (1984 ANA Okinawa Campaign ad). *Source*: Inside front cover of *Okinawa*: *Minami wa rizōto paradaisu*.

be rendered literally as something like "pleasingly warm, the body's smiling/laughing," but that does not begin to unpack the puns and suggestion typical of much Japanese ad copy. The character 快 (*kai*) can denote a pleasurably warm sensation (usually written adjectivally as 快い, *kokoroyoi*) resulting from balmy weather, but more generally it can be a nice, pleasing (warm) feeling stemming from emotional rather than physical warmth. There are also undertones of sexual desire in the pleasure felt—the English idiomatic use of "hot" for "sexy" comes close in this instance. *Kai* is also homonymic with the character for sea, 海, which is pictured in the background upon which 快 is written. The pleasing feeling (*kai*) is thus identified with the sea (*kai*). This wordplay can be extended further with the close resemblance of *kaikan* (快感, pleasurable feeling; also, in a sexual context, orgasm) to *kaigan* (seashore), which the campaign girl is walking along while her smiling face and upper body are turned to the viewer. Doubling *kai* also lends it an onomatopoeic dimension, as if *kai kai* is the sound of the smiling/laughing body. Placed parallel to the girl's body and against the sea, this tagline creates a series of associations swirling around sea, sand, and sex. Okinawa qua Hawaii is even slipped in with the reference to the campaign girl's place of residence. If it were not already clear that this is an Okinawa for the youthful, the ANA ad has a bright yellow stamp (mimicking a *hankō* chop) that reads in black letters "OKINAWA Seishun Burando" (OKINAWA Youth Brand). Within ten years, the seemingly innocuous and nature-oriented Expo '75 blue sea theme had metastasized into an unabashed branding of Okinawa as a "hot" beach resort haven through sophisticated and well-financed Okinawa tourism-promotion campaigns engineered by the private and public sectors and joint partnerships between them (in what constitutes the "third sector" in the Japanese context since the 1980s.)[21]

The ANA Okinawa campaigns that ultimately produced this branding of Okinawa began as soon Okinawa reverted to Japan in 1972 and intensified after the marine expo within the broader context of general tourism marketing strategies to sell Okinawa to consumers while not alienating skeptical local residents, especially those who had previously opposed the idea of the marine expo on the grounds that it would bring unwanted and unsustainable (over)development. To achieve this goal, the advertising giant Dentsū, which was responsible for the Okinawa campaign's media image, initially appealed to the locals' pride in their (premodern) history and culture as something to share with visitors instead of blatantly casting Okinawa as simply a beach resort destination. Focusing on Okinawa's longer history and cultural products, especially its Ryukyu Kingdom heritage, diminished the presence of war-related history and the U.S. military bases in tourism publications and advertisements. There was no getting around the tourist draw of the sacred ground in the south, but it was politely placed in the background, as demonstrated in *Okinawa: Minami wa, rizōto paradaisu*. While Okinawa's history and culture was being pitched to locals as reason to support the idea of Okinawa as "Japan's Hawaii," the image of Okinawa's natural environment cultivated during the marine expo was transformed into the well-manicured, picturesque, tropically themed beach resort under the umbrella concept of "Fantasia Okinawa." At the same time that Dentsū was crafting the "Discover Japan" campaign for domestic rail tourism on the mainland, it was applying the same principles to "Fantasia Okinawa," namely that the "discovery" of such travel was ultimately of one's self.[22] As the word "fantasia" suggests, the discovery of one's self in Okinawa involved dreams, imagination, romance, and life outside the everyday, according to Dentsū's campaign concept. This campaign was a call to discover one's exotic self, to experience leisure and recreation a bit outside the ordinary and even to indulge one's self in that experience.

All Nippon Airways began the use of "campaign girls" for promoting the "Tropical Okinawa" campaign in 1978, and with them came the unabashed depiction of beach resort leisure and bronzed female bodies—young women in swimsuits lounging, frolicking, and catering to a heterosexual male gaze. Campaign themes and catchphrase copy from the late 1970s to late 1980s represent variations on this basic image, worlds away from Okinawa's pre-Reversion image. The catchphrase for 1978, for example, "Moete kuru. Okinawa" (Catching fire. Okinawa) suggested warm weather, hot bodies, and the growing popularity of Okinawa as tourist destination. The "Kongari Okinawa" (Beautifully Browned Okinawa) campaign the following year explicitly focused on tanned female bodies with the catchphrase "Tōsuto musume ga dekiagaru" (The toast girl is ready), likening a tanned young woman to a piece of toasted bread coming out of the toaster. The 1980 catchphrase, "Hadaka ikkan, Makkuroneshia hito," relied on the idiom *hadaka ikkan* (with nothing but one's own naked body; i.e., stripped of all possessions) and wordplay between *makkuro* (tanned almost black) and Micronesia to connect Okinawa with a sense of primitive nakedness among South Pacific islanders (think nineteenth-century, idealized Tahitians), while displaying on the campaign poster the near nakedness of the campaign girl (and *Heibon Punch* men's magazine pinup girl) Yuki Makkente posed with fishing rod in hand. The ad understandably drew protests from Okinawans. The print advertising and television commercials ANA and its competitor JAL produced during this decade rarely deviate in theme and general appearance: long shots of unidentified strands of beach with sea-line foam or small waves in the background and a bikinied woman in the foreground. She is sometimes kicking up sand and water alone, sometimes with males trailing in hopeless longing for her suntanned body. One TV commercial in the year of the "Kai, kai, karada ga waratteru" print ads (1984) featured a woman running in slow motion in profile along the shore in ankle-deep water with two Dalmatian dogs acting as proxies for human males chasing at her side. As if to animate scenes straight out of *Okinawa: Minami wa, rizōto paradaisu*, the 1987 ANA "Sports Resort Okinawa" TV commercial promoting the newly opened ANA Manza Beach Hotel consists of quick edits of the typical bikinied young woman diving, swimming, and wind sailing, interspersed with images of her rolling in the beach sand and shallow water, with smiles and cleavage facing the camera.

The one-dimensional quality of this Okinawa tourism advertising from the major carriers that had come to spearhead resort development in Okinawa by the mid-1980s had a substantial impact on the transformation of Okinawa's seashore to "the beach" and on the transformation of the face (and body) of the people associated with Okinawa. As previously noted, rare was the depiction of a beach or sea populated by leisure-seeking tourists before this time. The seashore was a scenic, not recreational, spot, or else it was shown as the site of local work or ritual. The people who might appear in a seaside scene were nearly always Okinawans or sometimes American military and their dependents. Tourists as such had not yet colonized Okinawan beaches. The first ANA Okinawa campaign poster immediately after Reversion is revealing of this transformation from the depiction of iconic scenery and local people to the trope of the mainland tourist playing on the beach. Designed for the "Kira Kira Okinawa" (Sparkling Okinawa) campaign, it depicts a smiling, ordinary-looking woman (that is, not an obviously sexed-up mainland model) dressed in shorts and blouse splashed with a colorful Ryukyuesque pattern walking toward the viewer in ankle-deep ocean (no visible sand) and holding a large woven basket on her hip as if she's gathering seashells or kelp. It is actually a rather tasteful and gently beautiful image. Unlike the campaigns from 1978 on, there is no obvious display of sexualized suntanned female bodies lounging on the sand or frolicking in the surf. On the contrary, the "Kira Kira Okinawa" campaign has more in common with pre-Reversion images of locals happily working the seashore while at the same time foreshadowing the surf-and-skin trope of later, post–Expo '75 campaigns. The other iconic female faces of early Okinawa tourism—tour bus guides narrating the drama of battle sites, the girls of the Himeyuri Student Nurses Corps, and traditionally costumed Ryukyuan dancers—became even further removed as the mainland colonization of Okinawa tourism in general and of Okinawa's beaches in particular progressed after Reversion and through the 1980s. Only with the Ryukyu Kingdom boom that accompanied the opening of the rebuilt Shuri Castle in 1992 (see chapter 4) did one see something other than the beach and bikinis that dominated Okinawa tourism advertising during the previous decade.

## RESORT BEACHHEADS

The so-called Resort Law (officially, Sōgō Hoyōchi Seibi Hō, or the Comprehensive Health Resort Development Law) of 1987 accelerated the appearance of large, gated hotel complexes on Okinawa's shores. A record number of various resorts in general were built throughout Japan by the summer of the following year, and the floodgates were opened for the full-fledged beach resort development of some of Okinawa's most appealing shoreline, much of it along Onna Village's lengthy west-facing coast and all the way up north to Nago and the Marine Expo Park. Such development would have likely occurred over time in any case, but, as Miki Takeshi chronicled in 1990, the "trigger" for the then current resort boom in Okinawa was no doubt the Resort Law that offered developers tax incentives and a fast track for the approval of construction permits.[23] Coming at the crest of the bubble economy, the Resort Law has since been criticized for stimulating unchecked development harmful to the environment, being out of step with local development plans, and ignoring principles of supply and demand. Okinawa Prefecture's direct response to the opportunities envisioned in the Resort Law found expression in the March 1990 *Rizōto Okinawa masutā puran: Sekai ni hokoreru "toropikaru rizōto OKINAWA" no keisei o mezashishite* (Resort Okinawa Master Plan: Aiming for the Formation of a World-Class "Tropical Resort Okinawa"), discussed briefly in chapter 3 in the context of the tropicalization of Okinawa's landscape. The maps, graphs, charts, tables, and text dissecting the land, resources, and rationale for the creation of a prefecture-wide "Tropical Resort Okinawa" are as meticulous as they are idealized in their vision. From a map placing Okinawa along with Hawaii and Australia's Gold Coast as one point in a "Golden Triangle of Resorts" embracing all of the South Pacific, to a prefectural map marking fourteen resort zones from Iriomote Island to the south to Izena and Iheya islands in the north, to a very detailed map of sightseeing spots labeling all named beaches and golf courses in addition to the usual war-related and established attractions such as the Southeast Botanical Gardens and Ryukyu Mura, *Resort Okinawa Master Plan* presents a vision of a multilayered anatomy of Okinawa as one vast tourist site and presages Governor Ōta Masahide's famous "Tourism Prefecture Declaration" (*Kankō Ritsuken Sengon*) of November 1, 1995.[24]

While briefly mentioning Okinawa's cultural heritage as tourism resource and acknowledging the existence of the Peace Memorial Park zone in Mabuni and U.S. bases in the central part of Okinawa Island, the clear focus of *Resort Okinawa Master Plan* as described in text and image is the further shaping of the seashore into world-class beach resorts. The plan exemplifies what Miki identifies as the "three-point development set" for completing the transformation of Okinawa shoreline into a high-value tourism commodity after the Resort Law went into effect: hotel, beach, and marina all come to be designated under another new concept and catchphrase taken from the English—"waterfront" (*uātāfuronto*). The typical scenario of waterfront development in Okinawa involves large private developers approaching local government agencies to secure access to public land for their projects.[25] In other words, the agency, planning, and ownership of large-scale beach resort projects stem largely from outside local channels, flowing from a mainland Japanese investment source. In these cases there is minimal oversight of how the coastal space is shaped and ultimately used. As a result, beachfronts are groomed and fitted with guest facilities to meet guest expectations for a (generic) beach resort (lifeguard towers, changing rooms, refreshment stands, water sport equipment rentals, etc.) Once-public shoreline comes under the management of private enterprise, usually with majority interests based outside Okinawa Prefecture.

The other pattern of development involves public agencies having a plan that they present to a private enterprise for joint development, often through third-sector arrangements in which, in the Japanese business context, public and private sectors invest in joint corporations. The plan for Cape Busena outlined in *Resort Okinawa Master Plan* is an example of projects proposed by the state—in this case Okinawa Prefecture—and carried out by private firms. As Okinawa's primary response to opportunities opened up by the Resort Law, the plan targets as one concrete project the creation of a major world-class beach resort and international convention area on Cape Busena. Within the introductory pages of *Resort Okinawa Master Plan*, which include shots of sunbathers, swimmers, and windsurfers at Moon Beach and Manza Beach Resort, appears an aerial shot of this striking peninsula that juts out in a curve into clear blue sea just south of Nago City. The photograph is not unlike the U.S. wartime reconnaissance photos of Okinawa in its intention to size up the point of invasion. Indeed, in its presentation of data and discussion of "strategic" uses of resources, *Resort Okinawa Master Plan* appears as a civilian battle plan, shorter and more colorful but comparable to the U.S. Tenth Army Operation Iceberg plans for the invasion of Okinawa in spring 1945.

Carried out according to plan, one beachhead of a renewed invasion of resort development was established in grand fashion: the multimillion-dollar Busena Terrace Beach Resort was completed in 1997, and one of its adjunct facilities, the Bankoku Shinryōkan (Bridge between Nations Hall), was built as the convention site for the G-8 summit in 2000. Examination of photos of Cape Busena's shoreline before and after construction of Busena Terrace reveals an expansion and shaping of the beach that fronts the primary resort area. At the far end of the sandy strand are a small marina, pier, and boathouse to dock glass-bottom boats that tour the surrounding sea and are open to the general public. Just across the shuttle bus road that encloses the beach are an expansive palm-lined swimming pool complex, tennis courts, and putting greens before one reaches clusters of high-end cottages and hotel rooms. The effect of the sea, beach, stands of palm trees, manicured hibiscus hedges, and plantings of other tropicalesque foliage is truly stunning—the picture-postcard image of a world-class beach resort. The only other thing that visibly remained the same on Cape Busena from before construction is the Underwater Observation Tower that extends from the tip of the cape. A joint project funded and carried out by the Government of Japan, the Government of the Ryukyu Islands, and the Okinawa Tourism Development Corporation (the GRI quasi-governmental corporation and forerunner of the Okinawa Convention & Visitors Bureau [OCVB]), the Underwater Observation Tower has been a public attraction since 1970, planned in anticipation of Reversion.[26] It and the glass-bottom boat operation now form part of Busena Marine Park, which is open to the general public despite being geographically integrated with Busena Terrace Beach Resort. The Busena Marine Park is managed by the Okinawa Convention & Visitors Bureau, which has a satellite office at the site. Founded in 1996 as the major umbrella agency for the promotion of tourism, resorts, and conventions in Okinawa Prefecture, the OCVB also manages use of the Bankoku Shinryōkan and administers the Navy Underground Headquarters site. With branch offices in Tokyo, Osaka, Fukuoka, Seoul, and Taipei, its quasi-governmental status is a prime example of an integrated public-private (*kanmin ittaigata*) organization designed to oversee and coordinate the strategic development and promotion of tourism on a prefecture-wide scale. Operating between the prefectural government and private enterprise, the OCVB can be viewed as both a facilitator of and a check on unbridled beach resort construction. However, as long as annual goals for the prefecture include topping the previous year's number of tourists, it is difficult not to see the OCVB as collaborating in the proliferation of resorts that have established multiple beachheads on Okinawa's coastline.

The comparison of beach resorts such as Busena Terrace, ANA Manza Beach Hotel, and Yomitan's Hotel Nikko Alivila to foreign bases occupying fortified footholds on strategic soil is not so far-fetched. Some beach resorts, such as Moon Beach (former site of a U.S. military sanatorium) and the JAL Private Resort Okuma (site of a U.S. military rest and recreation center), are on attractive real estate that has been occupied by both American military and Japanese business interests, continuing the complaint that quality public swimming beaches for local families are dwindling. The commercial airline approach from mainland Japan to Naha International Airport down the west coast of Okinawa Island prompts this comparison as well—after relatively low-level views of the Manza Beach Hotel and the Alivila, Kadena Air Base suddenly appears in line with its runway and approach lighting system towers aiming out into the East China Sea. The location of the Hotel Nikko Alivila in particular is provocative. Literally on the beach where American troops landed in April 1945, about four kilometers north of the present U.S. Torii Station and about a kilometer away from the infamous Chibichirigama refugee cave where eighty-two villagers died in a "compulsory group suicide" shortly after the invasion, the resort complex embraces the curve of Nirai Beach across grassy fields quite apart from the local population. One could spend one's entire time at the Alivila and any of the other large beach resorts without venturing "off base" beyond the beach compound to interact with the locals. Those who do sightsee from the Alivila benefit from the unusually well-mixed cross section of history, culture, and recreation within or adjacent to Yomitan's municipal boundaries. In addition to the aforementioned war history and U.S. military presence are the Zakimi Castle Ruins World Heritage Site, Ryukyu Mura (see chapter 4), the Yachimun-no-sato pottery village, the traditional arts and crafts center featuring local fabric production, Cape Zanpa and the nearby Zanpa Golf Club, the diving spot at Cape Maeda, and Taiken Ōkoku Murasaki Mura (Hands-on Experience Kingdom Murasaki Village, the present name of the Ryūkyū no Kaze Studio Park). All of these tourist attractions are within easy striking distance from the Alivila for half-day sorties, but there is still a sense of being safely distanced from them while "on base" at the resort in a cocoon of creature comforts.[27] And, like the U.S. military, the inhabitants of beach resorts are temporary residents from overseas, cycling in and out on tours—some of them more than once—albeit for days not months or years. Finally, as discussed in chapter 5, many mainland tourists actively seek out association with American military personnel and base culture as one of the attractions of Okinawa, searching for souvenirs at military surplus stores and mingling among Americans at well-known shopping and entertainment areas as well as at the occasional open base festival.

In its capacity of selling Okinawa to potential visitors—95 percent of whom are Japanese from the mainland—the Okinawa Convention & Visitors Bureau has had, since its founding, a major role in shaping Okinawa's media image. Its official multilingual website, *Okinawa Monogatari* (Okinawa Story), is heavy on visualizing its tagline "Okinawa blue sea blue sky" (*Okinawa aoi umi aoi sora*), the phrase that gestated during the 1960s, was born from Expo '75, and is now so closely tied to "Okinawa" as to have the effect of a registered trademark. While presenting iconic historical and cultural content such as Shuri Castle, red-tiled roofs, and traditional crafts under the title of *champuru bunka* (mixed culture), scenes of blue sea and white-sand beaches are foregrounded whenever possible and form the greatest impression to the would-be visitor. Presentation of war-related sites, on the other hand, is limited to a short paragraph on the Peace Park in the "Southern Okinawa" section, and the history of war and occupation totals two sentences in the "History" subsection of the "Getting to Know Okinawa" section. Getting to know Okinawa now is more about getting to know the "Okinawa brand" (*Okinawa burando*), a relatively recent media buzz phrase that represents a maturity in the marketing of Okinawa both as destination to visit and as product to possess. "Blue sea blue sky"—the Okinawan formulation of "the beach"—is the foundation of the brand, with sky as an extra dimension. Its most conspicuous form manifests itself in the Okinawan version of the beach resort complex in its totality of tropical landscaping, sea-centered recreation, neo-Ryukyuan fusion dining, colorful drinks, and spa treatments featuring exotic herbal concoctions. In the resorts' proliferation across prime real estate as gated compounds generally off limits to the nonpaying public, they echo the U.S. bases that perforate other prime real estate across the island. But the beach concept in this instance is also, more indirectly, the "nature" from which spring brand products—from medicinal botanicals, tropical jams, sweet potato and sugar cane confections, and local seaweed to contemporary glassware, handwoven fabrics, "aloha wear," skincare ointments, and designer furniture. The brand aura glows with something fresh, natural, and eco-friendly, invoking, if not actually derived from, native sea, soil, and sky. It sometimes gestures to the tropical, sometimes to the Ryukyuan, sometimes to both.[28] A far cry from the image of the seashore in the early postwar period, this is the seashore as geographical feature shaped into beach as leisure resort and finally distilled into a consumable essence laced with a *champuru* of cultural extracts ranging from selectively packaged items of premodern heritage to the transplanted tropicals that, like the bases and beaches, have invaded and overtaken much of Okinawa Island.

## NOTES

1. Lena Lenček and Gideon Boskar, *The Beach: A History of Paradise on Earth* (New York: Viking Penguin, 1998), xx.
2. The northernmost natively occurring palm, the stumpy Mediterranean fan palm, reaches the south of France, whereas certain hardy species have been transplanted as far north as Scotland, Norway, and British Columbia.
3. Lenček and Boskar, *The Beach*, 217.
4. Senge Tetsuma, *Okinawa kankō shindansho* [A Diagnosis of Okinawa Tourism] (Naha: Okinawa Kankō Kyōkai, 1962), 46.

5. Okinawa Kankō Kyōkai, *Okinawa kankō jū shūnen shi* (Naha: Okinawa Kankō Kyōkai, 1964), 49.

6. *Kankō Okinawa*, no. 96 (July 1965): 4 (no author).

7. *Kankō Okinawa*, no. 22 (May 1959), cover.

8. *Kankō Okinawa*, no. 49 (August 1961): 5. It is unclear if the tennis court and ball field were ever added.

9. *Kankō Okinawa*, no. 14 (September 1958): 6–7.

10. Okinawa Kankō Kyōkai, *Okinawa kankō* (undated, but contents suggest 1958–1959), n.p.

11. Moon Beach's current incarnation can be glimpsed online at http://www.moonbeach.co.jp.

12. Okinawa Kankō Kyōkai, *Okinawa kankō: Sightseeing of Okinawa* (Naha: Okinawa Kankō Kyōkai, 1960).

13. Tomita Yūkō, *Burū gaido bukkusu 44: Okinawa* (Tokyo: Jitsugyō no Nihonsha, 1964), 49.

14. Figures are taken from Ishikawa Masahide, *Okinawa no kankō keizai* (Naha: Okinawa-ken Kankō Renmei, 1979), 21.

15. Gekkan Okinawa-sha, ed., *Mensōre Uchinā* (Naha: Gekkan Okinawasha, 1974), 96.

16. Cited by Tada Osamu, *Okinawa imēji no tanjō*, 69–70.

17. Okinawa Prefecture, *Okinawa-ken kankō shūkei ryokka keikaku* (Naha: Okinawa Prefecture, 1979), 23–31.

18. Matthew Allen, *Identity and Resistance in Okinawa* (Lanham, MD: Rowman & Littlefield, 2002), 208.

19. Matsutaka Akihiro, "90-nendai no Okinawa kankō ni kansuru kōsatsu," *Okinawa tandai ronsō* 14, no. 1 (March 1998): 137.

20. The competition between JAL and ANA for package tours actually began with city hotels built right before Marine Expo '75: JAL opened Okinawa Grand Castle Hotel in 1974, which ANA countered with the Harborview Hotel. The former currently exists on the way to Shuri Castle as the JAL Hotel Nikko Naha Grand Castle, while the latter is currently the Crowne Plaza ANA Harborview Hotel in Naha (and not in view of any harbor).

21. See Tada, *Okinawa imēji no tanjō*, 150–51, for a brief overview of the structure of business-government interests in post–Marine Expo Okinawa.

22. Tada, *Okinawa imēji no tanjō*, 154.

23. Miki Takeshi, *Rizōto kaihatsu: Okinawa kara no hōkoku* (Tokyo: San-ichi Shinsho, 1990), 7.

24. The full text of Ōta's declaration, in which he ties together Ryukyu Kingdom history, Okinawan arts and culture, natural environment (particularly sea and sun), and a natural peace-loving Okinawan spirit in a pitch for tourism to share with the world, can be found in "Okinawa kankō nyusu," no. 468 (November 15, 1995), available online at http://www.sokuhou.co.jp/backno/468.html.

25. "Okinawa kankō nyusu," 49.

26. E-mail communication with Okinawa Convention & Visitors Bureau representative Sugita Sayo, June 28, 2010.

27. I "infiltrated" the Hotel Nikko Alivila in June 1999 after visiting the Ryūkyū no Kaze Studio Park by walking through fields and up the beach. Once on the premises—and noticing that "inspection tours" (*kengaku*) were allowed—I asked if I could roam the grounds for a possible future stay, and the request was granted.

28. A special feature article on "those who make the Okinawa Brand" appears in the summer 2004 volume of the magazine *Champurū*. See *Champurū* Editorial Staff, "Okinawa, ima burando ō-koku he," *Champurū* 4 (Summer 2004): 4–20.

# Epilogue

## *Beyond Postwar, Beyond Okinawa Island*

Back to 1995, this time November 1, within five months of my first visit to Okinawa and the festivities surrounding the fiftieth anniversary of the end of the Battle of Okinawa, within only two months of the infamous September 1995 rape of a twelve-year-old Okinawan girl by three marines. On this day, at the opening ceremony of the inaugural Dai-Ryūkyū • Matsuri Ō-koku (Greater Ryukyu, Festival Kingdom), then governor Ōta Masahide—survivor of the Blood and Iron Youth Corps, university professor, author of several books on the Battle of Okinawa, and staunch antibase campaigner—delivered his famous "Tourism Prefecture Declaration" on a stage in front of the festival headquarters on Kokusai Dōri. As it was reported at the time,

> Governor Ōta read the text of his declaration and when he announced that Okinawa would be Japan's "Tourism Prefecture" [*kankō ritsuken*], drums boomed, bells reverberated, and confetti danced in the air.
>
> The festival was bustling afterwards as a thousand-person *eisā* parade engulfed the tourists on the street.[1]

This time the local people overwhelmed the tourists, not the other way around, as it had been since the 1980s beach resort invasion.

Ōta's declaration began with rhetorical gestures to Okinawa's premodern past, which, during the early 1990s "rediscovery" of the Ryukyu Kingdom in conjunction with the rebuilding of Shuri Castle and the airing of the Japan Broadcasting Corporation's television drama *Ryūkyū no kaze*, became boilerplate for the characterization and promotion of Okinawa in various contexts but especially in tourism. For both political and economic reasons, Ōta was perhaps the single most-influential popularizer of the image of a peaceful, weaponless Ryukyu Kingdom flourishing amid regional trade networks with neighboring countries and melding a distinct traditional culture through such contact:

> This here Okinawa, from ancient times, was a crossroads tying together over the sea numerous countries to continental Asia. Culture and wealth flowed from the four corners; at times the tumultuous history of many countries taught hard lessons. Even within this situation, people came into contact with foreign cultures and accepted them with enterprising spirits, creating a richly bountiful traditional culture by enhancing but without losing their own.

After this evocation of an idealized historical basis for hosting visitors, Ōta launched into a poetic paean of verse punctuated by prose commentary extolling the blessings of the abundant nature—sea, sun, and wind—that the gods have bestowed on Okinawa:

The wind sings across the richly reflective sea; plants dance on verdant Mother Earth;
the sun sparkles over all God's creatures great and small;
and time flows gently. . . .

. . . We rejoice together at having received life from these islands, treasuring heart-to-heart bonds and holding life dear above all else.
This place overflows in a bounty of sun and sea,
A verdurous isle of eternal youth where people are naturally kindhearted;
The *sanshin* resonates and drums beat out to the heavens,
A tropical rhythm shakes Mother Earth;
From the heroics of karate to dance, dragon boat races, and tug-of-war,
And then the bejeweled splendor of royal culture;
Young and old alike are cheerfully spirited and full of health,
To a long life!
Beckoning the blessings of this abundant nature and unique history and culture and looking toward a new generation, we nurture a spirit of independence and aspire to a tolerant and harmonious society.
Learning from our forbears who in the past constructed a bridge of nations [*bankoku no shinryo*] through trade, I hereby declare that we will construct a bridge of peace and friendship through tourism and redouble our efforts to build a hospitable, bountiful, and beautiful island [*churashima*] Okinawa overflowing with a kind and welcoming spirit.[2]

Cutting through the hyperbole of overwrought prose and verse not unexpected in public oratory from an academic turned politician, one can distill from this speech the three pillars of Okinawa tourism promotion in its contemporary form: distinct Ryukyuan heritage, unique *champuru* culture, and abundant beautiful nature characterized by sea, sun, sky, and wind.

Although a prolific researcher and critic of the Battle of Okinawa and a supporter of its memorialization, Ōta makes only a veiled and vague reference to that history ("the tumultuous history of many countries taught hard lessons"). He was by this time able to compartmentalize leisure tourism from war tourism. This separation of war-related sightseeing from the kind of tourism that Okinawa now offers as Japan's "Tourism Prefecture" represents not only an obvious change in the content of tourism from immediate postwar Okinawa; it is also a measure of the extent to which Okinawa, at least on an official level, has managed its wartime past and war's remainders. War tourism has become contained within a new peace memorial (the Cornerstone of Peace, unveiled June 23, 1995), a new archive (Okinawa Prefectural Archives, opened August 1, 1995), a new organization of "peace guides" (announced in June 1995), and a new museum (Okinawa Prefectural Peace Memorial Museum, opened on April 1, 2000, the fifty-fifth anniversary of the American invasion of Okinawa Island). Officially recognized and displayed in these sites, the Southern Battle Sites Tour has been institutionalized. The multiplex of memorial-museum-archive-peace tours acts to exhaust public treatment of the war, converting and redeeming it as perpetual peace act whereby reverence, education, and scholarship fulfill the obligation to face and acknowledge war loss. At the same time, tourism itself is cast as a "peace industry" that overcomes differences among peoples because of the inherent need for hospitality and friendly relations toward guests. No longer the prime attraction for visitors—the veteran, the bereaved, the patriot—who a generation ago had more direct connections with the Battle of Okinawa, war-related sites no longer need to be advertised as a part of Tourist Okinawa as they were until the 1970s. They have become a part of routine observance and historical interest that has no necessary connection to twenty-first-century tourism, to "the new generation" that Ōta invokes. The war is accounted for without having to foreground it among Okinawa's primary tourist attractions.

Governor Ōta's enthusiasm for tourism as the solution to Okinawa's longstanding economic woes was matched only by the energy he spent campaigning against the presence of military bases on Okinawa Island. For him, the two were connected, not in the context of bases as tourist sites as discussed in chapter 5, but as tourism displacing the bases economically and in some cases physically. In a 1996 interview with Tony Barrell and Rick Tanaka, in a response to a question about how to increase Okinawa's economic—and, by extension, political—autonomy, Ōta unhesitatingly answers, "Tourism!" and describes plans to turn Kadena Air Base into a civilian freight airport.[3] Comparable plans for turning Futenma Marine Air Station in Ginowan City into civilian business, living, and leisure space have also been floated ever since the U.S. announced in 1996 its (as of yet unfulfilled)[4] intention to move the base's function elsewhere. The most elaborate plan was mapped out and labeled "Ginowan Dream" in a display within the odd, globe-shaped Kakazu Observation Platform (see figure E.1). This pre-Reversion sightseeing spot, established in 1964 under sponsorship of the *Ryūkyū Shimpō* newspaper, offers a view of the air station tarmac from atop a small hill in nearby Kakazu Park. It figures in most peace tours of the island. Mainland officials are routinely taken there during trips in conjunction with the negotiations over the move of Futenma Marine Air Station because of its unobstructed view over the base's perimeter wall (see figure E.2). One of the strangest and most provocative of pre-Reversion sightseeing spots, the platform—paint peeling and covered with graffiti—is a giant globe in four sections with mainland Japan and Okinawa Island highlighted together in red but separated by the empty space between their respective sections. Given the mid-1960 date for the establishment of the platform, it is difficult not to see the connection by color but separation by space as commentary on Okinawa's geopolitical position at the time. The imagined "Ginowan Dream" once displayed on the top floor of the platform (seen left of center in figure E.2) depicted a Core Zone, Hotel Zone, Research Center Zone, Historical Recreation Zone, Residential Zones, and a Theme Park Zone that would fill the hole of the doughnut that the base has turned the city into. "Ginowan Dream" was, in its own way, a microcosm of the 1990 Okinawa Prefectural Master Plan, albeit with more emphasis on everyday living, leisure, and workspace for the locals over vacation space for visitors. The last time I visited the site in November 2009 the maps for "Ginowan Dream" had vanished, like the many other unrealized visions for Okinawa's postwar development.

The gradual distancing of the historical battlefield sites from the main attractions of Okinawa tourism—like the cordoning off of the military bases on the one hand and the parceling of beach resort property on the other—is an effect of the impulse to zone every available hectare on Okinawa Island. Such enthusiastic and detailed planning, which often remains forever in the planning stage, is perhaps required in a place of limited space and resources, but there is also behind it a technocratic urge to engineer the ideal built environment even when the plan is to set aside mountain forests in Yanbaru (northern Okinawa Island) and mangrove marshes on Iriomote Island (in the southern Ryukyus) for eco-tourists. The previous problem of not fully exploiting Okinawa's shoreline as "the beach" has turned into the problem of overexploiting Okinawa's sea and shores. And as tourist zones on Okinawa Island have filled—victims of their own success—and demand for an "authentic" Okinawan experience has increased, tourism development has moved beyond the borders of the main island and even further from the old battle sites and war monuments.

**Figure E.1.** Kakazu Observation Platform buzzed by aircraft from Futenma Marine Air Station. *Source*: Gerald Figal.

**Figure E.2.** Futenma Marine Air Station from the Kakazu Observation Platform. *Source*: Gerald Figal.

Ōta's call for the realization of "Tourism Prefecture Okinawa" in 1995 represented a continuation of the previous administration's prefecture-wide *Resort Okinawa Master Plan* dressed up in the rhetoric of regional heritage and cultural identity in a way so as to deflect critics of unfettered beach resort development. Like the master plan, it embraced the entire prefecture with its dozens of separate islands, recognizing that the future of Okinawa tourism—as analysts since the 1960s had foreseen—lay in the outlying islands. Kume Island to the west and the Yaeyama and Miyako Islands to the south, which had always been secondary to main island tourism for only those adventurous travelers seeking sanctuary from the congestion (of traffic, urban development, and U.S. military) on Okinawa Island, are now poised to reverse the priority of destinations in Okinawa tourism. Despite historical and cultural differences between the main island and the periphery, however, they are all typically advertised as part of the "Okinawa experience" in which the signified for "Okinawa" in this instance is usefully ambiguous: does it mean the prefecture as a whole or a core culture and unified identity emanating from Okinawa Island? The overlap here allows tourism promoters enough slippage to suggest that the most Okinawan of Okinawan experiences—experiences to this point almost solely defined by tourism as developed on Okinawa Island—is to be had in relatively less worked-over places like Kume, Miyako, Ishigaki, and Taketomi islands.

But selling these places as part of the Okinawa brand is, as Matthew Allen points out in the case of Kume, problematic as they fall victim to two layers of mediation driven by the tourist gaze. They are cast as an extension of "Okinawa," which itself has already been formed—some would say deformed—by years of catering to northern, mainland expectations for "the south country" (*nangoku*, i.e., the tropics):

> Marketing strategies and the perceived marketability of the tourism product drives the relationships between the purveyors of tourism culture and the consumers, and underscoring this relationship is the construction of a coherent "identity" of Okinawa. Whereas the visual images of Okinawa presented for consumption by the tourist market are those of "resort" and "exotica," the text of advertising Kume as a tourist destination relies on a two-pronged attempt to lure travelers to the island. It invokes not only the visually stimulating water and the implications this has for marine and leisure activities but also the island as a living example of "traditional" Okinawan life and culture; the subtropical Okinawan "experience."[5]

Allen notes recent initiatives by Kume islanders to reset the terms of cultural—as opposed to resort—tourism to Kume by aspiring to meet tourist expectations with material drawn from local Kume rather than generic

"Okinawan" culture. He describes this trend as reclamation of the island from "the colonial tourism economics of the mainland," but he could have also added to that the colonial tourism economics of the main island of Okinawa as well. Okinawa Island—like Shuri Castle in the days of the unified Ryukyu Kingdom—has dominated the definition of traditional Okinawan culture and the production of the contemporary Okinawa brand within the frame of the mainland tourist gaze. Allen's analysis of the Nikko Kume Island Resort, opened in 1990, reveals the fully matured version of beach as built environment that caters to mainland expectations of *Nangoku* Okinawa while pitching local authenticity. The advertising brochure for the resort rehashes clichés about the beauty of the surrounding sea and greenery that can be found at resorts on the main island while at the same time enumerating local selling points that distinguish Kume Island from other sites on Okinawa Island. Even so, those local selling points are still ultimately pulled within the orbit of a unified Okinawa. For example, Kume tourism makes claims to difference from Okinawa Island in that it was largely spared from war damage and thus has still intact "many cultural and historic artifacts, enabling visitors to fully enjoy a genuine Okinawan experience."[6]

It is the emphasis on the outlying Ryukyu Islands as presenting a "living example" of traditional and genuine Okinawa heritage—that is, old Ryukyu—that provides a principal pitch for the tourism there—that and the promise of less-crowded white-sand beaches and thicker tropical foliage. While Ishigaki Island, the central transit hub within the Yaeyama Islands to the south of Okinawa Island, can boast its share of "traditional" atmosphere and the picture-postcard white-sand beaches on Kabira Bay (recognized as one of the hundred most beautiful spots in Japan),[7] it is the small nearby Taketomi Island that represents the extreme version of this logic of "living history." With an area of only 6.3 square kilometers and a permanent population of about three hundred, Taketomi is routinely described in guidebooks—and by many Okinawans—as the place that possesses the most *Okinawarashisa* (Okinawaness) of all the Ryukyus, even though this description should at least be kept specific to Yaeyama. This claim of being a living example of old Ryukyu qua Okinawa arises from Taketomi's history of association with the folk craft (*mingei*) movement and from the locally supported and nationally endorsed 1987 Townscape Preservation Order (*Machinami Hozon*) that requires the maintenance of traditional architecture with red-tiled roofs, *himpun* (spirit walls), stone fences, and unpaved streets. As Amanda Stinchecum has documented, from the first gleanings of tourism development in the prewar period, to its slow growth during U.S. occupation, to a significant surge in visitors after Reversion and the 1975 International Marine Exposition, tourism to Yaeyama in general and Taketomi Island in particular has been closely identified with folk craft production, especially in the fiber arts of *bashōfu* (banana-fiber cloth) and *minsā* patterned weaving.[8] Whereas tourist attractions on Okinawa Island such as Ryukyu Mura, Murasaki Mura (Ryūkyū no Kaze Studio Park), and Okinawa World Bunka Ō-koku (Culture Kingdom) emphasize hands-on experience and "living history" through live performances and working artists and craftspeople within the confines of their respective parks, Taketomi Island strives to weave living history within the fabric of everyday life. It does not have a theme park; the entire island is, arguably, a theme park.

Taketomi's preserved townscape provides a "natural" stage for the active preservation of traditional Yaeyama arts and has directly contributed to the increase in visitors to the island. It is no coincidence, for example, that the number of tourists to Taketomi Island jumped over 30 percent (from 72,117 to 104,449) the year after its Tanedori Festival was designated an Important Intangible Cultural Asset by the Japanese Ministry of Culture in 1977. Similarly, after a steady downward trend from 1978 to 1984 (104,499 to 68,870) and slight up-and-down increase from 1984 to 1987, tourist numbers jumped approximately 20 percent the year after the Townscape Preservation Order went into effect and have increased dramatically ever since, reaching nearly half a million by 2009.[9] The island's preservation and presentation of a "live" Ryukyu village is widely credited for the disproportionate number of visitors it receives for its size compared to other Yaeyama destinations. Only its much larger, jungly neighbor, Iriomote, a primary target for recent eco-tourism and beachcombers, has routinely drawn larger numbers since the mid-1980s. Coincident with the enactment of the Resort Law and the subsequent beach resort boom from the late 1980s, Taketomi's turn to the preservation of "heritage homes" and traditional arts—rather than the establishment of resorts on its beautiful Kondoi Beach or on one of its famed star-sand beaches (*hoshizuna-no-hama*)[10]—ran counter to the predominant trend in Okinawa tourism development of the time. In the midst of this old-town revival, townscape preservation booster and director of the island's modest folk craft museum, Uesedo Yoshinori, has noted that the steep post–preservation order increase in tourism was an unplanned side effect, and it has, in turn, halted out-migration from Taketomi. The island's permanent population has actually been gradually increasing since the mid-1990s.[11] Uesedo considers the preservation of the old-style streets and homes a positive form of tourism development, one that is "natural," or at least not overtly artificial like the faux-tropical landscapes of beach resorts, public spaces, and hotel lobbies throughout the prefecture. However, one can argue—as I did in my conversation with him—that the imposition of strict building codes and purposefully sandy streets in the name of heritage preservation is quite artificial in its conscious attempt to create, in effect, a themed environment. Uesedo accepted the idea of the manmade quality of Taketomi's townscape and old Yaeyama/Okinawa atmosphere but balked at my suggestion that the island had been "theme-parked" (*tēmapākukasareta*). To him, placing Taketomi Island on the level of Ryukyu Mura did not seem appropriate, and in some respects he was correct—Taketomi is not Ryukyu Mura in the latter's overt commercial staging of Ryukyu culture. And yet, functionally, the two places are indeed comparable insofar as the gaze of the tourists they draw is directed toward an authentic display of Ryukyu heritage as Okinawan—if not, as Yanagita Kunio argued in his *Kaijō no michi* (The Road Overseas, 1961), Japanese—roots. In other words, despite the intention of the island's inhabitants, the act of touring the place prompted by promises of an authentic Okinawa/Ryukyu/Yaeyama experience has defined in practice its status as de facto theme park. This status does not necessarily discredit claims to authenticity that drive this kind of cultural and historical tourism. Adopting Erve Chambers's suggestion, introduced in the prologue to this study, that we focus more on the source of agency rather than on the contents of the product in determining touristic "authenticity," Taketomi's townscape is on that score authentic to the extent that its (re) creation has derived from the initiative of local residents. Questions arise, however, when the product of Taketomi's labors is generalized and marketed as the quintessence of "the Okinawa experience."

Writing in 1979, not long after national recognition of Taketomi's Tanedori Festival as an Important Intangible Cultural Asset, economic historian and Okinawa tourism watcher Ishikawa Masahide commented on the contemporary surge in tourism to Okinawa's outlying islands, characterizing the trend as a yearning for peacefulness, carefree simplicity, and "old Okinawa as it was" away from the clamor of urban life on the mainland.[12] If he had been writing today, he might well have included the escape from the clamor and congestion of Okinawa Island as well. It is beyond Okinawa Island and, in a sense, beyond its postwar burdens that, he seems to be saying, nostalgic visions of the good old days can be at least partially realized. More than once he invokes the word *heiwa* (peace) in the sense of quiet calm and the absence of conflict to characterize the appeal of the outer Ryukyu Islands as a tourist destination. It is a word that when read now cannot help but be caught up in the rhetoric of war redemption and tourism promotion that was prominent during Ōta's governorship and in the wake of the fiftieth anniversary of the Battle of Okinawa. In other words, it strikes the reader as loaded in a way Ishikawa might not have intended but that is nevertheless consistent with the long-standing concept of tourism in general as a "peace industry" and with the widespread deployment of "peace" as fundamental to Okinawa's public persona in particular. Foregrounded in the war (peace) tourism of battle sites, military bases, memorials, museums, and peace parks, idealized as the historical backdrop to Shuri Castle Park and the Ryukyu Kingdom boom, and planted within the grave site *bussōge* turned beach resort *haibisukasu*, peace seals the Okinawa brand, giving it a weighty historical and universal relevance in its implicit and explicit reference to (the) war while at the same time offering a flighty escape from the present toward a paradise perpetually deferred.

## NOTES

1. "Okinawa kankō nyusu," no. 468 (November 15, 1995), available online at http://www.sokuhou.co.jp/backno/468.html.

2. "Okinawa kankō nyusu."

3. Tony Barrell and Rick Tanaka, *Okinawa Dreams OK* (Berlin: Gestalten Verlag, 1997), 84.

4. As of this writing (September 2011), the latest news on the relocation plans is that the U.S.-Japan Security Consultative Committee has reaffirmed the moving of the functions of Futenma Marine Air Station to an offshore facility at Henoko in Nago over the protestations of local residents ("Defense White Paper 2011 Suggests That Relocating Futenma Outside of Okinawa Will Impair the Functions of the U.S. Marine Corps," *Ryūkyū Shimpō* [online English edition], August 3, 2011, http://english.ryukyushimpo.jp/2011/08/11/2271.

5. Matthew Allen, *Identity and Resistance in Okinawa* (Lanham, MD: Rowman & Littlefield, 2002), 216–17.

6. Allen, *Identity and Resistance in Okinawa*, 216.

7. Eriko Arita, "Resort to Sheer Pleasure on Ishigaki Island," *Japan Times Online,* June 20, 2010, http://search.japantimes.co.jp/cgi-bin/fv20100620a1.html. This article, which reads more like an advertisement than reportage, praises the resort facilities, food, and entertainment at the Club Med Kabira.

8. Amanda Stinchecum, "Yaeyama ni okeru kankō kaihatsu to minsā," in Hateruma Eikichi, *Minsā zensho* (Ishigaki, Okinawa: Nanzansha, 2009), 241–65.

9. Statistics cited in Stinchecum, "Yaeyama ni okeru kankō kaihatsu to minsā," 252.

10. The "star-sand" of Kajihama and Aiyaruhama beaches is actually formed by the shells of tiny crustaceans that wash up on the shore. Local laws prohibit the carting off of sand containing the shells but do allow the picking of individual specimens of star-sand.

11. Uesedo Yoshinori, "Machinami hozon," in the "Hae" (Southern Wind) column of the *Ryūkyū Shimpō*, Evening Edition, February 10, 1999. I visited Taketomi twice, in April and June 2001. On the second occasion, Uesedo gave me a tour of the museum and afterward over lunch discussed with me the history, theory, and practice of Taketomi's townscape preservation order of which he is a major advocate. See also Barrell and Tanaka's interview with him in *Okinawa Dreams OK*, 66–73.

12. Ishikawa Masahide, *Okinawa no kankō keizai* (Naha: Okinawa-ken Kankō Renmei, 1979), 235–39.

# Bibliography

*Archival material*: Archival documents from the Okinawa Prefectural Archives (OPA), including U.S. documents copied and stored there from the U.S. National Archives, are identified in notes by their OPA reference code. The only exception is when an OPA reference code for a U.S. National Archives document was not available, in which case the U.S. document location identifier (box and folder number), as indicated on the copy, is used. If documents in the archives are copies of published materials with clear publication data, then I have included them in the bibliography below.


Agriculture and Forestry Department, Government of the Ryukyu Islands. *Ringyō shiryō 7: Ryūkyū no ringyō*. Naha: Government of the Ryukyu Islands, 1966.

Akamine, Namaki. "Irei no Hi ni omou." In *Wakatake sōshūhen: Sōritsu 25 shūnen kinenshi*, edited by Okinawa-ken Izoku Rengō Kai Seisōnen-bu. Naha: Okinawa-ken Izoku Rengō Kai Seisōnen-bu, 1966.

Aldous, Christopher. "Achieving Reversion: Protest and Authority in Okinawa, 1952–70." *Modern Asian Studies* 37, no. 2 (2003): 485–508.

Allen, Matthew. *Identity and Resistance in Okinawa*. Lanham, MD: Rowman & Littlefield, 2002.

Angst, Linda Isako. "The Rape of a Schoolgirl: Discourse of Power and Gendered National Identity in Okinawa." In *Islands of Discontent: Okinawan Responses to Japanese and American Power*, edited by Laura Hein and Mark Selden, 135–57. Lanham, MD: Rowman & Littlefield, 2003.

Angst, Linda Irene. "In a Dark Time: Community, Memory, and the Making of Ethnic Selves in Okinawan Women's Narratives." PhD diss., Yale University, 2001.

Anonymous. "Dai-3-ji zen-Ryū ryokka suishin undō jikkai yōryō." *Midori*, no. 23 (November 1964): 6–8.

———. "Dai-4-ji zen-Ryū ryokka suishin undō jikkai yōryō." *Midori*, no. 35 (November 1967): 6–8.

———. "Haibisukasu no subete (jō): Sono rekishi to haikei." *Midori to seikatsu* 1, no. 4 (August 1982): 4–5.

———. "Hanauri henjō." *Okinawa Times* (Naha), April 2, 1983.

———. "Kankōdan no mita Okinawa." *Kankō Okinawa*, no. 41 (December 1964): 5.

———. "Sensō iseki • ibutsu, sensō kōkōgaku ni tsuite." *Kōkōgaku kenkyū* 41, no. 3 (1994).

———. "Shurijō fukugen wa kokumin no ganbō." *Okinawa Taimusu* (Naha), February 8, 1984.

———. "Tōnan Shokubutsu Rakuen no ayumi." Southeast Botanical Gardens. N.d. http://www.sebg.co.jp/about/ayumi.html.

Arasaki, Moriteru. *Kankō kōsu de nai Okinawa: Senseki, kichi, sangyō, bunka*. Tokyo: Kōbunken, 1998.

———. *Okinawa gendai shi*. Tokyo: Iwanami Shoten, 1996.

Barrell, Tony, and Rick Tanaka. *Okinawa Dreams OK*. Berlin: Gestalten Verlag, 1997.

Breyette, Gordi. "A History of the Southeast Botanical Gardens and Himeyuri Cactus Park." Unpublished internal document, n.d.

Butler, Richard. *Change in Tourism: People, Places, Processes*. London and New York: Chapman & Hall, 1995.

Chambers, Erve. *Native Tours: The Anthropology of Travel and Tourism*. Prospect Heights, IL: Waveland Press, 2009.

*Champurū* Editorial Staff. "Okinawa, ima burando ō-koku he." *Champurū* 4 (Summer 2004).

Chibana, Shoichi. *Burning the Rising Sun: From Yomitan Village, Okinawa: Islands of U.S. Bases*. Kyoto: South Wind, 1992.

Christy, Alan. "A Fantasy of Ancient Japan: The Assimilation of Okinawa in Yanagita's Kainan Shoki." *Productions of Culture in Japan, Select Papers* 10 (1995): 61–90.

———. "Representing the Rural: Place as Method in the Formation of Japanese Native Ethnology, 1910–1945." PhD diss., University of Chicago, 1997.

Clarke, Hugh. "The Great Dialect Debate: The State and Language Policy in Okinawa." In *State and Society in Interwar Japan*, edited by Elise K. Tipton, 193–217. London: Routledge, 1997.

Culler, Jonathan. "Semiotics of Tourism." *American Journal of Semiotics* 1, no. 1/2 (1981): 127–41.

Dai-32 Gunshireibugō Hozon • Kōkai Kentō Iinkai. *Dai-32 gunshireibugō no hozon • kōkai ni tsuite*. Naha: Dai-32 Gunshireibugō Hozon • Kōkai Kentō Iinkai, 1996.

Desmond, Jane C. *Staging Tourism: Bodies on Display from Waikiki to Sea World*. Chicago: University of Chicago Press, 2001.

Duits, Kjeld. "Ginza Streetcar." Old Photos of Japan. N.d. http://oldphotosjapan.com/photos/759/ginza-streetcar.

Easter, Travis V. "Step into an Enchanted Forest." *Okinawa Marine*, May 12, 2006.

Eldridge, Robert D. *The Origins of the Bilateral Okinawa Problem: Okinawa in Postwar U.S.-Japan Relations, 1945–1952.* London and New York: Routledge, 2001.

Feifer, George. *Tennozan: The Battle of Okinawa and the Atomic Bomb.* New York: Ticknor & Fields, 1992.

Field, Norma. *In the Realm of the Dying Emperor: Japan at Century's End.* New York: Vintage, 1991.

Figal, Gerald. "Bones of Contention: The Geopolitics of 'Sacred Ground' in Postwar Okinawa." *Diplomatic History* 31, no. 1 (January 2007): 81–109.

———. "Historical Sense and Commemorative Sensibility at Okinawa's Cornerstone of Peace." *Positions: East Asia Cultures Critique* 5, no. 3 (Winter 1997).

———. "How to *Jibunshi*: Making and Marketing Self-Histories of Shōwa among the Masses in Postwar Japan." *Journal of Asian Studies* 55, no. 4 (November 1996): 902–33.

———. "Waging Peace on Okinawa." In *Islands of Discontent: Okinawan Responses to Japanese and American Power*, edited by Laura Hein and Mark Selden, 65–98. Lanham, MD: Rowman & Littlefield, 2003.

Frenke, Robert C. "Okinawa Paradise." *Okinawa Marine*, February 29, 2008.

Gekkan Okinawa-sha, ed. *Mensōre Uchinā.* Naha: Gekkan Okinawasha, 1974.

Genka, Yoko. "Imag(in)ing Okinawa: Representations from Within and Without." PhD diss., George Mason University, 2004.

Gluck, Carol. "The Past in the Present." In *Postwar Japan as History*, edited by Andrew Gordon, 64–95. Berkeley and Los Angeles: University of California Press, 1993.

Gottdiener, Mark. *The Theming of America: American Dreams, Media Fantasies, and Themed Environments.* Boulder, CO: Westview Press, 2001.

Goya, Shigenobu. "Shurijō Fukugen Kisei Kai ni-jū-go no ayumi." *Shurijō fukugen kisei kai kaihō*, no. 17 (July 1998): 42–45.

———. "Sōritsu 25 shūnen o mukaete." *Shurijō fukugen kisei kai kaihō*, no. 17 (July 1998): 33.

Gushiken, Kanehiro. "Shirokotsu no yama to natta nanbu senseki." In *Shomin ga tsuzuru Okinawa sengo seikatsushi*, edited by Okinawa Taimususha, 41. Naha: Okinawa Taimususha, 1998.

Hallas, James H. *Killing Ground on Okinawa: The Battle for Sugar Loaf Hill.* Westport, CT: Praeger, 1996.

Hara, Tomoaki. *Minzoku bunka no genzai: Okinawa • Yonagunishima no "minzoku" he no manazashi.* Tokyo: Dōseisha, 2000.

Hayashi. "Ireitō shinsetsu okotowari." *Asahi Shimbun* (Tokyo), January 26, 1962.

Hein, Laura, and Mark Selden. *Islands of Discontent: Okinawan Responses to Japanese and American Power.* Lanham, MD: Rowman & Littlefield, 2003.

Heiwa kyōiku kenkyū iinkai, ed. *Aruku, miru, kangaeru Okinawa.* Naha: Okinawa Jiji Shuppan, 1986.

Hook, Glen D., and Richard Siddle, eds. *Japan and Okinawa: Structure and Subjectivity.* London: Routledge, 2002.

Humphrey (Yonetani), Julia. "Making History from Japan's Margins: Ōta Masahide and Okinawa." Canberra: Australian National University, 2002.

Inamine, Kunisaburō. "Kankō meguri no kansō." *Kankō Okinawa*, no. 31 (February 1960): 2.

Inouye, Frank T. "Requirements for Successful Development of Tourism in the Ryukyus." USCAR Tourism Committee, 1962. RG 260, Box 78 of HCRI-AO, Folder No. 8, U.S. National Archives.

Ishihara, Masaie. "Memories of War and Okinawa." In *Perilous Memories: The Asia-Pacific War(s)*, edited by T. Fujitani, Geoffrey M. White, and Lisa Yoneyama, 87–106. Durham, NC: Duke University Press, n.d.

———. *Okinawa no tabi: Abuchiragama to Todoroki no gō*. Tokyo: Shūeisha Shinsho, 2000.

———. "Watashi no sensō taiken chōsa to daigakusei to no kakari." *Okinawa Kokusai Daigaku shakai bunka kenkyū* 7, no. 1 (March 2004): 2–3.

Ishikawa, Masahide. *Okinawa no kankō keizai*. Naha: Okinawa-ken Kankō Renmei, 1979.

Itō, Kenichi, ed. *Ehagaki ni miru Okinawa: Meiji, Taishō, Shōwa*. Naha: Ryūkyū Shimpōsha, 1993.

Itō, Yushi. "Make no bunkazai—sensō iseki no jūyōsei." In *Bunkazaigaku ronshū*, edited by Bunkazaigaku ronshū kankiōkai. Nara: Bunkazaigaku Ronshū Kankiōkai, 1994.

Ivy, Marilyn. *Discourses of the Vanishing: Modernity, Phantasm, Japan*. Chicago: University of Chicago Press, 1995.

Iwata, Eisuke. *Midori*, no. 24 (March 1980): 3.

Kabira, Chōshin. *Midori to seikatsu* 1, no. 6 (n.d.): 33.

Kakazu, Hiroshi. *Island Sustainability: Challenges and Opportunities for Okinawa and Other Pacific Islands in a Globalized World*. Bloomington, IN: Trafford Publishing, 2009.

———. "Sustainable Island Tourism: The Case of Okinawa." *Yashi no mi daigaku*, n.d. http://www.yashinomi.to/pacific/pdf/Kakazu_02.pdf.

Kanda, Kōji. "Senzenki no Okinawa kankō o meguru imēji to aidentiti." In *Kankō no kūkan: Shiten to apurōchi*, edited by Kōji Kanda, 211–21. Tokyo: Nakanishiya Shuppan, 2009.

Kawahashi, Noriko. "Seven Hindrances of Women? A Popular Discourse on Okinawan Women and Religion." *Japanese Journal of Religious Studies* 27, no. 1 (Spring 2000): 85–98.

Kerr, George. *Okinawa: The History of an Island People*. Rev. ed. North Clarendon, VT: Tuttle Publishing, 2000.

Keyso, Ruth Ann. *Women of Okinawa: Nine Voices from a Garrison Island*. Ithaca, NY: Cornell University Press, 2000.

Kinjō, Washin. "Seinen-bu no arikata." In *Wakatake sōshūhen: Sōritsu 25 shūnen kinenshi*, edited by Okinawa-ken Izoku Rengō Kai Seisōnen-bu, 87. Naha: Okinawa-ken Izoku Rengō Kai Seisōnen-bu, 1985.

Kinjō, Yukikitsu. "Kankō ritsuken wa ryokka kara: Naha Kūkō kara shigaichi o hana to midori ni." *Midori to seikatsu* 4, no. 3 (July 1982): 31.

Kirshenblatt-Gimblett, Barbara. *Destination Culture: Tourism, Museums, and Heritage*. Berkeley and Los Angeles: University of California Press, 1998.

Kitagawa, Munetada, ed. *Kankō jigyō ron*. Kyoto: Minerva Shobo, 2001.
Kitamura, Tsuyoshi. *Sensha-tachi no sengoshi: Okinawa senseki o megure hitobito to no kioku*. Tokyo: Ochanomizu Shobo, 2009.
Laderman, Scott. *Tours of Vietnam: War, Travel Guides, and Memory*. Durham, NC: Duke University Press, 2009.
Lenček, Lena, and Gideon Boskar. *The Beach: A History of Paradise on Earth*. New York: Viking Penguin, 1998.
Loo, Tze May. "Treasures of a Nation: Cultural Heritage Preservation and the Making of Shuri Castle in Prewar Japan." PhD diss., Cornell University, 2007.
MacCannell, Dean. *The Tourist: A New Theory of the Leisure Class*. 1st ed. Berkeley: University of California Press, 1999.
Maehira, Bōkei. *Shurijō monogatari*. Naha: Hirugisha, 1997.
Matsukawa, Kunio. "Kankō to iu keredo." *Kankō Okinawa*, no. 91 (February 1965): 4.
———. "Shurijō fukugen no suishin." *Shurijō fukugen kisei kai kaihō*, no. 3 (July 1984): 12–13.
Matsutaka, Akihiro. "90-nendai no Okinawa kankō ni kansuru kōsatsu." *Okinawa tandai ronsō* 14, no. 1 (March 1998): 137.
McCune, S. *The Ryukyu Islands*. Harrisburg, PA: Stackpole Books, 1975.
Medoruma, Shun. "Droplets." In *Southern Exposure: Modern Japanese Literature from Okinawa*, edited by Michael Molasky and Steven Rabson, translated by Michael Molasky, 255–85. Honolulu: University of Hawaii Press, 2000.
Miki, Takeshi. *Rizōto kaihatsu: Okinawa kara no hōkoku*. Tokyo: San-ichi Shinsho, 1990.
Miyagi, Eishō. "Ryokka undō—watashi no mita Okinawa." *Midori*, no. 1 (January 1960): 27.
Molasky, Michael. *The American Occupation of Japan and Okinawa: Literature and Memory*. London and New York: Routledge, 1999.
Molasky, Michael, and Steven Rabson, eds. *Southern Exposure: Modern Japanese Literature from Okinawa*. Honolulu: University of Hawaii Press, 2000.
Naha International Airport. "Ibento gyararii." *Naha kūkō kokunaisen ryokyaku taaminaru biru*. http://www.naha-airport.co.jp/event.
Nelson, Christopher. *Dancing with the Dead: Memory, Performance, and Everyday Life in Postwar Okinawa*. Durham, NC: Duke University Press, 2008.
Nelson, John. "Social Memory as Ritual Practice: Commemorating Spirits of the Military Dead at Yasukuni Shrine." *Journal of Asian Studies* 62, no. 2 (May 2003): 443–67.
NHK Shuppan Kyokai, ed. *Ryūkyū no kaze, Dragon Spirit: NHK taiga dorama sutōrī*. Tokyo: NHK Shuppan, 1993.
Nihon Kankō Kyōkai Okinawa Chiiki Kankō Sōgō Chōsa Ii-in Kai. *Okinawa chiiki kankō kaihatsu no kansō keikaku*. Tokyo: Nihon Kankō Kyōkai, 1972.
Nonomura, Takao. *Natsukashiki Okinawa: Yamasaki Masatada ra ga aruita Shōwa shoki no genfūkei*. Naha: Ryūkyū Shimpōsha, 2000.
———. *Shurijō o sukutta otoko*. Naha: Niraisha, 1999.
Oguma, Eiji. *"Nihonjin" no kyōkai: Okinawa, Ainu, Taiwan, Chōsen, shokuminchi shihai kara fukki undō made*. Tokyo: Shinyōsha, 1998.

Ōhama, Sō. *Okinawa Kokusai-dōri monogatari: "Kiseki" to yobareta ichi mairu*. Gushikawa, Okinawa Prefecture: Yui Shuppan, 1998.

Ōhiro, Tatsuhiro, and Mineo Higashi. *Okinawa: Two Postwar Novellas*. Translated by Steve Rabson. Berkeley: Institute of East Asian Studies, University of California, Berkeley, 1989.

Okinawa Chiiki kagaku kenkyūjo, ed. *Okinawa no kenmin zō: Uchinanchu to wa nani ka*. Naha: Hirugisha, 1997.

Okinawa Heiwa Nettowāku. *Shin aruku, miru, kangearu Okinawa*. Naha: Okinawa Jiji Shuppan, 2000.

Okinawa Izoku Rengō Kai, ed. *Okinawa Izoku Rengō Kai 25-nen no ayumi*. Naha: Okinawa Izoku Rengō Kai, 1977.

Okinawa Kankō Kyōkai. *Okinawa kankō jū shūnen shi*. Naha: Okinawa Kankō Kyōkai, 1964.

Okinawa kokusai kaiyō hakurankai kyōkai, ed. *Okinawa kokusai kaiyō hakurankai kōshiki kiroku*. Tokyo: Okinawa Kokusai Kaiyō Hakurankai Kyōkai, 1976.

Okinawa Prefecture. *Okinawa-ken kankō shūkei ryokka keikaku*. Naha: Okinawa Prefecture, 1979.

———. *Okinawa-ken shūkei ryokka jissai keikakusho*. Naha: Okinawa Prefecture, 2002.

Okinawa Sōgō Jimukyoku. *Tēma pāku no dōnyū ni yoru kankō sangyō shinkō chōsa*. Naha: Kuniken LTD, 1998.

Okinawa Taimusush‌a, ed. *Shomin ga tsuzuru Okinawa sengo seikatsushi*. Naha: Okinawa Taimususha, 1998.

———. *Okinawa no shōgen, jōmaki*. Naha: Okinawa Taimususha, 1971.

Okinawa-ken Haebaru-cho Kyōiku Iinkai, ed. *Haebaru rikigun byōin gōgun I*. Haebaru: Okinawa-ken Haebaru-cho Kyōiku Iinkai, 2004.

Okinawa-ken Seikatsu Fukushi-bu Engo-ka, ed. *Okinawa no engo no ayumi: Okinawasen shiketsu 50 shūnen kinen*. Naha: Okinawa-ken Seikatsu Fukushi-bu Engo-ka, 1996.

Osaka Shōsen, ed. *Okinawa e*. Osaka: Osaka Shōsen, 1939.

Ōta, Masahide. *Essays on Okinawa Problems*. Gushikawa City, Okinawa: Yui Shuppan, 2000.

———. *Okinawa sen senbotsusha o inoru irei-no-tō*. Naha: Naha Shuppansha, 1985.

Ōta, Seisaku. *Omoide o zuikitsu ni nosete*. Naha: Kitajima Kenzō, 1970.

———. "Ryokka undō ni kyōryoku o." *Midori*, no. 1 (January 1960): 1–2.

Picard, Michel, and Robert E. Wood, eds. *Tourism, Ethnicity, and the State in Asian and Pacific Societies*. Honolulu: University of Hawaii Press, 1997.

Roberson, James E. "*Uchinā* Pop: Place and Identity in Contemporary Okinawan Popular Music." In *Islands of Discontent: Okinawan Responses to Japanese and American Power*, edited by Laura Hein and Mark Selden, 192–227. Lanham, MD: Rowman & Littlefield, 2003.

Robertson, Jennifer. *Native and Newcomer: Making and Remaking a Japanese City*. Berkeley and Los Angeles: University of California Press, 1991.

Rojek, Chris, and John Urry, eds. *Touring Cultures: Transformations of Travel and Theory*. London and New York: Routledge, 1997.

Ryūkyū Ōkoku jidai no shokubutsu hyōhon tenjikai jikkō iinkai, ed. *Ryūkyū Ōkoku jidai no shokubutsu hyōhon: Perī ga mochikaetta shokubutsu-tachi*. Urasoe City, Okinawa: Chitose Publishing, 1998.

*Ryūkyū Shimpō*, ed. *Shin Okinawa kankō meisho 100 sen*. Naha: Ryukyu Shimpōsha, 1995.

Safier, Joshua. "Yasukuni Shrine and the Constraints on the Discourse of Nationalism in Twentieth-Century Japan." Master's thesis, University of Kansas, 1997.

Sarantakes, Nicholas Evan. *Keystone: The American Occupation of Okinawa and U.S.-Japanese Relations*. College Station: Texas A&M University Press, 2000.

Senge, Tetsuma. *Okinawa kankō shindansho*. Naha: Okinawa Kankō Kyōkai, 1962.

Sensō Iseki Hozon Zenkoku Nettowaaku, ed. *Nihon no sensō iseki*. Tokyo: Heibonsha Shinsho, 2004.

———. *Sensō iseki kara manabu*. Tokyo: Iwanami Jyunia Shinsho, 2004.

Shima, Tsuyoshi. "Bones." In *Southern Exposure: Modern Japanese Literature from Okinawa*, edited by Michael Molasky and Steven Rabson, translated by William J. Tyler, 156–70. Honolulu: University of Hawaii Press, 2000.

Shimizu, Hajime, and Akiyoshi Murakami. "Sensō iseki shōsai chōsa to kindaika isan sōgō chōsa ni miru Okinawa-ken no sensō iseki no haaku jōkyō." *Nihon kenchiku gakkai gijutsu hōkoku shū* 13, no. 25 (June 2007): 311–12.

Shimojima, Tetsurō. *Chibichirigama no shūdan jiketsu: Kami no kuni no hate ni*. Tokyo: Gaijūsha, 2000.

Shinohara, Takeo. *Anettai chiiki no Okinawa ringyō no ayumi*. Naha: Ryūkyū Ringyō Kyōkai, 1984.

Shurijō fukugen kisei kai, ed. *Shurijō*. Naha: Naha Shuppansha, 1987.

Shurijō kenkyū gurūpu, ed. *Shurijō nyūmon: Sono kenchiku to rekishi*. Naha: Hirugisha, 1997.

Shurijō Kōen Jigyō ni Kakaru Jūmin no Kai. *Shurijō kōen keikaku hihan*. Shuri Kinjōchō: Shurijō Kōen Jigyō ni Kakaru Jūmin no Kai, 1989.

Smith, Valene L. *Hosts and Guests: The Anthropology of Tourism*. Philadelphia: University of Pennsylvania Press, 1989.

Smits, Gregory. "Romantic Ryukyu in Okinawan Politics: The Myth of Ryukyuan Pacifism." Annual Meeting of the Association for Asian Studies, San Francisco, April 2006.

———. "The *Ryūkyū Shobun* in East Asian and World History." In *Ryūkyū in World History*, edited by Josef Kreiner, 279–304. Bonn: Bier'sche Verlagsanstalt, 2001.

———. *Visions of Ryukyu: Identity and Ideology in Early-Modern Thought and Politics*. Honolulu: University of Hawaii Press, 1999.

Tada, Osamu. *Okinawa imēji o tabisuru—Yanagita Kunio kara ijū būmu made*. Tokyo: Chūō Kōron Shinsha, 2008.

Teruya, Seisho. "Shurijō fukugen no igi—mitsu shiten kara no shigen." *Shurijō fukugen kisei kai kaihō*, no. 10 (1991): 35–36.

Toguchi, Masao. "Kankō ishiki no kōjō to watashi." In *25-nen no ayumi*, edited by Okinawa Izoku Rengō Kai. Naha: Okinawa-ken Kankō Renmei, 1979.

Toma, Shiichi. "Senseki kōkōgaku no susume." *Nantō kōkōgaku dayori*, no. 30 (1994).

Tomita, Yūkō. *Burū gaido bukkusu 44: Okinawa*. Tokyo: Jitsugyō no Nihonsha, 1964.

Tomiyama, Ichirō. *Kindai Nihon shakai to "Okinawajin": Nihonjin ni naru to yū koto*. Tokyo: Nihon Keizai Hyōronsha, 1990.

———. *Senba no kioku*. Tokyo: Nihin Keizai Hyōronsha, 1995.

———. "The Critical Limits of the National Community: The Ryūkyūan Subject." *Social Science Japan Journal* 1, no. 2 (October 1998): 165–80.

Ueunten, Wesley. "Okinawan Diasporic Identities: Between Being a Buffer and a Bridge." In *Transcultural Japan: At the Borderlands of Race, Gender, and Identity*, edited by David Willis Blake and Stephen Murphy-Shigematsu, 159–78. New York: Routledge, 2008.

Uezu, Yasuhide. "Shurijō ni yuki ga furu: Sapporo yuki-matsuri o mite." *Shurijō fukugen kisei kai kaihō* (February 1984): 8.

Urry, John. *The Tourist Gaze: Leisure and Travel in Contemporary Societies*. London: SAGE Publications, 1990; 2nd ed., 2002.

Walker, Egbert H. *Flora of Okinawa and the Southern Ryukyu Islands*. Washington, DC: Smithsonian Books, 1979.

———. *Important Trees of the Ryukyu Islands*. Naha: U.S. Civil Administration of the Ryukyu Islands, 1954.

Weiner, Michael. *Japan's Minorities: The Illusion of Homogeneity*. London and New York: Routledge, 2009.

Yahara, Hiromichi. *The Battle for Okinawa*. Translated by Roger Pineau and Masatoshi Uehara. New York: Wiley, 1997.

Yamashiro, Zensan, ed. *Okinawa kankō kyōkai shi*. Naha: Okinawa Kankō Kyōkai, 1964.

Yamauchi, Masanao. *Sengo Okinawa tsūka hensen shi: Beikoku tōji jidai o chūshin ni*. Naha: Ryūkyū Shinpōsha, 2004.

Yanagita, Kunio. "Kainan shoki." In *Yanagita Kunio zenshū*. Vol. 1, 483–519. Tokyo: Chikuma Bunko, 1989.

Yonetani, Julia. "On the Battlefield of Mabuni: Struggles over Peace and the Past in Contemporary Okinawa." *East Asian History* 20 (December 2000): 145–69.

Yoshida, Kensei. *Democracy Betrayed: Okinawa under U.S. Occupation*. Bellingham: Center for East Asian Studies, Western Washington State University, 2002.

Yoshihama, Shinobu. "Okinawa-ken no okeru sensō iseki no hozon katsuyō: Sensō iseki no bunkazai shitei o shiten." *Okinawa Kokusai Daigaku shakai bunka kenkyū* 11, no. 1 (June 2008): 43–71.

Zaha and Kuba. "Okinawa sensai bunkazai nado fukugen ni kansuru koiinkai sanka no kiroku." *Shurijō fukugen kisei kai kaihō*, no. 2 (June 1983): 4.

Zukin, Sharon. *Landscapes of Power: From Detroit to Disney World*. Berkeley and Los Angeles: University of California Press, 1993.

———. *The Cultures of Cities*. Berkeley and Los Angeles: Blackwell Publishers, 1996.

# Index